RIBA Job Book
Ninth Edition

RIBA Publishing

© RIBA Enterprises Ltd, 2013
Reprinted 2014
Published by RIBA Publishing, 15 Bonhill Street, London EC2P 2EA

ISBN 978 1 85946 496 0

Stock code 80460

The right of Nigel Ostime to be identified as the Author of this Work has been asserted in accordance with the Copyright, Designs and Patents Act 1988.

British Library Cataloguing in Publication Data
A catalogue record for this book is available from the British Library.

Publisher: Steven Cross
Commissioning Editor: James Thompson
Project Editor: Alasdair Deas
Designed by Ben Millbank
Typeset by RIBA Publishing
Printed and bound by W&G Baird, Antrim
Cover image: © sxc.hu

RIBA Publishing is part of RIBA Enterprises Ltd.
www.ribaenterprises.com

CONTENTS

Foreword

Throughout its 50-year history the *RIBA Job Book* has been based on the RIBA Plan of Work. The changes it has gone through over that time are a reflection of the evolution of the project process and the various forms of building procurement. This edition reflects the most fundamental change to date; one that embraces the current themes of collaboration within project teams, aligned to advances in information technology, and the continued importance of environmental sustainability.

While it has changed in quite significant ways, the RIBA Plan of Work 2013 still provides stage-by-stage guidance to assist the architect and other members of the project team in managing the building design and procurement process from inception to completion. Indeed, it now adds further advice for work before the project has commenced and after it has been completed.

Set out in a clear, easy-to-use format, this ninth edition provides comprehensive information on the administration of an architectural project, with good practice guidance, action checklists and stage outputs. It is equally applicable to all forms of procurement and to all sizes of project and as such it will provide an accessible and vital resource for all practising architects, as well as students preparing for practice.

Angela Brady
President, RIBA

Preface to the ninth edition

This ninth edition of the *RIBA Job Book* is based on the new RIBA Plan of Work 2013. The broad features of the eighth edition have been maintained and the clear and consistent structure provides easy navigation through the project process. Each stage is set out in exactly the same way, reflecting the iterative nature of design.

The critical change is that this edition adopts the new stages of the RIBA Plan of Work 2013, with eight numbered stages instead of 11 stages denoted by letters. There are consequent adjustments to existing stage activities, as well as the addition of new ones, in particular with regard to Building Information Modelling (BIM) processes and the incorporation of the actions previously set out in the Green Overlay. The work stages in the RIBA Outline Plan of Work 2007 can be aligned with the RIBA Plan of Work 2013 stages as follows:

- Stage 0 is a new stage in which a project is strategically appraised and defined, reflecting the need to identify the Business Case before work is commenced, and includes activities associated with winning the commission. Some activities in Stage 0 are derived from Stage A
- Stage 1 combines the residual Stage A tasks with Stage B activities
- Stage 2 corresponds to Stage C
- Stage 3 is broadly matched to Stage D, but with enhanced coordination requirements, similar to the coordination activities previously carried out under Stage E, and reflecting the capabilities of contemporary computer software and BIM processes
- Stage 4 is broadly analogous to the residual activities from Stage E plus F1 and F2, preparation of detailed information for construction and including design work carried out by specialist subcontractors and work by the architect in checking subcontractors' or specialists' information
- Stage 5 maps to Stages J and K
- Stage 6 maps to Stage L and covers the defects liability period from the point of issue of the Practical Completion certificate up to issue of the final certificate as well as post-handover activities such as Soft Landings and initial Post-occupancy Evaluation
- Stage 7 is a new stage that covers Post-occupancy Evaluation and facilities management activities throughout the life of the building up to its eventual demolition. This stage provides the opportunity for architects to provide additional services facilitated by managing the BIM model. It also leads back to Stage 0, where refurbishment and alteration of a building will provide new project opportunities.

Within the Procurement task bar, tendering can occur at any time from Stage 2 to Stage 4, so the advice previously set out within Stages G and H has been put into a separate chapter titled: 'Contractor Engagement'. Procurement in the RIBA Plan of Work 2013 also covers assembly of the project team and these activities are set out under Stage 1.

The *RIBA Job Book* sets out the stages in the order they appear in the RIBA Plan of Work 2013. Each starts with a facsimile of the Plan itself, followed by eight main sections: Core Objectives; the 'three Ps': Procurement, Programme and (Town) Planning; Suggested Key Support Tasks; Sustainability Checkpoints; Information Exchanges; and UK Government Information Exchanges.

It is inevitable that in getting used to the revised nomenclature and adjustments to certain activities, architects will make comparisons between the old and new stages. However, the RIBA Plan of Work 2013 provides an opportunity to fully embrace modern methods of working, without the baggage of decades' worth of amendments. Architects and other construction professionals are encouraged to put old practices behind them and embrace the new. Only in this way will we be able to take full advantage of what the RIBA Plan of Work 2013 has to offer.

The *RIBA Job Book* contains advice not just for the architect but for the other members of the project team, particularly for those who are undertaking project management and contract administration activities. It should be noted that in this book and the RIBA Plan of Work 2013, the 'design team' comprises all of the professional consultants appointed, via a Professional Services Contract, in relation to a project, and 'project team' means the full team appointed to design, construct and, where appropriate, maintain a building, and other parties directly involved in the process, including the client.

As with the eighth edition, this edition of the *RIBA Job Book* is accompanied by a website (which has also been revised and updated): www.ribabookshops.com/jobbook. The website contains free downloadable action checklists and template forms, enabling the creation of project plans for individual projects. The ability to use the electronic checklists in conjunction with the hard copy explanatory notes makes this publication a practical project management tool, enabling the original concept of the RIBA Job Book, created 50 years ago, to be realised using modern technology.

Acknowledgements

The author would like to thank Dale Sinclair, who has led development of the RIBA Plan of Work 2013 and who has contributed to the development of this edition of the *RIBA Job Book*. He would also like to thank Adrian Dobson, Jane Duncan, Ruth Reed, Roland Finch, Richard Teale, Koko Udom and Peter Caplehorn for their advice, Bill Gething for his contribution regarding Sustainability Checkpoints and Gary Clark and BSRIA for the information on Soft Landings.

About the author

Nigel Ostime is an architect with 25 years' experience in the construction industry. He is currently principal of **whiteroom** architecture, having previously been a director at 3DReid.

He has wide experience in the design and delivery of complex projects, including numerous large-scale developments in aviation, utility infrastructure, commercial offices, high-end residential, retail, town-centre mixed-use and industrial/ distribution buildings. He has delivered planning permissions on sensitive sites, both urban and rural, and has expertise in the management and coordination of multidisciplinary consultant teams through all project stages.

He has a long-standing interest in the process of design and specifically a knowledge-led, 'lean' approach to project work, developed at 3DReid, that ensures all the necessary information and skills are fed into the project at the right time to consistently provide the best solutions with the greatest efficiency. **whiteroom** architecture also focuses on the benefits of collaboration with other specialists in the construction industry as well as the core issues of design quality, value and sustainability.

Nigel is an active member of the RIBA and chairs both the Client Liaison Group, which provides an interface between the Institute and client representative bodies, and the Future Leaders Group, which develops and implements an education programme for business-focused, post-Part 3 skills for architects.

He was co-author of the previous edition of this book (2008) and of the current edition of the *Architect's Handbook of Practice Management* (RIBA Publishing, 2010). He was also a member of the editorial board of the fourth edition of the *Metric Handbook* (Architectural Press, 2012) and a member of the steering group for the government-sponsored Creative Industries KTN Beacon Project on the future of digital tools for designers (2010).

He lives in north London with his wife, three children and six bicycles.

Introduction

How to use this book

The *RIBA Job Book* can be used either on its own or in tandem with the companion website www.ribabookshops.com/jobbook (see below), from which you may download editable electronic documents related to the book, free of charge.

This edition follows the new stages in the RIBA Plan of Work 2013 (reproduced inside the back cover). The structure of the book is similar to the eighth edition, with the chapters set out consistently, but each stage now precisely reflects the layout of the Plan of Work. Each chapter starts with a facsimile of the relevant stage of the Plan itself and a general description of the stage activities. The chapters are then split into eight main sections, relating to each of the eight task bars for each stage in the RIBA Plan of Work 2013:

1. Core Objectives
2. Procurement
3. Programme
4. (Town) Planning
5. Suggested Key Support Tasks
6. Sustainability Checkpoints
7. Information Exchanges
8. UK Government Information Exchanges

Core Objectives sets out the principal activities for each stage.

The 'three Ps' are a set of activities that can take place at different times depending on the needs of the project, the approach to risk and the form of procurement. The activities in Procurement, Programme and (Town) Planning vary widely from project to project and so the RIBA Plan of Work 2013 allows users to generate their own bespoke practice- or project-specific RIBA Plan of Work by selecting from a pull-down list.

The proposed procurement route can be selected to generate a practice- or project-specific RIBA Plan of Work that includes the specific procurement and tendering activities required at each stage.

The procurement strategy, or certain client demands, may dictate that a number of stages need to occur simultaneously or overlap. The Programme task bar allows a bespoke practice- or project-specific Plan of Work to be created to illustrate and highlight these stages. More importantly, this task bar underlines the need for every project to have a Project Programme that sets out the durations for each stage and any supporting activities.

The pull-down options of the (Town) Planning task bar allow the user to determine whether the planning application will be made at the end of Stage 2 or Stage 3 and the stage(s) when any conditions attached to a planning consent will be addressed. This will vary depending on the nature of the planning consent, the conditions imposed, the type of project and the contractual relationships. This task bar also takes into account the length of time required to conclude any conditions attached to the planning consent prior to construction commencing. On some projects these may need to be resolved prior to the building contract being let, whereas on others, such as a conservation project, they may continue to be discharged during construction. The Project Programme should make these durations clear, as well as the period required by the planning authority to consider any application.

The Suggested Key Support Tasks task bar sets out activities required to achieve the Sustainability Aspirations – particularly reduced carbon emissions related to the building – and those required to embed Building Information Modelling (BIM) into the process. It also sets out key tasks in relation to statutory requirements, such as those relating to Building Regulations submissions, project and design management protocols, roles and responsibilities, and construction health and safety, and ensures that the team is properly assembled and that buildability, health and safety, logistics and other construction considerations are considered early in the process. This is achieved through preparation of the Project Execution Plan and Construction Strategy.

In the book, the activities relating to Suggested Key Support Tasks are set out under the following headings:

- Information required
- Brief
- Appointment
- Client
- Project team
- General matters (i.e. those not covered under other headings)
- Inspections/tests
- Consultations, approvals and consents
- Cost planning.

 Throughout the book, activities related to BIM are highlighted in the margin.

The Sustainability Checkpoints section sets out those activities previously listed in the *Green Overlay to the RIBA Outline Plan of Work* (2011). In the RIBA Plan of Work 2013 it is selectable and can be 'switched' on or off when compiling a project- or practice-specific Plan of Work, but the activities are all noted in this book.

The Information Exchanges task bar schedules the outputs for the stage, and the UK Government Information Exchanges task bar notes the specific data drop points for public procurement work. This task bar is selectable and can be switched on or off in a bespoke project- or practice-specific Plan of Work.

All terms used in the RIBA Plan of Work 2013 are capitalised in this book.

For a detailed explanation of how to use the Plan of Work 2013, refer to the RIBA publication *Guide to Using the RIBA Plan of Work 2013* (2013).

Useful notes provide background information and 'watch points'. The action checklists are supported by supplementary material to offer further guidance or to give examples of template forms.

Prior to commencing a stage all the actions should be reviewed as different projects will have different priorities.

The *RIBA Job Book* is not intended to constitute a quality management system in itself, but some parts of it, for example the action checklists and standard forms, may be relevant to an office quality system. It should always be remembered, however, that the RIBA Job Book checklists are not comprehensive, and though they may form a useful starting point they must be adapted to the specific needs of a particular practice.

The *RIBA Job Book* is coordinated with and cross-referenced to other RIBA documents and Good Practice Guides, which together form a suite of RIBA approved practice and guidance references.

The companion website – www.ribabookshops.com/jobbook

The companion website has been developed to allow architects to download, free of charge, a comprehensive set of editable template documents to help them consistently run their projects to a high standard. The templates may be completed electronically or printed out and completed manually to suit the preferred method of working. It is envisaged that a set of checklists will be used at the start of every new project as the project plan for that job. To use these templates safely and as intended it is important to refer to the introductory and supplemental guidance and background notes in the book.

Once downloaded, the action checklists may be edited electronically, allowing them to form the basis of the project plan. For each action in the checklists it is possible to record the date on which the action was undertaken or completed, and there is also space below to record notes on the activity, if relevant.

The numbering of the action checklists on the companion website mirrors that used in the book. The website also contains all the figures reproduced in the book.

BIM protocol

It is not the role of this book to set out Building Information Modelling (BIM) processes and procedures in detail, but it is important to recognise the growing importance of BIM in the construction industry, the importance of BIM as an influence on the Plan of Work 2013, and the broad activities that are required during the project process if BIM processes are followed. Evolving BIM technology is transforming modes of working in the construction industry in terms of how design data is generated, shared and integrated, which in turn creates a requirement for new protocols, activities and definitions.

Varying levels of 'maturity' of BIM use have been defined. Level 0 BIM is the use of 2D CAD files for Technical Design. Level 1 BIM acknowledges the increased use of both 2D and 3D information on projects and embraces the need for management processes to sit alongside design processes. Level 2 BIM requires the production of 3D information models by all key members of the design team, although not necessarily using a single project model. Level 3, or iBIM, involves collaborative use of a single, interoperable digital model by all members of the design team simultaneously.

The book has set out certain key actions that need to be carried out for projects where BIM is to be used at Level 2 and above, which require certain protocols to be followed, including appointing a project information manager and preparing a project BIM Execution Plan as part of the Project Execution Plan.

Information manager

The information manager has the responsibility of developing, implementing and updating the BIM Execution Plan; taking a lead in the planning, set-up and maintenance of the model and leading the design team with regard to development of the design model and the protocols used.

BIM Execution Plan

This document should set out: the parameters of the project; project team members; the BIM standards to be used; the deliverables from the model; the software to be used; the data exchange method; the file naming convention; a schedule of quality control checks; and a schedule of dates for review of the model by the design team.

Level of detail

Although CAD information is produced 'full size', when drawing are issued, whether as hard copy or electronically, the level of detail added to the drawing is dictated by the scale of the output. BIM changes this approach as such outputs are no longer required (although it is likely that 2D 'slices' through a model will continue to be used as contractual documents for some time). The matter therefore becomes one of purpose rather than scale. For example, if the model is being used for design discussions with a client, a relatively low level of detail is required, but if the BIM model is being handed over to a specialist subcontractor to develop the curtain walling, a high level of detail must be included.

For each project/model, a spreadsheet should be prepared setting out, by building element, the level of detail at each stage (Stages 0 to 7), alongside the author of that design.

Members of the design team should consult the information manager for advice on BIM protocols and procedures.

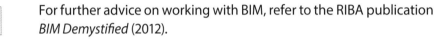 For further advice on working with BIM, refer to the RIBA publication *BIM Demystified* (2012).

STAGE 0

Strategic Definition

CONTENTS

Plan of Work and Stage Activities

Supplementary Material

Figures

RIBA
Plan of
Work
2013

Excerpt from the RIBA Plan of Work 2013

RIBA
Plan of
Work
2013

Stage 0

Strategic
Definition

Task Bar	Tasks
Core Objectives	Identify client's **Business Case** and **Strategic Brief** and other core project requirements.
Procurement Variable task bar	Initial considerations for assembling the project team.
Programme Variable task bar	Establish **Project Programme**.
(Town) Planning Variable task bar	Pre-application discussions *may be required to test the robustness of the* **Strategic Brief**.
Suggested Key Support Tasks	Review **Feedback** from previous projects.
Sustainability Checkpoints	• *Ensure that a strategic sustainability review of client needs and potential sites has been carried out, including reuse of existing facilities, building components or materials.*
Information Exchanges (at stage completion)	**Strategic Brief.**
UK Government Information Exchanges	Not required.

0

Summary

Stage 0 is used to ensure that the client's **Business Case** and the **Strategic Brief** have been properly considered before the **Initial Project Brief** is developed.

The **Strategic Brief** may require a review of a number of sites or alternative options, such as extensions, refurbishment or new build. By asking the right questions, the consultants, in collaboration with the client, can properly define the scope for a project, and the preparation and briefing process can then begin.

Mapping to RIBA Outline Plan of Work 2007

Stage 0 is a new stage in which a project is strategically appraised and defined before a detailed brief is created. This is particularly relevant in the context of sustainability, when a refurbishment or extension, or indeed a rationalised space plan, may be more appropriate than a new building. Certain activities in Stage 0 are derived from the former (RIBA Outline Plan of Work 2007) Stage A.

0.1	**Core Objectives**

Stage 0 is the stage when requirements are clarified and a strategy for action prepared. It is important at this stage to raise fundamental questions regarding the project; for example, whether there is a need for a new building, or whether adaptation and reorganisation of the client's existing premises might not satisfy existing needs. Key issues such as funding, budget, project duration and building lifespan should be addressed.

The use of Building Information Modelling (BIM) should be determined at the outset of the project or as soon as possible to attain the greatest benefit from it.

This stage may or may not involve other consultants; with larger or more experienced clients the process of appraisal may be handled by the client body itself. The stage should culminate in the Strategic Brief, which will form the basis of the Initial Project Brief to be delivered in Stage 1.

Stage 0 includes such studies as may be relevant to determine what services will be necessary and whether it is feasible to achieve the project aims within the defined constraints. Such studies may be undertaken initially by the client organisation with in-house expertise or by a project manager or architect before the appointment of other consultants. Professional advisers may be commissioned solely for Stage 0, particularly in the case of major projects where demonstrable impartiality and objectivity are required by a client body.

BIM

Stage 0 relates to the final stage, Stage 7, as Feedback from the completed project can be used to inform refurbishment or alteration of the building or other future projects of a similar nature. Stage 7 covers the in-use management of the building throughout its life until its eventual demolition. A BIM model can be used to assist in this and architects should seek opportunities to perform this service for their clients. Traditionally, once a building has been completed the architect has had little involvement in managing it as an asset or a facility, but this could change, with consequent benefits to the profession and the industry. As buildings become 'smarter' they also require greater technical understanding to run them efficiently and information technology can play a key part in this.

RIBA Client Advisers

RIBA Client Advisers are independent of the project team and monitor and help to manage the design process from its earliest stages. They give advice on the composition and selection of the project team and provide independent advice to help the client run the project efficiently and achieve best value and quality. Their work might include:

- strategic decision-making

- stakeholder consultation

- design brief development

- budget-setting

- feasibility studies

- procurement procedures

- appraisals of design proposals.

Client Advisers are selected by the RIBA from its membership and are evaluated and accredited on an annual basis. The RIBA maintains a register and provides shortlists of Client Advisers with the most appropriate skills and experience.

Securing the commission

Although not strictly part of the Strategic Definition process, there are some key matters to be considered in winning and then preparing to take on a commission. These are set out in this section of the book.

There is potential within the industry for the architect to perform a wide variety of roles. Great care is therefore needed to ensure that any commission is secured on the right basis – it can no longer always be assumed that 'the normal services will apply' or that there will be a common understanding between architect and client as to what the 'normal services' might mean. In any individual case the services will vary according to the expectations and requirements of the client.

In relation to any given project, the services will be affected by the nature and scale of the building project, the management structure set up for the project and the procurement method adopted. The architect could be engaged from inception through to completion, or perhaps for specific services at a single stage. Given this wide diversity of potential roles, it is important that the services to be provided in each case are identified accurately and with care.

The job or commission can be secured through a variety of methods. For example, it could be as a result of a direct approach made to a potential client or through an invitation to discuss and negotiate or to bid in competition. This might concern only the architect, or it might call for a joint submission, involving other professionals or partners from commerce and industry.

Where securing a commission is subject to competitive tendering, it is essential to know what criteria the client intends to apply when evaluating tenders, and what procedures will govern the submission. A careful assessment of the resources required will be crucial in order to make realistic costings and establish viability before tendering.

Whatever method of securing the commission is used, the importance of having an agreement in writing cannot be emphasised enough. It is a requirement of both the RIBA and the Architects Registration Board (ARB) codes of conduct, and it is normal practice to use one of the standard forms of agreement published by the RIBA. If these are not used then great care must be taken to allow for the effect of legislation, which directly regulates many aspects of an architect's appointment, particularly payment provisions and dispute resolution.

Sometimes, where the architect is contacted at a very early stage, the nature of the project and the scope of the services required may be so unclear that it is not practicable to use one of the standard forms. In these cases it may be better to agree the preliminary services by letter, but it is essential that the services are confirmed in writing.

A successful working relationship depends on the roles of all parties being established clearly from the outset, and without the ambiguities that so frequently lead to misunderstandings and conflict. The activities listed below could be relevant before the appointment of an architect, whether for full or partial services, under any RIBA Plan of Work 2013 stage or part of a stage, and are generally applicable regardless of procurement method.

 Refer to the *Architect's Handbook of Practice Management* (2010), Chapter 9 'The Architect's Appointment', *Assembling a Collaborative Project Team* (2013) and *Creating Winning Bids* (2013) for further guidance.

0.2   Procurement

0.2.1   Consider the likely composition of the design team and discuss this with the client.

 Which consultants are first to come on board will vary depending on the nature of the project. If there are complicated planning issues, a planning consultant may be necessary; if there are key environmental matters to be considered, an environmental engineer may be required; or if transport is a factor, a traffic engineer may be needed at an early stage to establish the viability of the project.

Usually the first consultants to join the architect are project managers (who are sometimes appointed before the architect) and cost consultants (although generally only with experienced clients). If the project is engineering-led, such as an infrastructure project, then civil, structural or other engineers will be present.

Sometimes, the client will be reluctant to take on more consultants until the viability of the scheme has been tested, to keep costs down. It is important to emphasise the value that other consultants can bring, even if their input is relatively light at the initial stages of a project.

See notes on RIBA Client Advisers under 0.1 Core Objectives.

0.3   Programme

> NOTE
>
> *There are no specific programming requirements at this early stage, but it is wise to consider the programme for undertaking any activities, including the pre-project assessments, so as to understand the time cost to your business. It is not unusual for clients to expect the architect to share the risks in this stage by working on a speculative basis, in which case it is even more important to measure time and cost. If this is the case it is nonetheless important to set out the basis of this work in a letter: an example can be found in Figure 0/3.*

FIG.

> NOTE
>
> *The Strategic Brief should define key dates for outcomes, phasing and so on.*

0.4   (Town) Planning

0.4.1 Identify whether there are any planning policy issues that might prevent the type of development proposed. You can consult the planning section of the local authority's website to find this out, or refer to the planning consultant if one has been appointed.

0.5   Suggested Key Support Tasks

The only action noted in the RIBA Plan of Work 2013 for this task bar is to review Feedback from previous projects. However, there is a wide range of activities that should be undertaken in Stage 0 that do not sit within the other headings.

0.5.1	**Information required**

0.5.1.1	Obtain information on the site, knowledge of best practice in the specific building sector(s) (residential, retail, education, etc.) and an outline of the client's needs or aspirations.
	You will also need to understand the planning policy context (see 0.4.1 above).

0.5.1.2	Make preliminary checks on the client: these are noted below in 0.5.4.

0.5.1.3	Other inputs, such as marketing material, etc., are noted below in 0.5.6.

0.5.2	**Brief**

0.5.2.1	Arrange a preliminary meeting, if appropriate, to discuss requirements. The initial meetings between client and architect will set the tone for the future working relationship. Clarify your respective roles and responsibilities.
	Consider your reaction to the client and the project:
	Are you in general sympathy with the client's needs and aspirations – if not, will this have an adverse effect on your work? Are the prospects good for building up an understanding with the client? This is the stage at which issues such as the importance of environmental sustainability, quality of the public realm or different approaches to assembling the project team and appointment of the contractor can be discussed.
	Be properly equipped with information about your practice and its work. Prepare a practice brochure with details of your track record, key personnel and a statement about your expertise and experience.
	Refer to the *Architect's Handbook of Practice Management* (2010), Chapter 5 'Marketing and Business Development'.
	Take care when offering pro-bono services or free advice. The duty of care that you owe is not related to the size of fee. Even if there is no fee, you might still have a duty in tort.

Do not be casual in your dealings and inadvertently let yourself in for more than you intended. Under certain circumstances informal dealings can be construed as giving rise to contractual relationships. A contractual duty, if breached, could result in loss and an ensuing claim.

Warn the client at once if design requirements, timing and budget seem unrealistic. Remember that a failure to warn could leave you open to allegations of negligence. Explain fully what you advise should be done and avoid jargon.

0.5.2.2   Establish the Strategic Brief.

The Strategic Brief should set out the objectives that the client wishes to achieve in the project. It will probably refer to functional requirements, environmental standards, levels of quality, lifespan and maintenance and may consist of anything from a broad preliminary statement of interest to a comprehensive set of technical requirements. This brief will form the basis for feasibility studies.

The Strategic Brief should also set out the Business Case for the initiation of a new building project. This may consist solely of a reasoned argument or it may contain supporting information, financial appraisals or other background information. It should also highlight initial considerations for the Project Outcomes. The Business Case might be prepared in relation to a number of sites or in relation to assessing refurbishment against new build.

For detailed notes on the briefing process refer to 0/SM4 and 1/SM1.   **0/SM4**
1/SM1

0.5.2.3	For some projects it may be beneficial to introduce the Design Quality Indicator (DQI) process.

DQI is a method of evaluating design and construction for both new build and refurbishment, involving the whole project team and the building users. It can be used at all stages of a building's development, but the earlier it is introduced, the greater the benefit derived. The DQI process establishes a platform from which stakeholders can agree common goals, interrogate designs and demand excellence from suppliers. It empowers a building's community by providing them with a structured way to talk about their building. By encouraging effective communication between suppliers and the eventual users of the building, the process helps to ensure that suppliers deliver excellent buildings that meet users' needs. It is an inclusive process and is at its most effective when the user group involved is as wide as possible.

Representatives from both the supply side and the demand side of a project take part. The supply side includes people responsible for delivering the building, such as the architects, the design team and contractors. The demand side includes the building's community and those people who will use the building.

DQI works through structured workshops and online tools. Presentations at the workshops brief an assessment group, formed from members of the building community, throughout the design and construction processes. The online tools give this assessment group a structure within which to consider a series of important issues relating to their building.

The workshops are mediated by a dedicated DQI facilitator, who is able to assess the results of the online tools and record the opinions of those present. The online tools take the form of questionnaires that provide instant results, which are used to generate discussion during each workshop.

The workshops should take place at all stages of a building project. Ideally, DQI should be put into practice at the first workshop held during the briefing stage and then continued throughout the project. In other situations it should be put into practice at the earliest stage possible.

For further information go to www.dqi.org.uk.

0.5.3	Appointment

0.5.3.1	Identify the likely role and nature of professional services needed. Will you be acting as lead designer, as project lead, as a design team member, as consultant to the employer client in design and build, as provider of information to the contractor client in design and build, or even as coordinator or manager for separate trades contracts? Make an appraisal and consider carefully the implications.	0/SM3

0.5.3.2	Examine carefully any terms or conditions proposed by the client. Consider whether the terms and conditions follow normal practice or whether there is any specially drafted wording that shows significant client bias.

NOTE *Be wary of conditions which might imply a level of services beyond that which can be reasonably provided for the fee.*

NOTE *Depending on the nature of the project, some preliminary design considerations may be necessary to establish the goals of Stage 0. You should take this into account when establishing the scope of work for this stage and agreeing it with the client.*

0.5.3.3	Check that there is no conflict with professional codes.

Box 0/1: Extracts from ARB Architects Code: Standards of Conduct and Practice 2010 version

Provisions of the Architects Code to be taken into account when forming a contract include the following:

4.4   You are expected to ensure that before you undertake any professional work you have entered into a written agreement with the client which adequately covers:

- the contracting parties;
- the scope of the work;
- the fee or method of calculating it;
- who will be responsible for what;
- any constraints or limitations on the responsibilities of the parties;
- the provisions for suspension or termination of the agreement;
- a statement that you have adequate and appropriate insurance cover as specified by the Board;
- your complaints-handling procedure (see Standard 10), including details of any special arrangements for resolving disputes (e.g. arbitration).

4.5   Any agreed variations to the written agreement should be recorded in writing.

4.6   You are expected to ensure that your client agreements record that you are registered with the Architects Registration Board and that you are subject to this Code; and that the client can refer a complaint to the Board if your conduct or competence appears to fall short of the standards in the Code.

4.7   You should make clear to the client the extent to which any of your architectural services are being subcontracted.

6.1   You are expected to carry out your work promptly and with skill and care and in accordance with the terms of your engagement.

6.2   You should carry out your professional work without undue delay and, so far is reasonably practicable, in accordance with any timescale and cost limits agreed with your client.

6.3   You are expected to keep your client informed of the progress of work undertaken on their behalf and of any issue which may significantly affect its quality or cost.

6.4   You should, when acting between parties or giving advice, exercise impartial and independent professional judgement. If you are to act as both architect and contractor you should make it clear in writing that your advice will no longer be impartial.

8.1   You are expected to have adequate and appropriate insurance cover for you, your practice and your employees. You should ensure that your insurance is adequate to meet a claim, whenever it is made.

10.1   You are expected to have a written procedure for prompt and courteous handling of complaints which will be in accordance with the Code and provide this to clients. This should include the name of the architect who will respond to complaints.

Refer to the *Architect's Handbook of Practice Management* (2010), Chapter 2 'The Profession' and *Law in Practice: The RIBA Legal Handbook* (2012).

0.5.3.4   Check what the client has asked for concerning indemnities, third party warranties, liability period, levels of professional indemnity cover, etc. and consider whether these are reasonable and acceptable. If being considered for the commission depends on evidence of professional indemnity (PI) insurance cover well in excess of that presently arranged, discuss with insurers the possibility of providing such cover as an interim measure, with the certainty of extending it if and when the commission is secured.

Take expert advice from a construction lawyer and insurers if the client seeks to impose onerous conditions.

0.5.3.5   If no terms are stipulated, draw up terms of appointment that could be proposed.

Consider the minimum and maximum levels of services which might be appropriate for the project, but, in order to remain competitive, keep strictly within the stated requirements when compiling the proposal.

Use one of the standard forms of appointment prepared by the RIBA (Standard, Concise or Domestic Agreement 2010 (2012 revision)) exactly as recommended in the guidance notes set out in Guide to RIBA Agreements 2010 (2012 revision) *(2012).*

If for some reason this is not possible, take expert advice on the terms to be proposed.

When setting out in writing the professional services you agree to carry out, make absolutely clear what is not included. Leave no room for misunderstandings, particularly when dealing with new or inexperienced clients.

With a consumer client, always arrange to meet and talk through the terms proposed in detail, and make sure your client fully understands them, otherwise, under the Unfair Terms in Consumer Contracts Regulations 1999, certain terms may not be considered to have been 'individually negotiated' and therefore become void.

0.5.3.6	Provide the client with the fee proposal, and be prepared to negotiate if appropriate.
	Price the client's stated requirements at the outset, no more and no less. You will need to be aware of prevailing market conditions, but if you quote a fee that is unrealistically low it might mean that you have to cut corners and so the quality of service you are able to provide will suffer accordingly. There are obvious risks in putting yourself under this kind of pressure.
	Take the time and trouble to explain fully to a client what you are proposing and why. For example, statutory obligations and necessary consents, Technical Design and procedures for appointing the contractor and subcontractors may well seem daunting to the uninitiated.
	Be realistic when negotiating. A successful negotiator knows how far to go and when to stop. The aim should never be to secure a commission at any price.

0.5.3.7	Decide whether to accept the commission if offered and confirm it in writing.

0.5.3.8	Submit appointment documents for signature before commencing work. Ensure that future review of the appointment is covered in case it is required. Where a standard form is used, follow the guidance notes exactly.
	Should it prove premature to enter into a formal memorandum at this point, when for example the extent of professional involvement cannot yet be determined, then enter into a preliminary agreement as an interim measure, clearly identified as such. See Figure 0/3.
	Keep adequate and appropriate records of all dealings connected with the project. Never sacrifice proper paperwork for the sake of assumed goodwill. File everything systematically, whether in hard copy or in digital form, so that items can be easily found and retrieved. It is essential to have fail-safe back-up arrangements to protect both work in progress and records which may be needed for future reference.
	Never assume that the commission is won until you have received written confirmation of acceptance.

0.5.4	Client

0.5.4.1	Identify the client, and the status and authority of any client representative.

Note whether an individual is acting in a private capacity or representing a charitable organisation, consortium or a company, etc. If a representative, then what authority is he or she acting under and with what power?

In the case of a commercial client, make certain precisely where the ultimate authority resides. For example, the client's company might exist within a parent body.

Where the client is two or more individuals or a family unit who have formed some kind of association, be sure that you know who has authority to make decisions, give instructions and make payments.

0.5.4.2	Understand whether the project is for direct occupation by the client or is a speculative development for sale or lease, and enquire about the potential involvement of any third party who may expect to be consulted, including funders.

NOTE

Bear in mind that working with a group of people on a community-type project, or with a user client for whom this is their first project, may entail a certain amount of extra work, including meetings outside of typical working hours.

0.5.4.3	Check the experience of the client. Some clients know exactly what is needed and what they can realistically expect from consultants, while some may never have built before.

NOTE

Be particularly careful in initial meetings with inexperienced clients. Remember that your legal duty of care can relate to the known experience or inexperience of your client.

0.5.4.4	Check the soundness of the client.

Make discreet enquiries about the prospective client's business record and financial position. Is there any known tendency to questionable business dealings or hasty resort to threats of legal action? What nature of client are they? What previous projects have they commissioned? What were they like to work with?

0.5.4.5   If appropriate, advise the client on the purpose, benefits and implications of implementing BIM on the project.

Agree the extent to which BIM will be used, including 4D (time), 5D (cost) and 6D (facilities management), following software assessment, and inform the design team.

4D (time) BIM

By adding 'time' to the information in the project model (by linking attributes in the model to a construction programme) it is possible for the contractor to review the construction of the building. For large, complex projects or those on challenging sites, this can be a particularly useful tool as it can be used to examine critical path activities, logistical issues such as deliveries and craneage, and to generally discuss and refine how the building is to be constructed. As interoperability improves it will become more straightforward to consider different buildability options, allowing a number of construction options to be prepared and rapidly translated into a 3D representation of the construction process.

If the model is updated to reflect activity on site, it can also be a useful tool for reviewing progress against the programme, highlighting where progress is behind. The model and project schedule can also be used to examine ways to make up time. Conversely, the contract administrator will be able to use the programme for assessing delays and any applications for an extension of time.

5D (cost) BIM

The ability of BIM models to contain cost information and quantity schedules allows the cost estimates for a given design to be produced faster. This allows option appraisals at the concept stage to be more accurately assessed and, because designers have cost information at their fingertips, the iterative design process will be accelerated, making it more likely that designs are aligned with the client's budget.

Consideration will need to be given to how cost consultants provide and integrate cost information into the model. Common methods of outputting area and quantity information – so that it can be converted into a robust cost plan that takes due cognisance of project-specific cost drivers and market trends – will have to be determined.

6D (FM) BIM

For many clients, their facilities management (FM) teams find 6D to be the most innovative and useful aspect of BIM. By harnessing the data in the model, the client will have a powerful tool for managing their assets. The principal means of achieving this is by adding data to the model as the project develops. For example, if the doors are specified descriptively then the performance data will be contained in the model at the outset; however, this will be replaced by the prescriptive data once the actual door to be used has been agreed. The door data tag will also contain information on the ironmongery and the maintenance information in relation to the door and each element contained in it. So, for example, if a trolley damages a door in a back-of-house corridor, the FM team will be able to use the model to ascertain the supplier of the damaged kick plate to order a new one and to use the supplier's operating data to repair the overhead door closer.

At a more strategic level, the 6D model might be used to hold energy performance data and be used as part of a data-driven Post-occupancy Evaluation (Soft Landings) process.

0.5.4.6 	Advise the client on the scope of service for the integrated team, both in totality and for each designer, including requirements for specialists and the appointment of an information manager. This is fundamentally a role required for projects where BIM is to be implemented.
0.5.4.7 	*You have a duty under the CDM Regulations to inform the client of the Regulations at the earliest opportunity. It is good practice to generate a standard letter that is always sent out with your first client correspondence.*

0.5.5	**Project team**

0.5.5.1	See note under 0.2.1 regarding bringing together the design team.

It is important to have the full design team appointed before dealing with planning application matters. The team might include, for example, ecologist, highways engineer, landscape architect (for landscape and visual impact assessment), transport consultant, archaeologist, heritage consultant and townscape consultant. The client should be advised on the need for the appointment of advisers and the coordination of their submissions prior to planning. This can be time consuming and potentially expensive if the client believes it is covered in the architect's fee.

0.5.5.2	Check whether any other architects were formerly involved with the project. If so, check that their appointment has been properly terminated and notify them in writing of your own appointment, when this has been formally concluded. See Figure 0/1.

0.5.5.3 A Design Responsibility Matrix should be prepared. This is a table that illustrates which member of the project team is responsible for each aspect of the design. The matrix provides early clarity regarding design responsibilities, which achieves a number of goals:

- It ensures that each designer is clear about their design responsibilities and the level of detail to be achieved for each aspect they are designing, enabling their drawings and specifications to be prepared accordingly.

- It makes certain that the contractor and any specialist subcontractors are aware of any design responsibility obligations to be included in the Building Contract.

- It allows fees to be properly apportioned and considered by each party.

- It reduces any ambiguities about responsibilities, minimising the possibility of disputes.

The Design Responsibility Matrix is of particular importance on a BIM project as it ensures that every party with design responsibilities is clear regarding the design information they will be contributing to the federated BIM model and the level of detail that the model will contain. The matrix is of particular importance to the lead designer who must ensure that the matrix allows them to undertake any design coordination obligations that are allocated to this role.

Refer to PAS 1192-2:2013: *Specification for Information Management for the Capital/Delivery Phase of Construction Projects using Building Information Modelling.*

0.5.6	**General matters**

0.5.6.1	Respond at once to approaches from potential clients and submit a practice statement if appropriate. If the project is of interest, ask for further particulars, including details of the selection process to be adopted.	0/SM1 0/SM2

Refer to the *Architect's Handbook of Practice Management* (2010), Chapter 5 'Marketing and Business Development'.

Avoid spending unnecessary time on 'long shots' or unsuitable commissions. In particular, avoid being drawn into giving free advice after the initial consultation.

0.5.6.2	Check the client's requirements for the submission. If competitive fee bidding is involved, make sure that it is on fair and equitable terms and that the given information is sufficient to permit preparation of a realistic bid. Confirm in writing any reservations or requests for further information.	 0/SM2

0.5.6.3	Agree a common policy between fellow consultants if the fee bid is to be a team effort. Agree compatible working methods, procedures and information format.

0.5.6.4	Assess carefully what the project will require in terms of practice resources before you quote a fee. Do you have the necessary skills and staff? Can they be made available for the particular programme? If it looks as if you will be overstretched, can you buy in skills or subcontract work? Figure 0/2 is a project resource planning sheet. Whether prepared manually or as a spreadsheet, this could provide essential information for a fee bid and be a useful tool for monitoring small jobs.

| 0.5.6.5 | Decide whether it is realistic to undertake the commission. Are you confident that the timetable, quality of services and budget can be met? What are the risks, and can they be traded off against likely benefits to the practice if the commission is won? |

| 0.5.6.6 NOTE NOTE | *It is important to note that the Construction (Design and Management) Regulations 2007 (CDM Regulations) apply to the project once you start to develop design elements that cannot or will not be changed. This is generally accepted as 'initial design' as described in the Approved Code of Practice. This will be the case irrespective of whether fees are being charged, and is even the case with competitions or bids.*

The duties under the CDM Regulations are imposed under criminal law, not contract law, and therefore the consequences for any breach are very serious and cannot be insured against. |

0.5.7   Inspections/tests

| 0.5.7.1 | There are no specific requirements for inspections/tests in this stage, but you should make yourself familiar with the site and its context, particularly in terms of planning policy and the key constraints and opportunities presented by the site. |

0.5.8   Consultations, approvals and consents

| 0.5.8.1 | There are no specific requirements for consultation, approvals and consents in this stage. |

0.5.9   Cost planning

| 0.5.9.1 | There are no specific requirements for cost planning in this stage, but an understanding of the likely capital cost parameters is necessary to assess the viability of a project. Seek advice from other consultants on this if necessary. You may find that they are prepared to offer advice on a speculative basis at this stage in order to gain an introduction to the client. |

0.6	**Sustainability Checkpoints**

Sustainability Checkpoint 0

 There are no specific tasks listed in the RIBA Plan of Work 2013; however, if the Sustainability Aspirations are likely to impact on how the project is defined then they should be considered and included in the Strategic Brief.

Sustainability aims

Establish the client's Sustainability Aspirations so that these can be properly taken into account in developing the Strategic Brief and Business Case.

Checkpoints

- Ensure that a strategic sustainability review of client needs and potential sites has been carried out, including reuse of existing facilities, building components or materials.

Key actions

- Review client requirements to distil their Sustainability Aspirations and the expected building lifespan against which capital costs and costs in use should be balanced.

- Identify potential for cost-effective enhancement of client aspirations.

- The client should consider appointing or identifying a client sustainability advocate (in a senior management position) and/or appointing a sustainability champion within the project team.

- Assess environmental opportunities and constraints of potential sites and building assets, including sufficient iterative modelling to support the conclusions of any Feasibility Studies.

- Initial consultation with stakeholders, identification of local planning sustainability requirements and appraisal of existing building, social, transportation, water, energy, ecological and renewable resources, including the need for pre-construction or seasonal monitoring or surveys, should be undertaken.

- Identify potential funding sources and their eligibility criteria.

- Review relevant current and emerging EU, national and local sustainability policies and legislation and analyse their implications for building, environmental and performance targets.

- Identify and understand the final occupants' needs in order to help to establish user patterns, energy profiles and the performance standards required.

- Obtain a letter from the planning authority to verify any sustainability requirements.

- The client should consider the formal adoption of a Soft Landings approach to the project (www.bsria.co.uk/services/design/soft-landings/).

- The client should consider appointing a Soft Landings champion.

- The client should consider the merits and protocols of using a BIM model to help deliver sustainability aims.

0.7	**Information Exchanges**

0.7.1	• Strategic Brief.
	• Report to the client on project viability, including planning policy, cost parameters and development appraisal.
	• Initial advice on likely consultant team.

0.8	**UK Government Information Exchanges**

0.8.1	There are no Information Exchanges at this stage.

PAS 91:2010 Construction related procurement. Prequalification questionnaires

Publicly Available Specifications (PASs) are sponsored, fast-track standards driven by the needs of the client organisations and developed according to guidelines set out by the British Standards Institution (BSI). Key stakeholders are brought together to collaboratively produce a

BSI-endorsed PAS that has all the functionality of a British Standard, for the purposes of creating management systems, product benchmarks and codes of practice. In not more than two years from the date of publication a PAS is reviewed to determine whether amendment or revision is required or whether it should be considered for conversion to a formal British Standard. A wide range of PAS documents are available from the BSI Shop, many as instant downloads and some free of charge. PAS 91 provides a set of questions for buyers to ask potential suppliers to enable prequalification for construction-related procurement. The BSI developed PAS 91 to specify the nature, content and format of a set of questions designed to test compliance with the core criteria essential for prequalification for construction tendering and to establish uniform requirements for their application and use. PAS 91 also specifies requirements for the consistent use of those questions, irrespective of the size or nature of the contract. It is intended that the questions are also used by assessment providers in their intermediary role between buyers and suppliers.

It is widely recognised that excessive prequalification activity adds unacceptable cost, bureaucracy and confusion to the construction supply chain. Unnecessary bureaucracy associated with prequalification diverts both buyers' and suppliers' resources and attention away from proportionate and effective risk management. Buyers and assessment providers should only require suppliers to provide the minimum paperwork necessary to demonstrate that the suppliers can provide a satisfactory response to the questions in the PAS 91 modules.

PAS 91 provides construction sector stakeholders with prequalification questions (PQQs), common questions relevant to construction-related procurement, which increase the scope for recognition between various types of PQQ activity, helping to significantly reduce duplication, unnecessary paperwork and cost for both buyers and suppliers. The document sets out the nature, content and format of a set of questions on core criteria essential to prequalification for construction tendering. In addition to setting out questions (the responses to which will be used to assess supplier suitability), the specification includes requirements for the selection, presentation and application of core criteria in a transparent and equitable manner.

To be eligible for prequalification it is necessary that suppliers demonstrate that they possess or have access to the governance, qualifications and references, expertise, competence, and health and safety/environmental/financial and other essential capabilities necessary for them to undertake work and deliver services for potential buyers. These 'areas of capability' are represented in the core question modules.

PAS 91 can be download free from the BSI Shop:
http://shop.bsigroup.com

Supplementary Material

0/SM1: Practice statement

Architects intending to approach, or who are being approached by, new clients need to have information about their practice ready to hand. General information might be immediately accessible from a practice brochure, or from entries in the RIBA Directory of Practices. In some cases where the practice has a quality management system, the quality manual will contain much relevant information and could be issued to the client. Detailed information required in the context of a particular project might need to be specially assembled. Some client bodies may require all this information in a specific format, but nearly all will expect information to be included about the following:

- practice name, addresses, telephone, fax, email
- status of practice: whether sole principal, partnership, company, etc.
- directors or partners: names, CVs, photos
- practice quality management systems, QA status
- practice health and safety policy
- practice environmental policy
- specialist skills in-house
- practice computer systems
- PI insurance arrangements (subject to insurer's agreement)
- building type experience
- recent commissions: details, illustrations, contact names
- overseas experience and completed commissions, if relevant
- languages in which the practice is fluent, if relevant
- consultants with whom the practice normally collaborates
- team being offered for the particular commission, with brief CVs
- membership of competence schemes under Safety Schemes in Procurement (SSIP), such as the Contractors Health and Safety Assessment Scheme (CHAS).

Refer to the *Architect's Handbook of Practice Management* (2010), Chapter 5 'Marketing and Business Development' for further guidance.

0/SM2: Selection process

The appointment of an architect may be handled directly by the client or indirectly through a project manager acting on the client's behalf. It could be for the full traditional services where the architect is project lead, including Building Contract administration, or for a limited appointment where the architect might be engaged as lead designer or simply to take on a design concept role. Regardless of the nature of the appointment or the procurement method adopted, the selection of an architect is likely to follow one of the following recognised procedures.

One-to-one negotiation

The architect is chosen on the basis of personal contact or recommendation, perhaps through interview. This procedure includes the following features:

- It is suitable for any project.
- It is particularly suitable where services required are not yet formulated or the project scope is unclear.
- The client can have the opportunity of professional help in preparing the Strategic Brief.
- Negotiations over services, terms and fees can be carried out using a standard schedule of services as a focus for discussion.

Competitive interview

The architect is chosen primarily on the basis of a presentation in some stipulated form. The main features include:

- The procedure is suitable for projects of any size.
- A limited number of architects are invited to make presentations.
- The architect can expect the client to supply a broad outline of the project and to state exactly what the presentation should cover.
- The presentation can be in written form only, or involve an interview, as stipulated by the client in the invitation. Any design content will not normally extend beyond broad concepts.
- After the presentation, the preferred firm can negotiate services and fees, etc.

Qualifications-based selection

The architect is chosen primarily on the basis of quality, by which is meant technical qualifications, design and performance potential and general suitability for the project in question. Refer to the RIBA publication *Guidance for Clients on Quality Based Selection* (1999). The guidance includes quality assessment forms and score sheets that can be used in the selection process.

After appropriate advertisement an initial list of firms is compiled from which a few are shortlisted for invitation for interview and discussion. The shortlisted firms are then ranked in order of preference. There is no mention of fees until the preferred firm is selected. If it proves impossible to agree a 'fair and reasonable' fee, negotiations with that firm are irrevocably terminated and fresh negotiations begin with the next preferred firm.

Quality/price selection

This system is similar to the above method but involves balancing quality and price at the outset. A ratio is agreed depending on the nature of the project, and indicative ratios are given as follows:

Type of process	Quality/price ratio
Feasibility studies and investigation	85/15
Innovative projects	80/20
Complex projects	70/30
Straightforward projects	50/50
Repeat projects	20/80

Quality criteria are then set out and weighted. (Note: If EC directives apply these will affect how this should be done.) Submitted tenders are then assessed for quality by marking each of the quality criteria and summing the marks using the agreed weightings to give a total quality score. Candidates meeting an agreed threshold are then interviewed and their quality scores adjusted. Their fees are then examined; the lowest is given a score of 100 and the others score 100 minus the percentage their fee is above the lowest fee. The final quality/price assessment is achieved by multiplying the quality and price scores by the quality/price ratio and adding them together to give a total score out of 100. The highest scoring candidate is awarded the contract.

Fee tender (without design)

The architect is chosen solely on the basis of the fee quoted; that is, the procedure is geared to the competitiveness of the fee.

- Unlikely to be suitable for more complex projects, and those under £500,000 capital value.
- A limited number of firms (say five or six) who accept invitations are sent tender documents. All must receive identical information.
- The information should state precisely which services are required and include an initial brief for the project.
- The tender may comprise a fee quotation and a resources schedule or other specified information.

- After receipt of satisfactory tenders, the client can be expected to enter into an agreement. There is little scope for negotiation; architects are required to act fairly and honestly with potential clients and competitors [Undertaking 3.4 of the RIBA Code of Professional Conduct].

Fee tender (without design) using the Two Envelope System

The architect is chosen both on the basis of technical qualifications and on a fee quoted. Each is considered separately.

- Unlikely to be suitable for projects of less than £500,000 capital value.
- A limited number of firms (say five or six) who accept invitations are sent tender documents. All must receive identical information.
- The information should state precisely which services are required and include an initial brief for the project.
- The criteria to be used when evaluating the tenders should be stated.
- Two envelopes will normally be provided for tender submissions, clearly marked:
  (1) 'Qualifications' (the technical submission)
  (2) 'Fee' (the tender and quoted figure in a form stipulated by the client).

The qualifications envelopes are opened first and the firms placed in order of preference. Then the fee envelope from the preferred tenderer (only) is opened in the presence of that firm. Negotiation might subsequently be needed to arrive at a fair and reasonable figure. The second envelopes of the other firms should remain sealed and be returned to those firms if negotiations with the preferred firm are successful. Undertaking 3.4 of the RIBA Code of Professional Conduct must be observed. Only in the event of failure to reach a satisfactory outcome should the fee envelope of the next preferred tenderer be opened.

Design submission with fee proposal

The architect is chosen both on the basis of a design submission and on a fee quoted. Each is considered separately under the Two Envelope System as described above.

- Suitable for larger projects (e.g. over £1 million).
- A limited number of firms (say three) who accept invitations are sent tender documents. All must receive full and identical information.
- The information should state precisely which services are required and include an initial brief for the project.
- Clients should expect to pay a fee to all tenderers who submit detailed design ideas, and this will usually restrict the number of invitations. Architects taking part in such an arrangement would be wise to secure a formal agreement with the client to this effect.

- Two envelopes will normally be provided for tender submissions, clearly marked:
  (1) 'Design Proposals'
  (2) 'Fee Tender'.

The design proposals envelopes from each of the tenderers are opened first and the firms placed in order of preference. Then the fee envelope from the preferred tenderer (only) is opened. Negotiation might subsequently be needed to arrive at a fair and reasonable figure. The second envelopes of the other firms should remain sealed and be returned to those firms if negotiations with the preferred firm are successful. Undertaking 3.4 of the RIBA Code of Professional Conduct must be observed. Only in the event of failure to reach a satisfactory outcome should the fee envelope of the next preferred tenderer be opened.

Design ideas competition

The architect is chosen solely on the basis of design ideas. The procedure does not involve fee tenders, since the fee is stated in the competition conditions.

- Suitable, in theory, for important projects regardless of size. In practice, application is likely to be restricted by the relatively high cost to both client and architect.
- The architect can expect the client to provide a project brief, to define the professional services required, and to appoint a panel of assessors. This requires professional input on the part of the client.
- Competition may be restricted to invited participants, and architects taking part in such an arrangement can expect to be paid a fee. A formal agreement with the client to that effect is advisable.
- Competition may be open, but there is obviously a high cost risk for architects who participate.

Competitions are best run according to the procedures detailed in the RIBA's *Design Competitions: Guidance for Clients*. Undertaking 3.4 of the RIBA Code of Professional Conduct prohibits architects from entering competitions which the RIBA has declared to be unacceptable. Guidance on architects' fees may be found in the RIBA publication *A Client's Guide to Engaging an Architect* (2013).

Credentials submission followed by a one-day design ideas competition

A number of practices (say ten) are asked to submit credentials on the basis of an outline brief for the proposed project. For ease of comparison the credentials are to be set out in a specific, predetermined format (e.g. ten sides of A4, including images) and with specific information (profile of the practice, relevant projects, brief CVs of intended team, etc.). Three of the practices are shortlisted and take part in a one-day design competition. This is held at the client's office, or at another suitable location with sufficient space and facilities. No preparation is required, or perhaps allowed.

On the day of the competition, the representatives of each practice (perhaps two or three people) – who will be the ones to deliver the project – are given a briefing by the client and the client's agents. Each practice is briefed individually, one after the other. They are then sent to separate rooms and given a period of time, say three to four hours, to prepare sketch designs and presentation material, following which they present their schemes. The commission is given to the practice that best meets the criteria set out in the briefing.

Fees are negotiated subsequently.

The advantages of this method include giving the client the opportunity to meet the individuals who will be developing the design and managing the project, observe them working under pressure (often a requirement in a commercial environment) and see how they are able to assimilate ideas and communicate them clearly and to keep the amount of time taken by all to a minimum while thoroughly addressing the process. It can also be an enjoyable and insightful process for all involved!

This method will work best where quality is ranked very much higher than cost and can be beneficial where the scope of the project is only loosely determined and needs further definition.

0/SM3: Outline of possible roles for the architect

Some of the more common roles for the architect are described below, with a brief summary of the likely duties under such a role. The detailed duties will be as set out in the appointment documents, and the RIBA Plan of Work 2013 can be used as a model when discussing the services to be provided.

A standard appointing document should preferably be used but this should never be sent 'cold' to a client. It should first form a focus for discussion on the professional services that need to be commissioned, and only then be completed as a formal confirmation of what has been agreed.

If a preliminary appointment is needed pending formal agreement about the full services to be provided, a letter can be used incorporating the appropriate references. A letter activating appointment for specific stages can often be used in conjunction with a formal appointing document. A variation in services already formally agreed, or additional services to be provided, can often be imported by a letter supplementing the original document. It is important to be meticulous over such matters, however, and to take legal advice where appropriate.

Appointment of architect as lead designer or project lead

The architect will normally act as lead designer and as such is responsible for coordinating and integrating the work of other design consultants and specialists. Although design management has emerged as a separate skill, and design managers are present as independently appointed consultants on some larger projects (or work as part of the contractor's team), the management and coordination of design information from all sources throughout the process should, in general, be regarded as a key component of the architect's role.

In the traditional or conventional appointment, and particularly on smaller projects, the architect will combine this role with that of project lead, including contract administration. On larger projects, the architect's commission is increasingly being confined to certain stages of the RIBA Plan of Work, or designated activities not necessarily to a Plan of Work format. Sometimes, particularly in construction management procurement arrangements, the role will be that of lead designer working under a project manager who is the first point of contact for the client and may take on the role of contract administrator. Sometimes the appointment will be for full services, but moving stage by stage. With arrangements where a more flexible approach to appointment is necessary, particular care is needed.

Typical duties

Typical duties of an architect acting as lead designer might include:

- directing the design process
- consulting the client about significant design issues
- informing the client of duties under the CDM Regulations
- investigating the feasibility of the requirements, and reporting
- advising the client about any limitations on the use of land or buildings
- preparing outline proposals, a scheme design, detail design drawings, etc.
- advising on the need for statutory and other consents, and preparing sufficient information for applications to be made
- preparing sufficient Technical Design to allow consultants and specialists to develop their proposals, coordinating these and integrating them into the overall scheme
- bringing contract documentation to a final state for inviting tenders.

If the architect is also project lead and contract administrator, the following might be added:

- advising on the need for and appointment of other consultants
- coordinating the work of other consultants
- advising on methods of procurement, and on tendering and the appointment of the main contractor
- administering the terms of the Building Contract and inspecting the performance of the contractor as necessary
- issuing further reasonably necessary information, issuing empowered instructions, and acting as certifier as the Building Contract requires, including issue of the final certificate
- arranging for the preparation of record information and manuals.

Appointment of architect as Client Adviser

Refer to 0.1 Core Objectives for details of the role of RIBA Client Advisers.

Appointment of architect as consultant in design and build

A majority of design and build contracts involve an architect. This role differs quite markedly from that in the traditional commission, in that the architect acts solely as a consultant to either an employer client or a contractor client at any one time. It is not uncommon for the architect to be engaged by both, but this would be sequential, never simultaneous, and would entail consultant switch or 'novation'. Even under this kind of arrangement it is often extremely difficult to separate clearly legal accountability and design responsibility. The degree of involvement with either the employer client or the contractor client will vary depending on the particular arrangements but the architect has no stated function in connection with the Building Contract.

Typical duties – employer client

Typical duties of an architect appointed as consultant to an employer client might include:

- advising on the initial brief
- informing the employer client of duties under the CDM Regulations
- carrying out a Site Appraisal
- advising on the appointment of other consultants
- advising on and taking part in discussions with statutory and other bodies
- preparing outline proposals and making application for outline planning permission
- advising on development of the brief for the Employer's Requirements
- developing design concept drawings as appropriate for the Employer's Requirements
- advising on tendering procedures
- advising on contract matters
- examining the Contractor's Proposals, including design and the contract sum analysis, and offering advice
- acting as the Employer's Agent under the Building Contract during the construction of the works
- visiting the site during construction and reporting back to the employer client
- advising the employer client on their obligations under the Building Contract and assisting in the drafting of statements
- inspecting the works on behalf of the employer client prior to Practical Completion and offering advice
- checking the contractor's as-built drawings and the operating and maintenance manuals
- advising the employer client on the Employer's Final Account and Employer's Final Statement as appropriate.

Typical duties – contractor client

Typical duties of an architect appointed as consultant to a contractor client might include:

- examining the Employer's Requirements and all available information, and discussing a strategy for tendering
- visiting the site and noting all relevant constraints
- checking arrangements for compliance with the CDM Regulations

- advising on the appointment of other consultants
- checking with authorities on statutory consents obtained and required
- advising on the need for specialist subcontractors
- fulfilling the role of lead designer
- providing the contractor client with sketches, specification notes, etc. for initial tendering purposes
- advising about limitations or inconsistencies in the Employer's Requirements
- providing the contractor client with drawings, specifications, samples, etc. to support the Contractor's Proposals
- after the Building Contract has been awarded, developing and amending drawings and other documents in the Contractor's Proposals for contract documentation
- developing design details
- applying for statutory and other necessary approvals
- preparing performance specifications and other detailed information for subcontractor tendering
- preparing Technical Design drawings, details, schedules and specification notes for the contractor client
- inspecting work during construction and reporting to the contractor client
- preparing additional drawings, etc. as necessary for submission to the employer in the event of change orders
- visiting manufacturers' workshops/factories as necessary and reporting to the contractor client
- assisting in the preparation of 'As-constructed' Information, operating and maintenance manuals, etc.
- inspecting the works prior to Practical Completion and advising the contractor client.

Appointment of architect as project manager

The project manager is the individual or firm primarily employed to look after the client's interests throughout the stages of a project in collaboration with the design team, including the cost consultant, and may be the project lead. The project manager's remit can be very wide, ranging from initially managing the brief through to managing the marketing or disposal of the completed project.

The project manager is usually responsible for the overall direction of the design team, specialists, contractor and subcontractors. Administering the Building Contract might be undertaken by the project manager or by a contract administrator working in close collaboration. The project manager's duties will vary considerably according to the nature of the project and the wording of the Building Contract. The appointment of a project manager might be appropriate in traditional procurement, design and build, or for a management contract.

The role of project manager, for which some architects might well have the skills and aptitude, should be seen as separate and distinct from the architect's traditional role. It should not be confused with what many architects think of simply as managing the project.

Typical duties

Typical duties of an independent project manager might include:

- assisting in the preparation and development of the brief
- informing the client of duties under the CDM Regulations
- arranging for feasibility studies and reports
- arranging for measures required by health and safety legislation
- preparing the project management structure and plan
- advising on the procurement method
- arranging the appointment of consultants and specialists
- checking PI insurances, warranties, etc.
- instructing consultants on feasibility studies, research, surveys
- coordinating the design process
- preparing and maintaining an overall cost plan
- organising communication and information systems
- arranging consultations/negotiations with statutory bodies
- arranging monthly reports to the client on cost and completion forecasts
- monitoring the performance, etc. of the consultant team
- arranging tender documentation
- organising prequalification checks on contractors
- evaluating tenders and preparing recommendations
- participating in the selection and appointment of the contractor
- arranging for the appointment of a construction supervisor/client's agent
- assembling contract documentation
- arranging for the appointment of an adjudicator and services as required
- issuing instructions and variation orders
- issuing extension of time notices
- preparing valuations and monitoring the budget
- arranging commissioning and witness tests
- developing a maintenance programme and staff training
- organising handover/occupation procedures
- issuing the Practical Completion certificate and preparing the final account
- organising maintenance manuals and 'As-constructed' Information
- planning facilities management
- advising on the marketing/disposal of the project
- checking that defects are remedied and issuing the final certificate.

The employment of an independent project manager who is not the architect is common on larger projects. In these cases it is important that the delineation of responsibilities between the architect and the project manager is very clear, both as it is documented in their respective contracts of appointment and as it is understood and practiced in day-to-day working relationships.

Appointment of architect as construction manager

The construction manager is the individual or organisation employed primarily to manage the construction stages of the project in collaboration with the consultant team, including the cost consultant. The appointee will be a specialist with contracting experience, paid by fee, and should preferably be appointed early (at the same time as the consultant team) so they can participate in initial discussions. However, in practice the construction manager is often not brought in until the pre-construction stages are well advanced. Construction of the project is carried out by trades contractors, each having a direct contract with the employer but working under the direction of the construction manager. Alternatively, the construction manager may enter into a management contract with the employer, and each trade contractor will then enter into a separate 'Works' contract with the construction manager. If the architect is to undertake this role, they would usually set up a company specifically for this purpose.

Services that can be provided by a construction manager are held by some people to include helping to establish the client's requirements at pre-construction stages. A construction manager may certainly make a positive contribution at project design stage, but duties will vary considerably according to the nature of the project, the timing of the appointment and the wording of the Building Contract.

Typical duties

Typical duties of a construction manager might include:

- arranging for meetings at design stages between client, consultant team and proposed trades contractors who will have a design responsibility
- recommending the most economical materials and methods to meet the requirements of specification and sound construction practice
- commenting on project drawings and project specification as appropriate, and advising on Technical Design for issue by trades contractors
- advising the design team on the division of the project into trades contracts
- advising on the need for works at pre-construction stages, e.g. exploratory, mock-ups, tests of particular components, etc.
- arranging as appropriate for checks of the outline cost plan, the preparation of a project cost plan and cash flow forecasts

0

- advising on measures necessary to satisfy statutory obligations, liaising with local and statutory authorities about construction and onsite matters, and monitoring compliance by trades contractors
- preparing a Project Programme showing lead times for trades contracts
- preparing detailed week-by-week programmes, and expanding and updating these during the progress of the works
- advising the client on insurances to be taken out in respect of the project
- preparing a schedule of tender events showing earliest start and anticipated finishing dates for all trades contracts
- preparing, in consultation with the design team, a suitable tender list of trades contractors, checking references and resource capability
- advising on tender procedures and participating in interviews, together with the client and design team as appropriate
- evaluating tenders and preparing recommendations
- advising the client on materials or plant to be ordered prior to placing trades contracts
- arranging for adequate information for setting out, and coordinating this as necessary
- issuing empowered instructions to trades contractors
- receiving, reviewing and coordinating information, shop drawings, etc. from trades contractors in consultation with the design team
- providing management, administration and planning of trades contracts operations; monitoring methods, progress and quality
- coordinating trades contracts operations in line with the project plan
- arranging regular meetings with trades contractors to monitor progress and ascertain information requirements; chairing regular site meetings, issuing minutes and providing the client with monthly reports
- preparing valuations and dealing with applications for payment from trades contractors
- preparing interim and final accounts for each trade contractor
- issuing certificates as required by the Building Contract, including at practical completion, in consultation with the design team
- arranging for commissioning and testing
- checking that defects are remedied
- obtaining from each trade contractor relevant records, as-built drawings and operating and maintenance manuals.

Acting in the role of the construction manager is unlikely to interest the majority of architects directly, as they will only rarely have the necessary experience, skills and aptitude, at least as far as projects of any size are concerned. Architects involved in this kind of procurement method are more likely to be acting as designer or lead designer under the direction of the construction manager.

However, architects sometimes find themselves handling smaller projects where there is no main contractor and the work is carried out by direct labour, sometimes volunteers, or through a series of separate trades contracts. If asked to organise such operations the architect might be acting as the construction manager, with all the attendant responsibilities for setting up the site, programming and coordination. This situation is not covered by standard appointing documents, and it would be well to check with insurers before undertaking to provide this kind of consultancy service. An appropriately drafted agreement would be needed.

Appointment of architect as CDM coordinator

Under the Construction (Design and Management) Regulations 2007 the client in most jobs will be under a statutory duty to appoint a CDM coordinator and a principal contractor.

Architects might wish to consider appointment as a CDM coordinator either on a job where they are also acting as the architect or one where architectural services are provided by others. In all cases an appointment as CDM coordinator should be seen as distinct from the provision of architectural services and the RIBA publishes a suitable form of appointment.

The CDM coordinator will need a sound knowledge of design and construction processes and practice and of health and safety matters relevant to the particular project and, as with the other duty holders, will need to provide evidence of their competence. The appointment is to be made as soon as is practicable after the client has sufficient information about the project to be able to assess the appointee's competence and adequacy of resources for health and safety.

Typical duties

The duties of a CDM coordinator, as set out in the Approved Code of Practice issued by the Health and Safety Executive (HSE), are:

- advising and assisting the client with their duties
- notifying the HSE
- coordinating health and safety aspects of design work and cooperating with others involved with the project
- facilitating good communication between client, designers and contractors
- liaising with the principal contractor regarding ongoing design
- identifying, collecting and passing on pre-construction information
- preparing/updating the Health and Safety File.

To this list could be added:

- advising the client on the competence and resources of designers as relevant to health and safety obligations
- ensuring so far as is reasonably possible that potential hazards are identified, eliminated or reduced at design stages
- ensuring that all design team members and others contributing to the design (e.g. specialists/subcontractors) cooperate over health and safety obligations
- attending pre-tender meetings with invited principal contractors to check adequacy of resources for health and safety obligations, and written health and safety policy statements
- advising the client on the competence and resources of contractors relevant to health and safety obligations
- checking that the principal contractor is provided with reasonably necessary health and safety information before construction commences
- appraising the principal contractor's initial construction phase health and safety plan and advising the client
- monitoring the principal contractor's development of, or changes to, the Construction Phase Plan following variations or additional work, and advising the client as necessary
- observing the principal contractor's compliance with the Construction Phase Plan during construction of the works, and advising the client if there are departures
- obtaining necessary information for the Health and Safety File during the design and construction stages
- advising the client on the safe keeping of the Health and Safety File and its future use.

The role of CDM coordinator is one which on major projects might be undertaken by an independently appointed architect who has undergone the necessary training. On simpler projects the architect as project lead might be well placed to take on the additional but separate role of CDM coordinator. However, this is a statutory appointment and the services to be provided need to be fully and precisely indicated. Any architect accepting such an appointment will need to understand fully the implications, be properly trained and have appropriate indemnity cover. It is a function which could attract considerable liability in the event of injury to persons, or losses to clients should the works be delayed because of incidents or intervention by the HSE.

Architects should remember that even where a minor or domestic job is not notifiable to the HSE and there is no CDM coordinator, the requirements on the designer under the CDM Regulations will still apply.

Refer to the HSE publication *Managing Health and Safety in Construction: Construction (Design and Management) Regulations 2007. Approved Code of Practice*, which is available to download free from the HSE website: www.hse.gov.uk.

Appointment of architect as party wall surveyor

Under the RIBA Forms of Appointment the architect may undertake various duties in respect of party wall matters. These are described in *The Party Wall etc. Act 1996: Explanatory Booklet* (available from: www.planningportal.gov.uk). The need for a party wall surveyor will only arise in the event of a dispute with an adjoining owner. If the architect is to act as the party wall surveyor, this should always be via a separate appointment.

NOTE

Item 8 of the RIBA Standard Agreement 2010 (2012 revision) services schedule provides for services in connection with party wall matters but this differs from the role of the party wall surveyor. While the owner is excluded from acting as a party wall surveyor, any other person including the architect may act in this role, as far as such a professional takes on the cloak of impartiality on appointment.

The party wall surveyor is a statutory appointment and the duties are as described or implied by the Act. In particular, the surveyor must uphold the rights and obligations of both parties, rather than serve the interests of the client alone.

The RIBA Standard Forms of Appointment are not suitable without significant modification. In addition to the quasi-arbitral nature of the role, some of the Act's specific requirements would conflict with the standard terms of appointment. For example, under the Act the appointment cannot be rescinded by the building owner, whereas the RIBA forms provide for termination. It is therefore preferable for the appointment to be by a specially drafted letter or document.

0/SM4: The briefing process

Compiling the brief and developing the design are activities which interact. Briefing is really a continuous process through to Stage 2 Concept Design, but for convenience it can be regarded as evolving through three distinct phases. The Strategic Brief is the starting point, and it should never be forgotten that the client is at the core of the process. An inexperienced client, perhaps on a smaller size project, might welcome the assistance of the architect in preparing the Strategic Brief.

The briefing process must be appropriate to the nature of the project. Some projects might depend upon planning and space standards which have already been widely researched and are generally available. Other projects might require considerable original investigation and extensive design studies. Such factors are likely to influence both the cost and duration of the design process, and the development of the brief.

The Strategic Brief

The Strategic Brief should set out the objectives which the client wishes to achieve in the project and will probably refer to functional requirements, environmental standards, levels of quality, lifespan and maintenance.

It may be anything from a broad preliminary statement of interest to a comprehensive set of technical requirements. It will rarely be sufficiently clear or detailed for design work but it should be seen as the basis for Feasibility Studies. The Strategic Brief should:

- state clearly the client's mission and objectives
- set out the client's needs
- indicate the impact of not meeting the needs
- identify the triggers for change
- place the client's needs in a historic context, e.g. a pattern of growth and change
- state what is expected in response to this statement
- state the sort of decisions needed and from whom.

Considerable further investigation and development work will be necessary to bring the Strategic Brief to the level of an Initial Project Brief by the end of Stage 1. However, it should be seen as an important part of developing the brief, and as such should be a formalised document to be agreed with the client.

The Initial Project Brief

The Initial Project Brief should be a document which covers the technical, managerial and design intentions, and shows how these requirements are to be met. It is likely to be the result of research and development involving all the design team, with additional expertise and advice from commissioned specialists. It will be the outcome of activities such as:

- feasibility studies
- site or building survey and studies
- research into functional needs
- accessibility audits
- environmental impact considerations
- statutory constraints
- cost appraisal studies.

It may include:

- the mission statement
- the context
- organisational structure and function
- overall scope and purpose of the project
- programme, including phasing
- statements on size and capacity requirements and functions to be accommodated
- global capital expenditure budget and cash flow constraints
- targets and constraints on operating expenditure and other whole-life costs
- internal and external environmental requirements
- technology to be incorporated or accommodated, including equipment, services and IT
- quality requirements for design, materials, construction and long-term maintenance
- what is expected in response to the brief
- how the success of the project will be measured
- statutory requirements.

A detailed checklist for the Initial Project Brief is given in 1/SM1.

The Initial Project Brief should be seen as a starting point for the development of the Final Project Brief and should be formalised by the end of Stage 1.

The Final Project Brief

The Final Project Brief should further define all design requirements. It should be prepared by the architect in collaboration with the client, and with coordinated contributions from all consultants and specialists, and the CDM coordinator. Development of this Final Project Brief will probably require:

- assembly of all relevant information
- design studies and investigations
- preparation of detailed design proposals
- preparation of a cost plan.

The Final Project Brief is the foundation on which the design will develop, and serves as a yardstick against which further design development can be measured. As such it is a factual record and a document of importance.

The Final Project Brief is the last stage in the briefing process. It can be equated with the end of Stage 2 and will be the basis for further detailed design work.

The Construction Industry Board report *Briefing the Team: A Guide to Better Briefing for Clients* states that the final brief should cover:

- the aim of the design, including prioritised Project Objectives
- the site, including details of accessibility and planning
- the functions and activities of the client
- the structure of the client organisation
- the size and configuration of the facilities
- options for environmental delivery and control
- servicing options and specification implications, e.g. security, deliveries, access, workplace
- outline specifications of general and specific areas
- a budget for all elements
- the procurement process
- environmental policy, including energy
- the Project Execution Plan
- key targets for quality, time and cost, including milestones for decisions
- a method for assessing and managing risks and validating design proposals.

A detailed checklist for the Final Project Brief is given in 2/SM3.

The Final Project Brief should be signed off by the client after approval. Any subsequent changes to the signed off Final Project Brief should be recorded, identifying their impact on the project and architect's services, and formally agreed with the client.

The steps outlined above are likely to be found in most projects of reasonable substance or complexity.

The briefing process is something that should always be developed systematically. It provides the framework within which the design can be developed and it is an indispensable part of quality management. However, on projects of a more domestic scale the design and briefing processes may be compressed. Nevertheless, sufficient time should be allowed for this work to be done thoroughly, and architects should resist jumping to quick design solutions which might not meet the client's requirements.

The process of brief development is iterative, and it should be accepted that clients sometimes wish to modify their requirements even after approval of the Final Project Brief. Major changes could lead to the abandoning of design work already completed, or could at least have a significant effect upon cost, time and statutory consents. It is therefore essential to have an identifiable approved Final Project Brief to start with, and to have Change Control Procedures as part of the quality management plan. This will enable the client to be aware of the implications of changes to the Final Project Brief before final instructions are given.

Refer to Figure 3/1 Specimen design change notice and record.

0/SM5 RIBA Agreements

The RIBA suite of Agreements has been updated to reflect the RIBA Plan of Work 2013. The suite comprises:

- Standard Agreement
- Concise Agreement
- Domestic Project Agreement
- Sub-consultant Agreement.

The Agreements are available in both paper and electronic versions and are accompanied by *Guide to RIBA Agreements 2010 (2012 revision)* and other supplementary documents.

Each Agreement comprises the selected Conditions of Appointment (Standard, Concise, Domestic, Sub-consultant), related components, a schedule or schedules of services and notes on use and completion and model letters for business and domestic clients. Selection of the appropriate agreement will depend on the complexity of the project and the risks for each party.

There are Architect and Consultant versions of the Standard, Concise and Domestic Project Agreements. Consultant versions are suitable for any profession as standalone agreements or as companion agreements to the architect versions. They are particularly suitable for multidisciplinary consultant teams to ensure that all the consultants are on the same contract terms.

For very small projects, under £100,000 in value, the use of an appropriate letter contract may sometimes be a suitable alternative to a standard appointment agreement, but great care is needed to ensure that all the essential elements of an appointment agreement are covered. The RIBA publishes *A Guide to Letter Contracts for Very Small Projects, Surveys and Reports* (2012), which provides model letters and guidance on their use. The professional codes of conduct of the ARB and the RIBA both require that a written appointment agreement is in place before any work is commenced on the provision of services.

Standard Agreement

The Standard Agreement 2010 (2012 revision) is suitable:

- for a commission where detailed contract terms are necessary
- for a wide range of projects and most procurement methods
- where the client is acting for business or commercial purposes
- where the commission is for work to the client's home where the size or value of the project merits its use. This would be appropriate where the Building Contract has been negotiated with the client as a 'consumer' (a consumer

is a natural person acting for purposes outside his or her trade, business or profession).

A Standard Agreement will comprise:

- the Standard Conditions of Appointment
- Standard Agreement 2012: Schedules (2012 revision – RIBA Plan of Work 2013 compatible version), which include Project Data, Role Specifications, Design and Other Services and Fees and Expenses
- a formal memorandum of agreement or a letter of appointment
- other schedules which may be used to replace or supplement those in Schedules (RIBA Plan of Work 2013 compatible version).

For further advice refer to *Guide to RIBA Agreements 2010 (2012 revision)*.

Concise Agreement

A Concise Agreement (2012 revision) is a suitable basis:

- for a commission where the concise contract terms are compatible with the complexity of the project and the risks to each party
- where the client is acting for business or commercial purposes.

A Concise Agreement will comprise:

- the Concise Conditions of Appointment
- Small Project Services Schedule 2010 (2012 revision – RIBA Plan of Work 2013 compatible version)
- Fees and Expenses Schedule 2010 (2012 revision)
- Concise Agreement 2010: Notes: Part 1 Use and Completion; Part 2 Model Letter (2012 revision).

For further advice refer to *Guide to RIBA Agreements 2010 (2012 revision)*.

Domestic Project Agreement

A Domestic Project Agreement is a suitable basis where:

- the commission relates to work to the client's home, provided that the client has elected to use these conditions in their own name, i.e. not as a limited company or other legal entity
- the contract terms are compatible with the complexity of the project and the risks to each party and have been negotiated with the client as a consumer.

A Domestic Project Agreement will comprise:

- the Domestic Project Conditions of Appointment
- Small Project Services Schedule 2010 (2012 revision)
- Fees and Expenses Schedule 2010 (2012 revision)
- Domestic Project Agreement 2010: Notes: Part 1 Use and Completion; Part 2 Model Letter (2012 revision).

For further advice refer to *Guide to RIBA Agreements 2010 (2012 revision)*.

Sub-consultant Agreement

A Sub-consultant Agreement is a suitable basis where:

- a consultant wishes or perhaps is required by the client to appoint another consultant (thus, a sub-consultant) to perform part of the consultant's services, and
- the contract terms are compatible with the (head) agreement between the consultant and the client, with the complexity of the project and the risks to each party.

The agreement is not for use where the client appoints consultants or specialists directly.

The appointment of a sub-consultant may arise where the first consultant is unable, for whatever reason, to perform part of the services under the head agreement with the client, or where the client has appointed the consultant as the sole consultant responsible for the whole of the design and management process – a 'one stop shop'.

A Sub-consultant Agreement will comprise:

- the Sub-consultant Conditions of Appointment
- Sub-consultant Agreement 2010: Notes: Part 1 Use and Completion; Part 2 Model Letter (2012 revision)
- Fees and Expenses Schedule 2010 (2012 revision).

For further advice refer to *Guide to RIBA Agreements 2010 (2012 revision)*.

Electronic and print formats

All the RIBA Agreements 2010 (2012 revision) and their components are available as electronic files for downloading at: www.ribabookshops.com/agreements, together with a range of additional schedules, guides and supplements that are not available in print.

There is a series of other components that supplement or replace core components provided with each agreement:

- Access Consultancy Services Schedule (2012 revision)
- Contractor's Design Services Schedule (2012 revision)
- Contractor's Design Services Schedule: Notes: Parts 1–4 (2012 revision)
- Initial Occupation and Post-occupation Evaluation Services Schedule (2012 revision)
- Multi-disciplinary Design Services Schedule (2012 revision)
- Master Planning Services Schedule (2012 revision)
- Historic Building or Conservation Project Services Schedule (2012 revision)
- Small Historic Building or Conservation Project Services Schedule (2012 revision).

There is a series of Supplementary Agreements:

- Draft Third Party Rights Schedule (2012 revision)
- Draft Warranty by a Sub-consultant (2012 revision)
- Public Authority Supplement (2012 revision).

A series of electronic guides is also available:

- *A Guide to Access Consultancy Services*
- *A Guide to Initial Occupation and Post-occupation Evaluation Services*
- *A Guide to Working with an Architect: Repair and Alteration of Historic Buildings*
- *A Guide to Working with and Architect: Repair and Alteration of Places of Worship.*

Table 0/1:

RIBA Agreements 2010 (2012 revision) – electronic components and their printed equivalents

ELECTRONIC *Only available at www.ribabookshops.com/agreements*	PRINTED equivalent
Conditions and guides are supplied as locked PDFs. *Other components, eg Notes, Schedules and Model Letters, are supplied in Rich Text Format (RTF), which can be customised using most commonly used word-processing software, such as MS Word, to meet project requirements or modified to match the house style of the practice.*	
Standard Agreement 2010 (2012 revision) – Architect	
Two selections online	*One pack comprising five separate printed documents*

• Standard Conditions of Appointment for an Architect 2010 (2012 revision)
• Core component bundle:
  – Memorandum of Agreement for the Appointment of an Architect (2012 revision)
  – Standard Agreement 2010: Schedules (2012 revision – RIBA Plan of Work 2013 compatible version): Project Data; Services; Fees and Expenses
  – Standard Agreement 2010: Notes: Part 1 Use and Completion; Part 2 Model Letter (2012 revision)
	• Standard Conditions of Appointment for an Architect 2010 (2012 revision)
	• Memorandum of Agreement for the Appointment of an Architect (2012 revision)
	• Standard Agreement 2010: Schedules (2012 revision – RIBA Plan of Work 2013 compatible version): Project Data; Services; Fees and Expenses
	• Standard Agreement 2010: Notes: Part 1 Use and Completion; Part 2 Model Letter (2012 revision)
	• Changes since 2010 Edition

Standard Agreement 2010 (2012 revision) – Consultant	
Two selections online	*One pack comprising five separate printed documents*

• Standard Conditions of Appointment for a Consultant 2010 (2012 revision)
• Core component bundle:
  – Memorandum of Agreement for the Appointment of a Consultant (2012 revision)
  – Standard Agreement 2010: Schedules (2012 revision – RIBA Plan of Work 2013 compatible version): Project Data; Services; Fees and Expenses
  – Standard Agreement 2010: Notes: Part 1 Use and Completion; Part 2 Model Letter (2012 revision)
	• Standard Conditions of Appointment for a Consultant 2010 (2012 revision)
	• Memorandum of Agreement for the Appointment of a Consultant (2012 revision)
	• Standard Agreement 2010: Schedules (2012 revision – RIBA Plan of Work 2013 compatible version): Project Data; Services; Fees and Expenses
	• Standard Agreement 2010: Notes: Part 1 Use and Completion; Part 2 Model Letter (2012 revision)
	• Changes since 2010 Edition

Concise Agreement 2010 (2012 revision) – Architect	
Two selections online	*One pack comprising four separate printed documents*

• Concise Conditions of Appointment for an Architect 2010 (2012 revision)
• Core component bundle:
  – Small Project Services Schedule 2010 (2012 revision – RIBA Plan of Work 2013 compatible version)
  – Concise Agreement 2010: Notes: Part 1 Use and Completion; Part 2 Model Letter 2010 (2012 revision)
  – Fees and Expenses Schedule 2010 (2012 revision)
	• Concise Conditions of Appointment for an Architect 2010 (2012 revision) (including Small Project Services Schedule, 2012 revision – RIBA Plan of Work 2013 compatible version)
	• Concise Agreement 2010: Notes: Part 1 Use and Completion; Part 2 Model Letter (2012 revision)
	• Fees and Expenses Schedule 2010 (2012 revision)
	• Changes since 2010 Edition

Concise Agreement 2010 (2012 revision) – Consultant	
Two selections online	*No printed equivalent*

• Concise Conditions of Appointment for a Consultant 2010 (2012 revision)
• Core component bundle:
  – Small Project Services Schedule 2010 (2012 revision – RIBA Plan of Work 2013 compatible version)
  – Concise Agreement 2010: Notes: Part 1 Use and Completion; Part 2 Model Letter (2012 revision)
  – Fees and Expenses Schedule 2010 (2012 revision)	

Domestic Project Agreement 2010 (2012 revision) – Architect	
Two selections online	*One pack comprising four separate printed documents*

• Domestic Conditions of Appointment for an Architect 2010 (2012 revision)
• Core component bundle:
  – Small Project Services Schedule 2010 (2012 revision)
  – Domestic Project Agreement 2010: Notes: Part 1 Use and Completion; Part 2 Model Letter (2012 revision)
  – Fees and Expenses Schedule 2010 (2012 revision)
	• Domestic Conditions of Appointment for an Architect 2010 (2012 revision) (including Small Project Services Schedule)
	• Domestic Project Agreement 2010: Notes: Part 1 Use and Completion; Part 2 Model Letter (2012 revision)
	• Fees and Expenses Schedule 2010 (2012 revision)
	• Changes since 2010 Edition

Table 0/1 (continued)

ELECTRONIC *Only available at www.ribabookshops.com/agreements*	PRINTED equivalent
Domestic Project Agreement 2010 (2012 revision) – Consultant	

Two selections online
• Domestic Conditions of Appointment for a Consultant 2010 (2012 revision)
• Core component bundle:
  – Small Project Services Schedule 2010 (2012 revision)
  – Domestic Project Agreement 2010: Notes: Part 1 Use and Completion; Part 2 Model Letter (2012 revision)
  – Fees and Expenses Schedule 2010 (2012 revision)
	No printed equivalent

Sub-consultant Agreement 2010 (2012 revision)	

Two selections online
• Conditions of Appointment for a Sub-consultant 2010 (2012 revision)
• Core component bundle
  – Sub-consultant Agreement 2010: Notes: Part 1 Use and Completion; Part 2 Model Letter (2012 revision)
  – Fees and Expenses Schedule 2010 (2012 revision)
	One pack comprising four separate printed documents
	• Conditions of Appointment for a Sub-consultant 2010 (2012 revision)
	• Sub-consultant Agreement 2010: Notes: Part 1 Use and Completion; Part 2 Model Letter (2012 revision)
	• Fees and Expenses Schedule 2010 (2012 revision)
	• Changes since 2010 Edition

Other Components (in editable format)	
Selected one by one online, as needed	*No printed equivalents of Other Components – although note that sample versions are reproduced in RIBA Agreements 2010 (2012 revision) Electronic-only Components*
Access Consultancy Services Schedule 2010 (2012 revision)	
Contractor's Design Services bundle: • Contractor's Design Services Schedule 2010 (2012 revision) • Contractor's Design Services Schedule: Notes Parts 1-4 (2012 revision)	
Historic Building or Conservation Project Services Schedule 2010 (2012 revision)	
Initial Occupation and Post-occupation Evaluation Services Schedule (2012 revision)	
Master Planning Services Schedule 2010 (2012 revision)	
Multi-disciplinary Design Services Schedule 2010 (2012 revision)	
Small Historic Building or Conservation Project Services Schedule 2010 (2012 revision)	
Supplementary Agreements (in editable format)	
Selected one by one online, as needed	*No printed equivalents of Supplementary Agreements – although note that sample versions are reproduced in RIBA Agreements 2010 (2012 revision) Electronic-only Components*
DRAFT Third Party Rights Schedule (2012 revision)	
DRAFT Warranty by a Sub-consultant (2012 revision)	
DRAFT Public Authority Supplement (2012 revision)	
Guides (in non-editable format)	
Selected one by one online, as needed	*No printed equivalents of Guides*
A Guide to Access Consultancy Services	
A Guide to Consumer Rights and Building Contracts	
A Guide to Working with an Architect: Repair and Alteration of Historic Buildings	
A Guide to Working with an Architect: Repair and Alteration of Places of Worship	

Figure 0/1:

Specimen letter to architect formerly engaged on project

IVOR B'ARCH Architects LLP

Prospect Drive, Thawbridge BS17 2ZX

T: 0100 012 023
F: 0100 012 024
E: mailto:ivor@b_arch.com

We understand that you were engaged by [the clients] to work on this
project but that the arrangement has been properly terminated.

Under Rule 3.5 of the RIBA Code of Professional Conduct we are obliged to notify
you that [the clients] have now appointed us as architects for this project.

We would be pleased to have your written confirmation that there are no
matters outstanding which should be drawn to our attention at this stage.

Figure 0/2:

Specimen project resource planning sheet

Job no: Job title:

Project resource planning sheet

Budget cost		Commencement					Completion			
		Estimated number of site visits								

Stage		0	1	2	3	4	5	6	7	
Start										
Finish										
Staff name/grade	£ per hour	Hours	Hours	Hours	Hours	Hours	Hours	Hours	Hours	Total
Ivor Barch partner	100	32	32	64	64	20	80	20	20	33,200
C. Smith architect	60	32	64	160	320	400	360	80	40	87,360
W. Blaggs assistant	40	16	320	320	640	800	180	40	20	93,440
Stage total										
Expenses										
Total										

1. Estimate duration of Stages with start and finish entries.

2. List staff assigned to job, grade, unit rate and estimated hours under Stages. Rates should include for overheads, profit and reserves.

3. Enter estimated expenses likely to be incurred against headings such as car milage, travel fares, subsistence, etc.

Figure 0/3:

Specimen letter confirming preliminary agreement

IVOR B'ARCH Architects LLP

Prospect Drive, Thawbridge BS17 2ZX

T: 0100 012 023
F: 0100 012 024
E: mailto:ivor@b_arch.com

We are writing about the terms of our appointment for this project.

You have asked us to undertake some preliminary services so that
the project may proceed, and we confirm these as follows:

_____

_____

It is understood that if you subsequently instruct us to undertake
other preliminary services, you will confirm this in writing. All these
services will be charged on a time basis at the following rates:

Principals	£ _____ per _____
Senior architectural staff	£ _____ per _____
Other architectural staff	£ _____ per _____
Administrative staff	£ _____ per _____

In addition, the following expenses will be charged:

_____

_____

Invoices will be submitted monthly. VAT is chargeable, where applicable,
at the current standard rate on all fees and expenses.

For the above services to be provided effectively, you will also need to appoint:

_____

_____

You should note that other financial commitments at this stage may include:

_____

_____

We will provide these services on the basis of the conditions included in the Form
of Agreement, a copy of which is enclosed [if appropriate at this stage].

We envisage that this preliminary appointment will continue for approximately
_____ months while we conclude the principal Agreement. When the principal
Agreement has been entered into, this appointment will be subsumed into
it, and fees invoiced under this letter will rank as payments on account.

Please confirm your acceptance of the appointment set out in this
letter by signing the enclosed copy and returning it to us.

Preparation and Brief

1

RIBA
Plan of
Work
2013

Excerpt from the RIBA Plan of Work 2013

RIBA
Plan of
Work
2013

Stage 1

Preparation
and Brief

Task Bar	Tasks
Core Objectives	Develop **Project Objectives**, including **Quality Objectives** and **Project Outcomes**, **Sustainability Aspirations**, **Project Budget**, other parameters or constraints and develop **Initial Project Brief**. Undertake **Feasibility Studies** and review of **Site Information**.
Procurement Variable task bar	Prepare **Project Roles Table** and **Contractual Tree** and continue assembling the project team.
Programme Variable task bar	Review **Project Programme**.
(Town) Planning Variable task bar	Pre-application discussions *may be required during this stage to discuss and determine the suitability of* **Feasibility Studies**.
Suggested Key Support Tasks	Prepare **Handover Strategy** and **Risk Assessments**. Agree **Schedule of Services**, **Design Responsibility Matrix** and **Information Exchanges** and prepare **Project Execution Plan** including **Technology** and **Communication Strategies** and consideration of **Common Standards** to be used. *The support tasks during this stage are focused on ensuring that the project team is properly assembled and that consideration is given to the handover of the project and the post-occupancy services that are required.*
Sustainability Checkpoints	• *Confirm that formal sustainability targets are stated in the* **Initial Project Brief**. • *Confirm that environmental requirements, building lifespan and future climate parameters are stated in the* **Initial Project Brief**. • *Have early stage consultations, surveys or monitoring been undertaken as necessary to meet sustainability criteria or assessment procedures?* • *Check that the principles of the* **Handover Strategy** *and post-completion services are included in each party's* **Schedule of Services**. • *Confirm that the Site Waste Management Plan has been implemented.*
Information Exchanges (at stage completion)	**Initial Project Brief**.
UK Government Information Exchanges	Required.

1

Summary

Several significant and parallel activities need to be carried out during Stage 1 Preparation and Brief to ensure that Stage 2 Concept Design is as productive as possible. These split broadly into two categories:

— developing the **Initial Project Brief** and any related **Feasibility Studies**
— assembling the project team and defining each party's roles and responsibilities and the **Information Exchanges**.

The preparation of the **Initial Project Brief** is the most important task undertaken during Stage 1. The time required to prepare it will depend on the complexity of the project.

When preparing the **Initial Project Brief**, it is necessary to consider:
— the project's spatial requirements
— the desired **Project Outcomes**, which may be derived following **Feedback** from earlier and similar projects
— the site or context, by undertaking site appraisals and collating **Site Information**, including building surveys
— the budget.

A project **Risk Assessment** is required to determine the risks to each party. The development of the procurement strategy, **Project Programme** and, in some instances, a (town) planning strategy are all part of this early risk analysis.

The importance of properly establishing the project team cannot be underestimated, given the increasing use of technology that enables remote communication and project development using **BIM**. For Stage 2 to commence in earnest, it is essential that the team is properly assembled.

Mapping to RIBA Outline Plan of Work 2007

Stage 1 merges the residual tasks from the former Stage A with the Stage B tasks that relate to carrying out preparation activities and briefing in tandem.

1.1   Core Objectives

For the majority of commissions the architect as designer is well placed to undertake Feasibility Studies, advise on alternative design and constructional approaches, and identify what might be imposed by legislative and other constraints.

Although it will have been considered in Stage 0, Stage 1 begins the actual process of team assembly. This will continue throughout Stage 2 but it is essential to have the composition of the complete team, and their various roles, agreed at an early stage and identified, whenever possible, in the appointment agreement. The RIBA Plan of Work 2013 can be used as a model to identify the services needed. The architect engaged as project lead would play a key role in this process. Alongside setting up the team, it is at this stage that partnering agreements may be finalised and project quality control systems put in place.

Stage 1 is present in all procurement routes. With design and build, the client must prepare a clear brief, which may form part of, or evolve into, the Employer's Requirements under the design and build contract. The architect may be appointed by the client to assist in its preparation or (less common), if the contractor has been approached at an early stage, may be engaged by the contractor to assist in preparing feasibility proposals or studies for the client.

Under the Standard Agreement 2010 (2012 revision) the preparation of the Initial Project Brief is the responsibility of the client and is 'received' by the architect at the start of Stage 2, although the architect may contribute to its development through the preparation of studies, etc. If the architect is to be responsible for the preparation of this document, this must be identified in the terms of appointment as an 'Other Service'.

1.2	**Procurement**

1.2.1	Explain to the client the options for procurement and note any matters which could affect the particular choice.
1.2.2	Check with the client whether tendering for the particular project is likely to be subject to legislative control. This could have an effect on procurement methods and procedures.
1.2.3	Consider the project's risk profile in terms of Procurement as well as Programme and (Town) Planning.
1.2.4	When acting for contractor clients in design and build, establish who carries the liability for design and to what extent. The contractor might not be insured against failures of design, and the liability might extend beyond the normal professional duty to exercise reasonable skill and care.

When acting for employer clients in design and build, be wary if asked to check the Contractor's Proposals against the Employer's Requirements, and avoid 'approving' drawings submitted by the contractor or subcontractors.

NOTE

Take expert advice on whether terms proposed by the client comply with current legislation, unless it is clear that they follow those currently recommended by the RIBA. It is particularly important to check that terms regarding payment, notices and dispute resolution comply with the Housing Grants, Construction and Regeneration Act (1996) as amended by the Local Democracy, Economic Development and Construction Act 2009, and that a provision to deal with the Contracts (Rights of Third Parties) Act (1999) has been incorporated.

Remember that the law requires a professional to exercise reasonable skill and care. Resist any attempt to get you to guarantee what might not be attainable, or covered by your professional indemnity (PI) insurance, e.g. that a building will be 'fit for the purpose intended' or other form of performance warranty, or to extend liability through additions such as 'every' or 'professional' skill and care.

Resist entering into collateral agreements with third parties or giving indemnities which impose greater liabilities than those which arise out of the agreement already entered into with your client.

1.3	Programme

1.3.1   Develop the Project Programme.

NOTE   *It is vital to develop this tool and to refer to it regularly throughout the life of the project. It will start as a 'high-level' strategic tool, but more detail will be added to it as the project progresses. It can be used to assess the in-house resource requirements and the overall durations of each stage in the design process. It can then be used to measure progress, particularly if activities are linked and a critical path set out as a result. It can also be linked to other project team members' programmes, and where the design team is working collaboratively, a single, integrated Project Programme can be developed.*

The contractor will be responsible for maintaining and managing the Construction Programme.

1.3.2   Set up procedures for regularly checking progress against the timetable for services, and for taking corrective action if necessary.

1.4	(Town) Planning

1.4.1   Develop the town planning strategy.

Check the planning situation with the local planning authority.   **1/SM3**
For example:

- whether there is any existing relevant permission, approval or consent which is still current – obtain the original notices if possible

- whether the proposed work requires planning permission, and if so which applications would be relevant

- whether there are special circumstances that need to be taken into account (e.g. listed building, conservation area, enterprise zone, development corporation)

- whether an environmental impact assessment will be expected, or might be helpful

- whether there is a known existence of hazardous substances or conditions due to earlier uses, likelihood of archaeological remains, etc.

- whether there are plans for compulsory purchase or any land take proposals (e.g. for road improvements) which could affect use of the site.

1.4.2   Hold preliminary discussions with the planning officer to discuss key issues arising from the above checks. Establish the approach of the planning officer towards the principle of development as proposed and enquire whether serious difficulties might be expected. Establish the measure of consultation that the planning officer would welcome or expect.

NOTE   *It is advisable to seek the opinion of the local authority planning officer at an early stage in design development. Some authorities charge for this service, but it will give valuable feedback before the greater cost of developing the design and making a full application and will help to manage risk in the planning process. The officer will give advice on planning policy and the likely outcome of an application. They may make recommendations to improve the chances of success if this is thought necessary. The process usually requires a set of drawings and other supporting information to be sent, with the fee, following which a meeting will be arranged. A formal response will usually be issued shortly after the meeting, although it should be noted that the planning committee will not always follow the officer's recommendation.*

The more information that is submitted, the greater the detail of advice you will receive in response, but it is important not to present the proposals as a finished design but rather as design options, exploring a range of solutions that could meet the client's brief. This will tend to elicit the most beneficial response and demonstrate a willingness to involve the authority as a stakeholder. Matters such as planning policy, the local built environment, access and egress, bulk and massing of the proposal, building materials and sustainability targets should be explained.

www.planningportal.gov.uk is a useful source of advice for all matters related to planning and making planning applications.

Refer also to the RIBA Good Practice Guide Negotiating the Planning Maze *(2009).*

Outline planning submission and pre-application planning consultation   **1/SM3**
are part of the services under the Standard Agreement 2010 (2012
revision). You would be expected to select the relevant box (item 10) or
mark it with 'T' for time-based services or 'LS' for lump sum. If further
services other than those mentioned above are required when applying
for outline planning permission, this would need to be identified
under Part 3 'Other Services', so unless such services are included in the
appointment it will be necessary to obtain client authorisation.

Refer to the RIBA Good Practice Guide Negotiating the Planning Maze
(2009) for advice on when an outline application is appropriate.

1.4.3	Prepare an application for certificates (e.g. lawful development) if appropriate.

1.4.4	Submit applications (if instructed by the client) with relevant documents, including a cheque from the client for the appropriate fee.

1.5   Suggested Key Support Tasks

1.5.1   Information required

1.5.1.1	Check that all information necessary during Stage 1 is available, which might include the following:

- the Strategic Brief, to include the client's requirements, budget,   **0/SM4** project timetable and timetable for services

- information about the site and/or existing buildings, to be supplied by the client; legal aspects to be verified by the client

- further information from the client, e.g. accommodation schedule, manufacturing process, equipment, plant layout, safety policy

- information relating to the user client, e.g. security, particular needs, access audits

- studies previously undertaken relevant to this project or site, e.g. social surveys, traffic or transport studies

- if available, Health and Safety File with information on site hazards or references to work carried out previously

- Ordnance Survey maps, site and/or building survey drawings

- documents referring to local history of site, plus possibly the political and social context, etc.

- environmental data, such as weather records, maps of the area, environmental studies, contaminated land investigations

- notes, sketches and photographs made during initial visits

- contributions, information and recommendations from consultants and specialists if they have been appointed

 - agreed Building Information Modelling (BIM) strategy.

NOTE *If procurement is through design and build for a contractor client, include the Employer's Requirements as issued to tenderers.*

1.5.2   Brief

| 1.5.2.1 | Collate information from the cost consultant, other consultants and specialists. |

| 1.5.2.2 | Develop the client's requirements into an Initial Project Brief, or assist the client in developing an Initial Project Brief. |

 Preparation of the Initial Project Brief is the most important task undertaken during Stage 1 and the time required to prepare it will depend on the complexity of the project.

1/SM1

When preparing the Initial Project Brief, it is necessary to consider:
- *the project's spatial requirements*
- *the desired Project Outcomes, which may be derived following Feedback from earlier and similar projects*
- *the site/context, and*
- *the budget.*

| 1.5.2.3 | Develop the Project Objectives, including Quality Objectives and Project Outcomes, risk profile, Sustainability Aspirations, Project Budget, other parameters or constraints. |

| 1.5.2.4 | Undertake site appraisals and collate Site Information, including building surveys. |

1.5.2.5   Consider the relationship between brief, site/context and Project Budget.

1.5.3   Appointment

1.5.3.1   Establish the scope, content and context for Stage 1 activities.

 Put this information into context, particularly if material produced is likely to be acted upon by others taking over subsequent stages.

1.5.3.2   Check the appointing documents with respect to services and fees:

- if the extent of professional services for Stage 1 is not yet settled, agree this with the client and confirm in writing

- if the methods and levels of charging for Stage 1 are not yet settled, agree these with the client and confirm in writing.

Because the project requirements, construction costs and architectural services are not fully defined at this stage, the fees for Stage 1 are often based on true costs rather than on a fixed sum or percentage fee.

1.5.3.3   Establish, if possible, whether this is to be a continuing involvement for full services or is likely to be a partial service confined to this stage.

1.5.3.4   Check with your professional indemnity insurers whether the project seems likely to call for services outside those covered by the policy. For example, the architect might find it necessary to engage other consultants directly, might be called upon to give advice on self-build operations, or might act as manager for a series of separate trades contracts. Cover could also be called into question because of the nature or scale of operations, or because of stipulations by the client as to the amount or duration of cover required.

If the architect is to engage sub-consultants directly, check their competence and resources, particularly with regard to the CDM Regulations. Consider the use of RIBA Sub-consultant Agreement 2010 (2012 revision).

1.5.3.5	Assess the office resources needed for Stage 1 and ensure that they are available and adequate.	
1.5.4	**Client**	
1.5.4.1	Check the identity of the client's representative, project team, personnel and authorised agents.	
	Check that the client has made organisational arrangements to deal with questions, supply information and take decisions. Under the RIBA Standard Agreement – or a letter of appointment with the RIBA Concise Agreement – the client's representative is to have authority to act.	
1.5.4.2	Obtain from the client the project requirements, budget and timetable and any other project data being supplied by the client. Check these carefully, question incompatibilities and agree priorities.	0/SM4
1.5.4.3	Alert the client straight away to key issues that may be missing from these requirements and will need to be addressed in the Initial Project Brief, such as strategy for accessibility, security policy and environmental policy.	1/SM1
1.5.4.4	Advise the client on the need to appoint a cost consultant and other consultants or specialists. Confirm who will make the appointments, the basis of agreements and the scope of such services. List the other consultants in the appointment agreement and any project quality plan.	
	NOTE *Be clear about the professional services needed. If other consultants and specialists are needed, be prepared to explain their roles and responsibilities. The guidance to the RIBA Plan of Work 2013 may be a useful tool at this stage for mapping out the tasks that must be performed and identifying who will perform them, although it should be noted that it may not list all appointments that are needed.*	
	Refer to Assembling a Collaborative Project Team *(2013).*	
	NOTE *Try to secure the client's consent that all professional appointments are on mutually interlocking agreements with similar, if not identical, contractual conditions. RIBA Agreements are available in Architect and Consultant versions with identical conditions, but Schedules of Services may be required for some disciplines.*	1/SM2

| 1.5.4.5 | Advise the client on statutory and other legal obligations, including: | 1/SM3 1/SM4 |

Advise the client on statutory and other legal obligations, including:

- the need for various approvals under national legislation concerned with planning and building, and the additional requirements of any local legislation or legislation for the particular building type which might apply

- the fees payable to the relevant authority at the time of these applications

- the obligations of a client under the CDM Regulations, and other health and safety legislation, as appropriate

- the need to appoint a CDM coordinator, where the law requires this

- the duties of the client as building owner under the Party Wall etc. Act 1996, including the possible need to appoint a party wall surveyor and the rights of adjoining owners to appoint their own surveyors

- possible duties of the client under Part IIA of the Environmental Protection Act 1990, if the site may contain contaminated land.

1.5.4.6 Provide proof of competence to the client.

Refer to *Managing Health and Safety in Construction: Construction (Design and Management) Regulations 2007* Approved Code of Practice, available to download free from the HSE website: www.hse.gov.uk.

1.5.4.7 Check whether any information provided by the client is confidential, and enquire whether the client wishes to ensure confidentiality for the project. If not, and publicity is sought, is this likely to involve wider consultation, e.g. presentations to a user client or local amenity bodies?

1.5.4.8 Establish procedures for the client to 'sign off' briefs, designs, etc. at relevant stages.

Be strict about keeping to deadlines for reports and other submissions to the client.

Set firm dates for approvals, instructions to proceed and the supply of information.

1.5.5	Project team

1.5.5.1   Assemble the project team and define the members' roles and responsibilities and the Information Exchanges.

The importance of properly establishing the project team cannot be understated given the increasing use of technology, which enables remote communication and project development using BIM. For Stage 2 to commence in earnest, it is essential that the team is properly assembled. The tools necessary to achieve this, and to produce the various documents required to accompany each team member's appointment, are considered in greater detail in the guidance to the RIBA Plan of Work 2013.

Refer to Assembling a Collaborative Project Team *(2013).*

The RIBA Plan of Work 2013 advocates the definition and establishment of the project team during Stage 1. This ensures that the roles and responsibilities of each organisation are clear before commencement of Stage 2 Concept Design. The publication *Guide to Using the RIBA Plan of Work 2013* (2013) provides advice on this process.

1.5.5.2   Where appropriate, and in accordance with the project's Technology Strategy, appoint an information manager, whose role should include the following:

- explaining to the client the benefits and implications of implementing BIM

- advising on the extent to which BIM should be used on the project

- determining the roles and responsibilities of each member of the project team with regard to the BIM process and the model

- leading the other consultants in preparing the BIM project plan

- defining and communicating the BIM inputs and outputs

- in conjunction with the other consultants, reviewing and signing off the model at agreed stages

- issuing data from the model at the appropriate times

- liaising with the contractor, subcontractors and suppliers to integrate their design data into the model

- agreeing and implementing 'Soft Landings' (see Stage 6)
- arranging for the model to be passed on to the client's facilities manager at practical completion (unless the architect is to maintain a role in this regard).

For further advice on working with BIM, refer to the RIBA publication *BIM Demystified* (2012).

1.5.5.3	If appointed as information manager, prepare BIM protocols and agree them with the other members of the design team. Define the responsibilities of the other members of the design team in this regard.
1.5.5.4	Define long-term responsibilities, including ownership of the model.
1.5.5.5	Define BIM inputs and outputs and scope of Post-occupancy Evaluation (Soft Landings).
1.5.5.6	Establish or review project quality management procedures together with relevant procedures for all design team members.
1.5.5.7	Confirm the design team composition and identify a project lead.
1.5.5.8	Identify the functional relationship between the project lead and the project manager (if appointed) and establish the authority of the project lead and lead designer.
1.5.5.9	Identify the need for a Project Execution Plan and agree its format with the client and design team.
1.5.5.10	Check the scope of professional services agreed with other consultants as they are appointed.
1.5.5.11	Confirm the agreed policy for consultants and specialists concerning accountability, warranties, PI insurance, etc.
1.5.5.12	Appraise the client's requirements and agree inputs to the stage by design team members.

1.5.5.13	Confirm the stage timetable for services and note its relationship to the project timetable as agreed with the client. The timetable should show critical points by which information from the client and design team members will be required.
1.5.5.14	Establish arrangements for communication between the client's representative, the CDM coordinator, the project manager and the lead designer.
1.5.5.15	Agree working methods and procedures with the design team members, including: • means for integrating and coordinating effort and inputs • compatibility in systems, software, etc. Refer to 'BIM protocol' on page 7.
1.5.5.16	Establish a programme and pattern for design team meetings. Figure 1/1 is a specimen agenda for an initial design team meeting.
1.5.5.17	Establish procedures for regular reporting to the client. *Procedures for design team members should be clearly set out and closely followed throughout the project.*
1.5.6	General matters
1.5.6.1	Set up an in-house project team.
1.5.6.2	Establish who will lead the office design unit. Identify personnel, roles, accountability and lines of communication and reporting within the office and with the external project team and the client.
1.5.6.3	Establish office administration procedures.
1.5.6.4	Open project files and allocate a job number to the project in accordance with office practice. Check with the client the full project title to be used.

1.5.6.5	Begin to compile a record of all key persons involved in the project, together with addresses, phone numbers, e-mail, etc. Check that names, titles or descriptions are correct. Circulate to all concerned.
1.5.6.6	Review how in-house quality management procedures will be applied to the project. These may include the preparation of a Project Execution Plan in an appropriate form.

A Project Execution Plan provides a mechanism to link the specific requirements of the project to an office quality management system which might already exist. It will not necessarily mean the development of a new document or procedures over and above those that already exist.

1/SM6

Refer to the *RIBA Quality Management Toolkit*.

1.5.6.7	Review the Site Information and undertake Feasibility Studies.
1.5.6.8	Prepare the Handover Strategy.

The Handover Strategy includes the requirements for phased handovers, commissioning, training of staff or other factors crucial to the successful occupation of a building. On some projects, the Building Services Research and Information Association (BSRIA) Soft Landings process is used as the basis for formulating the strategy and undertaking Post-occupancy Evaluations.

Refer to www.bsria.co.uk/services/design/soft-landings.

Refer to the Post-occupancy Evaluation (POE) activities listed in chapter 'Stage 6' (see pages 284, 287, 288 and 291).

1.5.6.9	Agree the Schedule of Services, Design Responsibility Matrix and Information Exchanges.
1.5.6.10	Prepare the Project Execution Plan, including the Technology Strategy.

1.5.6.11	Monitor office expenditure against fee income:
	• set up office procedures for recording time spent on the project, by whom and the rates chargeable, and for noting expenses and disbursements incurred
	• set up procedures for regularly checking expenditure against the office job cost allocation.

| 1.5.6.12 | Arrange for regular reports to be provided to the client on fees and expenses incurred, and for accounts to be submitted at agreed intervals. |

| **1.5.7** | Inspections/tests |

| 1.5.7.1 | Identify the scope of and commission BIM surveys and investigation reports. |
| BIM | Advise the client about other surveys needed and act as authorised. If independent surveyors are to do this, brief them fully. |

| 1.5.7.2 | Obtain maps, studies and other contextual material. |

| 1.5.7.3 | Make an initial visit to the site and/or existing building. Make a photographic record, notes and sketches as appropriate. File information and make an initial appraisal. | **1/SM5** **Fig. 1/2** |

| 1.5.7.4 | Check for any reference in previous use or history of the site to contamination or the presence of hazardous substances, geological problems, underground services, etc. In particular be aware of the Control of Asbestos Regulations 2012. Existing buildings should have a survey kept on file with a person appointed to manage it. Refer to the HSE website: www.hse.gov.uk. |

| 1.5.7.5 | Advise the client, if appropriate, to authorise special surveys to investigate potential health and safety problems if contaminated land is found to be present. |

1.5.7.6	Inspect information provided by the client, including the Health and Safety File, if applicable.

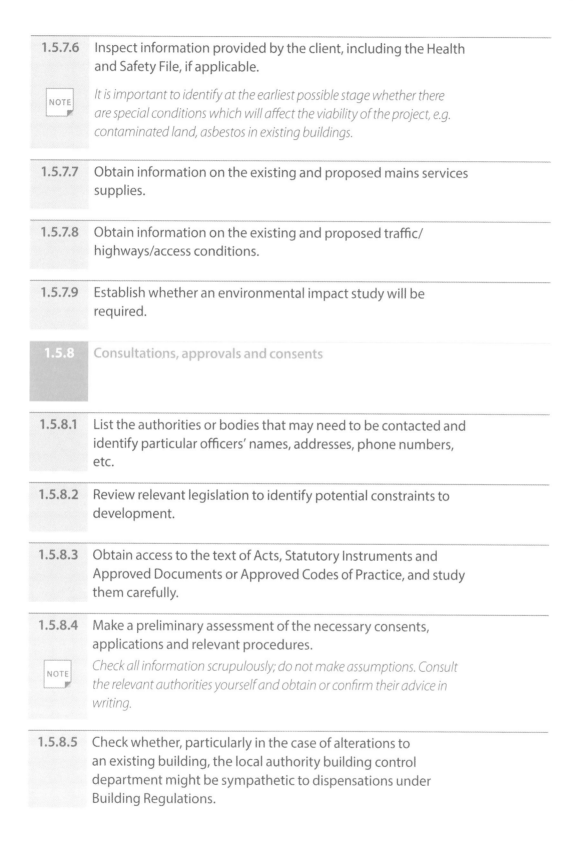

It is important to identify at the earliest possible stage whether there are special conditions which will affect the viability of the project, e.g. contaminated land, asbestos in existing buildings.

1.5.7.7	Obtain information on the existing and proposed mains services supplies.

1.5.7.8	Obtain information on the existing and proposed traffic/highways/access conditions.

1.5.7.9	Establish whether an environmental impact study will be required.

1.5.8   Consultations, approvals and consents

1.5.8.1	List the authorities or bodies that may need to be contacted and identify particular officers' names, addresses, phone numbers, etc.

1.5.8.2	Review relevant legislation to identify potential constraints to development.

1.5.8.3	Obtain access to the text of Acts, Statutory Instruments and Approved Documents or Approved Codes of Practice, and study them carefully.

1.5.8.4	Make a preliminary assessment of the necessary consents, applications and relevant procedures.

Check all information scrupulously; do not make assumptions. Consult the relevant authorities yourself and obtain or confirm their advice in writing.

1.5.8.5	Check whether, particularly in the case of alterations to an existing building, the local authority building control department might be sympathetic to dispensations under Building Regulations.

| 1.5.8.6 | Check any concerns that the fire authority, police or military might have, particularly in an area of high sensitivity, which might influence development or design. |

| 1.5.8.7 | Check whether there are restrictions on site development potential due to mains or cables either below ground or overhead, and whether or not the site is subject to easements or wayleaves. |

| 1.5.8.8 | Check the position and capacity of mains drainage and services supplies from statutory undertakers. |

Alert the client at a very early stage if it appears that there may be issues concerning the development that may require approval/agreement of adjoining owners, e.g. whether rights of light, boundaries, rights of way, such as for fire escapes or access, will be affected. These will normally be dealt with by the client's solicitors, but they may take a considerable time to negotiate.

| 1.5.8.9 | Check whether notices under the Party Wall etc. Act 1996 may be needed. |

| 1.5.8.10 | Check whether third parties, e.g. landlord, estate surveyor, lessees, adjoining owners, etc., will need to be consulted. Initiate preliminary consultations if authorised by the client. |

| 1.5.8.11 | Consult with user groups as authorised. |

Consultations with users and some third parties do not form part of the services under the RIBA Standard Agreement unless identified under Part 3 'Other Services'. Third parties mentioned by the agreement and therefore not requiring identification under 'Other Services' include landlords and freeholders and others in that class (item 12) and those involved in negotiations in connection with statutory approvals (item 11).

| **1.5.9** | **Cost planning** |

| 1.5.9.1 | Together with other consultants, review the client's budget figures and identify the sums included for actual construction work. |

1.5.9.2 Review the client's requirements, programme and budget to assess compatibility. If they are not in balance, report this to the client and seek clarification on priorities.

1.5.9.3 Alert the client to the possible effects on the cost of the project of inflation and the application of VAT. If necessary, recommend that the client take appropriate professional advice on VAT implications.

1.5.9.4 Review with other consultants possible sources of funding or grant aid and, if instructed, help to prepare a case or application. This might take the form of assistance from government departments, statutory bodies, local authorities, English Heritage, etc. or charitable trusts. There are many organisations with limited funds which may nevertheless be useful in aggregate. Financial assistance is often subject to conditions that could affect design and specification proposals.

1.5.9.5 Provide information for financial appraisal.

The report on cost implications should be structured under appropriate headings. It will normally be prepared by the cost consultant, if appointed. On jobs where there is no cost consultant, cost estimates may need to be prepared by the architect – the appointment must make this clear.

1/SM7

1.6 Sustainability Checkpoints

Sustainability Checkpoint 1

 During Stage 1 the Sustainability Aspirations should be considered and included in the Initial Project Brief. The Handover Strategy impacts the assembly of the project team, and the RIBA Plan of Work 2013 encourages the consideration of handover and in-use activities at this stage to ensure that appropriate Schedules of Services are prepared and adequate budgets included in the Project Budget.

Sustainability aims

During Stage 1, the Sustainability Aspirations should be considered and included in the Initial Project Brief, defining criteria to be met as appropriate. A budget, procurement route and design process should be established that will promote the realisation of those aspirations and a project team with the required resources, skills and commitment assembled.

Checkpoints

- Confirm that formal sustainability targets are stated in the Initial Project Brief.

- Confirm that environmental requirements, building lifespan and future climate parameters are stated in the Initial Project Brief.

- Have early stage consultations, surveys or monitoring been undertaken as necessary to meet sustainability criteria or assessment procedures?

- Check that the principles of the Handover Strategy and post-completion services are included in each party's Schedule of Services.

- Confirm that the Site Waste Management Plan has been implemented.

Key actions

- State the internal environmental conditions and formal sustainability targets.

- State the building lifespan and future climate parameters.

- Undertake early stage consultation, surveys or monitoring as necessary to meet sustainability criteria or assessment procedures.

- Define the involvement of the design team after Practical Completion.

- Start the Site Waste Management Plan.

- Commission surveys of existing buildings to be retained (including condition, historic/townscape significance, materials and components for recycling), services, noise, vibration, renewable energy resources, ecology, geology, etc. as required to inform the brief.

- Review options for formal assessment of aspects of sustainability and/or energy performance (e.g. BREEAM, LEED, Passivhaus). If the project is a component of a larger scheme, ensure that targets support and are consistent with any overarching sustainability assessment methodologies. Establish a timetable for associated assessor appointment and early stage actions.

- Include a simple description in the Initial Project Brief of the internal environmental conditions that the client requires.

- Involve the client's facilities management team and review past experience (both good and bad) in a spirit of openness in order to set environmental and performance targets or Project Outcomes that are useful, measurable and challenging but achievable and unambiguous. Energy use and carbon emissions targets should include both regulated and unregulated use.

- Agree how to measure performance in use, what incentives there will be to achieve Project Outcomes and what action is appropriate if anything falls short.

- Develop potential energy strategies, including estimated energy demand calculations, options for renewables and implications for building or site design (e.g. whether there is sufficient plant space).

- Develop water efficiency strategies to establish similarly robust performance targets.

- Set out sustainable drainage systems (SuDS) and surface water retention requirements.

- Develop a brief for specialist environmental sub-consultants (e.g. wind monitoring consultants, ecologists).

- Consider climate change adaptation criteria and future performance standards.

- Set out any future uses or reconfiguration to be accommodated.

- Ensure that the competence of potential design team members matches the client's Sustainability Aspirations. The team should be balanced, with members of similar competence and commitment and with complementary contracts of engagement.

- Client to implement the Site Waste Management Plan to enable designers to record decisions made to reduce waste as the project progresses.

1.7   Information Exchanges

1.7.1   Material produced by the conclusion of Stage 1 might include the following:

- Feasibility Studies and reports

- the Initial Project Brief

- a report to the client on studies to define the feasibility of the client's requirements. The report should analyse and appraise needs, give an environmental assessment and offer possible options, together with recommendations for the way forward – this might include conceptual drawings and diagrams

- a cost appraisal which is sufficiently detailed to enable a cost strategy to be devised

- where appropriate, a report on the condition of the fabric of an existing (perhaps historic) building, and suggestions for future uses

- where appropriate, proposals developed sufficiently to allow an application for outline planning permission.

The information exchanged at the end of a stage can vary and the RIBA Plan of Work 2013 advocates that during Stage 1 the Information Exchanges at the end of each stage are agreed along with the level of detail to be produced.

The Feasibility Study reports to the client will establish the basis upon which the project should proceed. It may be that the job is not feasible at all, or that the client's requirements, programme and cost limits cannot be reconciled. Make sure your reports are comprehensive, soundly researched and objective.

> **NOTE**
>
> *If procurement is through design and build, the reports should include:*
>
> * *for an employer client: initial suggestions for the Employer's Requirements*
>
> * *for a contractor client: a report to the client on the Employer's Requirements as received, and related matters pending preparation of the Contractor's Proposals.*

1.8 UK Government Information Exchanges

1.8.1 Information Exchanges are required.

Supplementary Material

1/SM1: Initial Project Brief checklist

An Initial Project Brief checklist relevant at the end of Stage 1 might include the following:

General

- agreed project BIM protocols
- the client's objectives, requirements and established priorities and criteria
- quality standards
- the client's environmental policy
- life expectancy of building and components
- user client's considerations
- access requirements, including disabled access
- security requirements
- health and safety policy
- budgets for security, energy and maintenance including cleaning (i.e. costs in use)
- detailed functional requirements of direct client/user client
- site history, topography and geology
- preferred spatial relationships and orientation
- studies previously commissioned
- plans for future expansion
- exact location of boundaries
- other parties known to have expressed an interest, e.g. English Heritage, the CABE team at the Design Council.

Planning and building considerations

- known constraints arising from previous consents or conditions
- likelihood of planning gain or Section 106 agreement
- impact of the local development plan
- leasehold/freehold interests and party walls, rights of light, access or other known easements.

Environmental

- services below ground and known restrictions on development
- likely parking requirements
- likelihood of archaeological or antiquarian discoveries
- known road widening or development plans

- known problems with the site, e.g. geological conditions, hazardous substances, presence of contaminated land
- known problems with the buildings, e.g. presence of asbestos.

Financial

- funding or institutional requirements or restrictions
- approximate cost per square metre if speculative development
- grants, subsidies or information relating to tax advantages, e.g. VAT.

1/SM2: Design team appointments and working

Appointments

When acting as project lead, the architect should advise the client on the appointment of other consultants and specialists as necessary. The appointment and payment of consultants and specialists are matters best dealt with directly by the client; the services required should be identified in detail and recorded. The conditions of appointment for all consultants should be compatible and, preferably, share a common basis.

It is very important for the architect to know precisely what is included in the appointment terms of all consultants, so as to be able to minimise any overlap or duplication and to coordinate effectively the work of all the members of the design team. It is also desirable to ensure that all members are appointed under compatible conditions with a common policy concerning responsibilities, insurance, collateral agreements, etc.

The RIBA Plan of Work 2013 serves as a useful source for the services that may need to be carried out and could be referred to as the team is being appointed.

Depending on the nature and size of the project, a wide range of specialists and/ or consultants may be needed at some stage. For example:

Surveyors

- cost consultant
- land surveyor
- building surveyor
- party wall surveyor.

Engineering consultants

- civil engineer (including geotechnics)
- structural engineer.

Building services consultants

- mechanical (heating and ventilation) engineer
- electrical engineer
- lighting consultant
- public health consultant.

Other consultants and specialists

- information manager
- planning consultant
- CDM coordinator
- landscape consultant
- acoustic consultant
- conservator
- health and safety consultant
- access consultant
- fire engineering consultant
- interior design consultant
- facilities management consultant
- security adviser.

Of these, the appointments most likely to be relevant at Stage 1 are set out below.

Refer also to the *Architect's Handbook of Practice Management*, Chapter 1, Section 1.6 'Key Roles in the Construction Industry'.

Cost consultant

Standard conditions of engagement are published by the Royal Institution of Chartered Surveyors (RICS) relating to a wide range of services. These need to be examined carefully to establish which services are to be provided for the particular appointment.

Structural engineer

Standard conditions of engagement and a number of different forms of agreement are published by the Association of Consulting Engineers (ACE). Normal services for structural work are arranged broadly in accordance with the RIBA Plan of Work 2013 stages. These need to be examined carefully to establish which services are to be provided for the particular appointment.

Building services engineer

Standard conditions of engagement are published by the ACE. The basic range of services can include for Full Duties, Abridged Duties or Performance Duties. The conditions need to be examined carefully to establish which services are to be provided for the particular appointment.

With engineering services, architects are reminded that:

- 'working drawings' as understood in architectural terminology are not produced by mechanical and electrical (M&E) consultants

- 'builder's work' drawings are for the architect to arrange, making sure that requirements for holes, shafts, access, insulation, etc. are properly coordinated and integrated into the design
- 'coordination drawings', where commissioned, should show detailed layouts and their relationship to plant rooms, spaces, structure, etc.
- 'installation drawings' (or 'shop drawings') are produced by the subcontractors or suppliers, and may be expected to show only general lines of pipework, fabrication and equipment installation details for comment by the engineering services consultant prior to fabrication or installation.

It is normally the architect's responsibility to coordinate and integrate the work of consultants and specialists into the overall design. To this end, architects will need to inspect drawings submitted by specialists (refer to Stage 5). However, contract documents should clearly place the responsibility for coordination of work being carried out on site with the main contractor.

Sub-consultants

If the architect is to appoint sub-consultants directly, great care must be taken to check their competence and resources with respect to health and safety regulations and their PI insurance provisions. The RIBA Sub-consultant Agreement 2010 (2012 revision) should be used wherever possible.

Information manager

Refer to 1.5.5.2.

Consultant team roles and responsibilities

It is good practice to table the Design Responsibilities Matrix at the earliest opportunity. This identifies all the main project activities and specifies which consultant will have prime responsibility for which activity. It can also identify whether there are any secondary roles. Its prime objective is to clearly set out who is doing what, which may then lead to any gaps or overlaps in services being identified. This matrix needs to be shared with the client and agreed and signed off by the whole team.

Cost consultant

The cost consultant can assist the architect in assessing economic site use and advising on procurement methods. They can analyse Cost Information from other similar projects, local levels of building costs and cost trends, etc., and can judge whether the client's budget is realistic and compatible with other stated requirements.

The cost consultant should cooperate with the CDM coordinator, liaise with other consultants and specialists, attend consultant team meetings and prepare the financial appraisal for the feasibility report.

Structural engineer

The structural engineer can advise the architect about local conditions relevant to the site, such as soil and geotechnical factors, roads, sewers, water supply, etc. They can:

- obtain existing information and interpret it
- identify hazards and hazardous substances
- arrange for site, structural and drainage surveys
- advise on alternative structural solutions
- prepare cost planning information for the cost consultant
- prepare design criteria and calculations
- advise on structural aspects of party walls, temporary structures and demolition work.

The structural engineer should cooperate with the CDM coordinator, liaise with other consultants and specialists, attend consultant team meetings and contribute to the feasibility report.

Building services engineer

The building services engineer should cooperate with the CDM coordinator, and liaise with the architect and the structural engineer to study climatic conditions, energy use and conservation, emissions problems, etc., and should consult relevant authorities as necessary.

The building services engineer can:

- provide details of load and space requirements for services
- prepare Feasibility Studies, estimates, forecasts and maintenance cost options
- assist in dealings with statutory bodies
- prepare outline schemes
- prepare energy management studies and reports
- prepare design criteria and calculations
- advise on installation options and cost implications
- advise on energy, cost/benefit and running costs.

Information manager

Refer to 1.5.5.2.

The information manager should all attend design team meetings and contribute to the feasibility report.

Design team meetings

The design team will probably need to be enlarged during the development of the project. However, it is essential that it is formally constituted with a proper definition of responsibility and clearly accepted roles. Regular consultant team meetings are important to review progress and to record decisions.

A specimen agenda for the initial design team meeting is shown as Figure 1/1, and although the list of items will need modifying as the project progresses, the main headings should remain consistent throughout. In this way the history of each aspect of job administration will be automatically recorded and can be easily traced.

A system of regular reporting can be established. For example, the client's representative will report under the heading 'Brief', the architect under 'Site' and 'Approvals', the cost consultant under 'Cost control', and so on. The chair for these meetings is usually the project lead, or the architect acting as project lead.

1/SM3: Inspections, planning permission, other consents and approvals

Consents may have to be obtained at any time during Stages 1 to 6 from authorities, organisations or persons having jurisdiction over, or rights affecting, the project, or who are affected by the project. Consents that could affect feasibility should be applied for during Stage 1.

Depending on the nature of the project, the procurement method, the site and the amount of information available, each application for consent should be made at the earliest possible time in order to avoid abortive work, although it is usual for planning applications to be made at the end of Stage 3.

Before initiating applications for consents:

- Explain fully to the client what consents are necessary and what is likely to be involved.
- Discover whether the client has contacts or lines of communication with authorities or individuals concerned.
- Inform the client about fees payable directly by them.
- Inform the client about the likely timescale for processing applications and the degree of consultation.
- Make it clear to the client that architects do not obtain consents, this being beyond their power, but that they prepare submissions or make applications on behalf of their clients in accordance with the agreement for professional services.
- Discover or confirm:
  - the existing allocated or established use of the site
  - whether the proposal is deemed to be 'development' under the Town and Country Planning Acts and so requiring planning permission
  - the planning history of the site, noting important issues such as the dates and decisions of any earlier planning permissions for the site
  - the effect on the site and the proposals of any policy statements or guidelines contained within the local development plan for the area
  - whether the local authority has identified the site as containing contaminated land
  - any likely limitations to the proposals or impositions on the developer through the use of Section 106 agreements or other planning conditions, such as Community Infrastructure Levy, etc.

Check which of the following applications are relevant to determine whether a planning application is necessary:

- for certificate of lawful development
- for mining or working of minerals

- for hazardous substances consent
- for outline planning permission
- for full planning permission to develop land
- for listed building consent
- for conservation area consent
- for approval of 'conditions' on a planning permission
- for varying or discharging conditions attached to listed building consent or conservation area consent
- for varying or revoking conditions attached to a planning permission
- for approval of reserved matters following an outline planning permission
- for a scheduled monument consent
- for a certificate of immunity from listing
- to fell or lop a tree
- to establish the need for an environmental impact assessment
- to display signs and advertisements under the Control of Advertisements Regulations.

1/SM4: Health and safety checklists

Legislation

The principal legislation is the Health and Safety at Work etc. Act 1974, which sets out general duties on the part of both employers and employees. These were reinforced with the introduction of the Management of Health and Safety at Work Regulations 1999.

The Workplace (Health, Safety and Welfare) Regulations 1992 are relevant at Stage 1. Although they place a duty on employers in respect of workplaces under their control, there are implications for the way in which new workplaces are designed and fitted out. This can be in respect of planning (e.g. traffic routes, escalators, room dimensions, sanitary provisions), finishes (e.g. floors, wall surfaces) and installations (e.g. lighting, heating, ventilation). The Regulations are concerned not only with the initial provision of safe conditions for staff but also with safety for cleaning and maintenance. The Workplace Regulations have been incorporated within the CDM Regulations.

The RIBA provides guidance on safety for personnel visiting building sites (see Figure 1/2). This should be issued to staff and strictly observed.

The Construction (Design and Management) Regulations 2007 ('the CDM Regulations') implement EU Directive 92/57/EEC, which requires that account be taken of the general principles of prevention concerning health and safety during the stages of project design organisation, construction and future maintenance. The CDM Regulations impose statutory duties on designers and contractors on all projects. They also impose duties on clients, except for domestic clients undertaking work on their own residences solely for their own occupation. Where construction work, other than for domestic clients, will be of more than 30 days' duration or where more than 500 person days of construction work are involved the Health and Safety Executive (HSE) must be notified by means of an F10 form and a CDM coordinator appointed.

A Client's Guide to Health and Safety for a Construction Project (2008) might be sent to an inexperienced client at the initial approach, together with the practice's competence pack.

The architect's role

The architect, when acting as lead designer or 'designer' (as referred to in the CDM Regulations) should carefully study the text of the Regulations and the Approved Code of Practice. It would also be wise to check the following:

- that the client is aware of their legal duty to appoint a CDM coordinator 'as soon as practicable', and a principal contractor – the client must be satisfied as to the competence and resources of both concerning health and safety matters
- that the client is aware of their legal duty to make available a Health and Safety File in respect of work previously carried out, and other relevant information concerning the site or premises
- that any sub-consultants employed directly by the architect have the necessary competence and resources
- that inspections and surveys of site or buildings cover all matters which might indicate potential health and safety hazards – this is a designer's duty, and if a detailed survey is thought necessary, the client must be prepared to pay for it
- that when undertaking risk assessments, proper consideration is given to eliminating or reducing potential health and safety hazards when planning site layouts or development – this will include the way that the contractor's operations on site are to be planned
- that there is full cooperation between the lead designer and all others having a design input (including consultants and specialist subcontractors) with regard to health and safety matters
- that there is full cooperation with the CDM coordinator over the production of information which may be relevant for the pre-construction information
- that the CDM coordinator is invited to attend design team meetings, and to comment as appropriate
- that in all design development the issues of safe specification, safe buildability and safe maintenance and cleaning are kept fully in mind
- that the pre-construction information is part of the tender documentation supplied to the principal contractor and subcontractors
- that tenders are carefully examined to make sure that the selected principal contractor has the necessary competence and resources available to deal with health and safety matters, and that price and programme reflect this
- that the building contract contains provisions for compliance with health and safety regulations, and for the contractor to cooperate with the CDM coordinator and provide 'as-built' information, etc.
- that the client is aware that no work must start on site before a Construction Phase Plan has been produced by the principal contractor as a management document for the works
- that a copy of any architect's instruction or variation with health and safety implications is passed to the CDM coordinator, so that the Construction Phase Plan can be updated accordingly
- that relevant information is passed to the CDM coordinator from time to time for possible inclusion in the Health and Safety File

- that work cannot commence on site without welfare provisions being in place.

Refer to the HSE publication *Managing Health and Safety in Construction: Construction (Design and Management) Regulations 2007, Approved Code of Practice*, which is available to download free from the HSE website: www.hse.gov.uk.

The CDM coordinator

Where this function is discharged by the architect on smaller contracts, it should be seen as a separate appointment, made via a separate appointing document and with an identifiably separate fee.

Where an independent CDM coordinator is to be appointed, an architect not otherwise involved in the project might be a suitable person. In all cases such appointments should only be considered by architects who have undergone proper training, fully understand the risks and have appropriate insurance cover.

Lead designers or project leads working on a project where an independent CDM coordinator has been appointed would do well to check that this appointee:

- gives proper notice to the HSE initially
- cooperates effectively in structuring information for the pre-construction information
- makes a thorough evaluation of health and safety aspects of the principal contractor's tenders, and is prepared to advise the client impartially
- is thorough but reasonable in evaluating the acceptability of the Construction Phase Plan from the principal contractor and as updated from time to time
- will prepare the statutory Health and Safety File for deposit with the client at the conclusion of construction, and will explain to the client their obligations concerning its safekeeping and future use
- approaches the role from a proportionate and practical perspective.

These may not be statutory duties, but such checks are very much in the spirit of the legislation and certainly demonstrate the use of reasonable skill and care.

The health and safety notice

Except where the project is for a domestic client, the HSE must be notified of projects where construction work is expected to:

- last more than 30 working days, or
- involve more than 500 person days, for example 50 people working for more than 10 days.

All days on which construction work takes place count towards the period of construction work. Holidays and weekends do not count if no construction work takes place on these days.

Where a small project that is not notifiable requires a short extension, or short-term increase in the number of people, there is no need to notify the HSE. However, if the work or the scope changes significantly so that it becomes notifiable, the HSE should be informed.

The information that has to be sent to the HSE is set out in Schedule 1 to the CDM Regulations.

A standard form (F10) can be completed and submitted electronically online or downloaded for manual completion. This is normally submitted by the CDM coordinator as soon as possible after their appointment. If the principal contractor is not appointed at that time then another, updated, notification must be made after they have been appointed. Any missing information must be notified once it becomes available, and the notifier should make clear that it relates to an earlier notification.

Pre-construction information

The pre-construction information provides information for those bidding for or planning work, and for the development of the Construction Phase Plan. The level of detail in the information should be proportionate to the risks involved in the project.

The HSE's Approved Code of Practice on the CDM Regulations notes the following topics for consideration when drawing up the pre-construction information, where the topic is relevant to the work proposed.

1   Description of project

(a)   project description and programme details including:
  (i)   key dates (including planned start and finish of the construction phase), and
  (ii)   the minimum time to be allowed between appointment of the principal contractor and instruction to commence work on site

(b)   details of client, designers, CDM coordinator and other consultants
(c)   whether or not the structure will be used as a workplace (in which case, the finished design will need to take account of the relevant requirements of the Workplace (Health, Safety and Welfare) Regulations 1992)

(d)   extent and location of existing records and plans.

2   Client's considerations and management requirements

(a)   arrangements for:
   (i)   planning for and managing the construction work, including any health and safety goals for the project
   (ii)   communication and liaison between client and others
   (iii)   security of the site
   (iv)   welfare provision

(b)   requirements relating to the health and safety of the client's employees or customers or those involved in the project such as:
   (i)   site hoarding requirements
   (ii)   site transport arrangements or vehicle movement restrictions
   (iii)   client permit-to-work systems
   (iv)   fire precautions
   (v)   emergency procedures and means of escape
   (vi)   'no-go' areas or other authorisation requirements for those involved in the project
   (vii)   any areas the client has designated as confined spaces
   (viii) smoking and parking restrictions.

3   Environmental restrictions and existing onsite risks

(a)   Safety hazards, including:
   (i)   boundaries and access, including temporary access – for example narrow streets, lack of parking, turning or storage space
   (ii)   any restrictions on deliveries or waste collection or storage
   (iii)   adjacent land uses – for example schools, railway lines or busy roads
   (iv)   existing storage of hazardous materials
   (v)   location of existing services particularly those that are concealed – water, electricity, gas, etc.
   (vi)   ground conditions, underground structures or water courses where this might affect the safe use of plant, for example cranes, or the safety of groundworks
   (vii)   information about existing structures – stability, structural form, fragile or hazardous materials, anchorage points for fall arrest systems (particularly where demolition is involved)
   (viii) previous structural modifications, including weakening or strengthening of the structure (particularly where demolition is involved)
   (ix)   fire damage, ground shrinkage, movement or poor maintenance which may have adversely affected the structure
   (x)   any difficulties relating to plant and equipment in the premises, such as overhead gantries whose height restricts access

(xi) health and safety information contained in earlier design, construction or 'as-built' drawings, such as details of pre-stressed or post-tensioned structures

(b)   health hazards, including:
(i)   asbestos, including results of surveys (particularly where demolition is involved)
(ii)   existing storage of hazardous materials
(iii)   contaminated land, including results of surveys
(iv)   existing structures containing hazardous materials
(v)   health risks arising from client's activities.

4   Significant design and construction hazards

(a)   significant design assumptions and suggested work methods, sequences or other control measures

(b)   arrangements for coordination of ongoing design work and handling of design changes

(c)   information on significant risks identified during design

(d)   materials requiring particular precautions.

5   The Health and Safety File

Description of its format and any conditions relating to its content.

Construction Phase Plan

The Construction Phase Plan sets out how health and safety is to be managed during the construction phase. The level of detail should be proportionate to the risks involved in the project.

The HSE's Approved Code of Practice on the CDM Regulations notes that the following topics should be included in the Plan, where the topic is relevant to the work proposed.

1   Description of project

(a)   details of client project description and programme details including any key dates

(b)   details of client, CDM coordinator, designers, principal contractor and other consultants

(c)   extent and location of existing records and plans that are relevant to health and safety on site, including information about existing structures when appropriate.

2   Management of the work

(a)   management structure and responsibilities

(b)   health and safety goals for the project and arrangements for monitoring and review of health and safety performance

(c)   arrangements for:
   (i)   regular liaison between parties on site
   (ii)   consultation with the workforce
   (iii)   the exchange of design information between the client, designers, CDM coordinator and contractors on site
   (iv)   handling design changes during the project
   (v)   the selection and control of contractors
   (vi)   the exchange of health and safety information between contractors
   (vii)   site security
   (viii)   site induction
   (ix)   on-site training
   (x)   welfare facilities and first aid
   (xi)   the reporting and investigation of accidents and incidents, including near misses
   (xii)   the production and approval of risk assessments and written systems of work

(d)   site rules (including drug and alcohol policy)

(e)   fire and emergency procedures.

3   Arrangements for controlling significant site risks

(a)   Safety risks, including:
   (i)   delivery and removal of materials (including waste) and work equipment taking account of any risks to the public, for example during access to or egress from the site
   (ii)   dealing with services – water, electricity and gas, including overhead powerlines and temporary electrical installations
   (iii)   accommodating adjacent land use
   (iv)   stability of structures while carrying out construction work, including temporary structures and existing unstable structures
   (v)   preventing falls
   (vi)   work with or near fragile materials
   (vii)   control of lifting operations
   (viii)   the maintenance of plant and equipment
   (ix)   work on excavations and work where there are poor ground conditions

(x)   work on wells, underground earthworks and tunnels

(xi)   work on or near water where there is a risk of drowning

(xii)   work involving diving

(xiii)   work in a caisson or compressed air working

(xiv)   work involving explosives

(xv)   traffic routes and segregation of vehicles and pedestrians

(xvi)   storage of materials (particularly hazardous materials) and work equipment

(xvii)   any other significant safety risks

(b)   health risks, including:

    (i)   the removal of asbestos

    (ii)   dealing with contaminated land

    (iii)   manual handling

    (iv)   use of hazardous substances, particularly where there is a need for health monitoring

    (v)   reducing noise and vibration

    (vi)   work with ionising radiation

    (vii)   exposure to UV radiation (from the sun)

    (viii)   any other significant health risks.

4   The Health and Safety File

(a)   layout and format

(b)   arrangements for the collection and gathering of information

(c)   storage of information.

The Health and Safety File

The Health and Safety File, a document for which the CDM coordinator should assume responsibility, is to be deposited with the client at the completion of the contract. It will probably be assembled from information acquired gradually and steadily as the works progress. The client might need briefing as to its purpose, safekeeping and future use.

The Health and Safety File should contain the information needed to allow future construction work, including cleaning, maintenance, alterations, refurbishment and demolition, to be carried out safely. Information in the file should alert those carrying out such work to risks, and should help them to decide how to work safely.

The file should be useful to:

(a)   clients, who have a duty to provide information about their premises to those who carry out work there

(b)   designers during the development of further designs or alterations

(c)   CDM coordinators preparing for construction work

(d)   principal contractors and contractors preparing to carry out or manage such work.

The file should form a key part of the information that the client, or the client's successor, is required to provide for future construction projects under regulation 10 of the CDM Regulations. The file should therefore be kept up to date after any relevant work or surveys.

The scope, structure and format for the file should be agreed between the client and CDM coordinator at the start of a project. There can be a separate file for each structure, one for an entire project or site, or one for a group of related structures. The file may be combined with the Building Regulations Log Book, or a maintenance manual providing that this does not result in the health and safety information being lost or buried. What matters is that people can find the information they need easily and that any differences between similar structures are clearly shown.

What you must do

Clients, designers, principal contractors, other contractors and CDM coordinators all have legal duties in respect of the Health and Safety File:

(a)   CDM coordinators must prepare, review, amend or add to the file as the project progresses, and give it to the client at the end of project

(b)   clients, designers, principal contractors and other contractors must supply the information necessary for compiling or updating the file

(c)   clients must keep the file to assist with future construction work, and

(d)   everyone providing information should make sure that it is accurate, and provided promptly.

A file must be produced or updated (if one already exists) as part of all notifiable projects. For some projects, for example redecoration using non-toxic materials, there may be nothing of substance to record. Only information likely to be significant for health and safety in future work need be included. The NHBC Purchaser Manual provides suitable information for developers to give to householders. You do not have to produce a file on the whole structure if a project only involves a small amount of construction work on part of the structure.

The client should make sure that the CDM coordinator compiles the file. In some cases, for example design and build contracts, it is more practical for the principal contractor to obtain the information needed for the file from the specialist contractors. In these circumstances the principal contractor can assemble the information and give it to the CDM coordinator as the work is completed.

It can be difficult to obtain information for the file after designers or contractors have completed their work. What is needed should be agreed in advance to ensure that the information is prepared and handed over in the required form and at the right time.

The contents of the Health and Safety File

When putting together the Health and Safety File, you should consider including information about each of the following where they are relevant to the health and safety of any future construction work. The level of detail should allow the likely risks to be identified and addressed by those carrying out the work:

(a)   a brief description of the work carried out
(b)   any residual hazards which remain and how they have been dealt with (for example, surveys or other information concerning asbestos; contaminated land; water bearing strata; buried services etc.)
(c)   key structural principles (for example, bracing, sources of substantial stored energy – including pre- or post-tensioned members) and safe working loads for floors and roofs, particularly where these may preclude placing scaffolding or heavy machinery there
(d)   hazardous materials used (for example lead paint; pesticides; special coatings which should not be burnt off etc.)
(e)   information regarding the removal or dismantling of installed plant and equipment (for example, any special arrangements for lifting, order or other special instructions for dismantling etc.)
(f)   health and safety information about equipment provided for cleaning or maintaining the structure
(g)   the nature, location and markings of significant services, including underground cables; gas supply equipment; fire-fighting services etc.
(h)   information and as-built drawings of the structure, its plant and equipment (for example, the means of safe access to and from service voids, fire doors and compartmentalisation etc.).

The file does not need to include things that will be of no help when planning future construction work, for example:

(a)   the pre-construction information, or Construction Phase Plan
(b)   construction phase risk assessments, written systems of work and COSHH assessments
(c)   details about the normal operation of the completed structure
(d)   construction phase accident statistics
(e)   details of all the contractors and designers involved in the project (though it may be useful to include details of the principal contractor and CDM coordinator)

(f)   contractual documents

(g)   information about structures, or parts of structures, that have been demolished – unless there are any implications for remaining or future structures, for example voids

(h)   information contained in other documents, but relevant cross-references should be included.

Some of these items may be useful to the client, or may be needed for purposes other than complying with the CDM Regulations, but the Regulations themselves do not require them to be included in the file. Including too much material may hide crucial information about risks.

Summary of the duties under the CDM Regulations

A summary of the duties and how they are applied is set out below:

Clients (excluding domestic clients)

All construction projects (Part 2 of the Regulations)
• Check competence and resources of all appointees.
• Ensure there are suitable management arrangements for the project including welfare facilities.
• Allow sufficient time and resources for all stages.
• Provide pre-construction information to designers and contractors.

Additional duties for notifiable projects (Part 3 of the Regulations)
• Appoint CDM coordinator.*
• Appoint principal contractor.*
• Make sure that the construction phase does not start unless:
    – there are suitable welfare facilities, and
    – the Construction Phase Plan is in place.
• Provide information relating to the Health and Safety File to the CDM coordinator
• Retain and provide access to the Health and Safety File

(* There must be a CDM coordinator and principal contractor until the end of the construction phase.)

CDM coordinators

Additional duties for notifiable projects (Part 3 of the Regulations)
• Advise and assist the client with their duties.
• Notify HSE.
• Coordinate health and safety aspects of design work and cooperate with

others involved with the project.
- Facilitate good communication between client, designers and contractors.
- Liaise with principal contractor regarding ongoing design.
- Identify, collect and pass on pre-construction information.
- Prepare/update Health and Safety File.

Designers

All construction projects (Part 2 of the Regulations)
- Check client is aware of their duties.
- Eliminate hazards and reduce risks during design.
- Provide information about remaining risks.

Additional duties for notifiable projects (Part 3 of the Regulations)
- Check CDM coordinator has been appointed.
- Provide any information needed for the Health and Safety File.

Principal contractors

Additional duties for notifiable projects (Part 3 of the Regulations)
- Plan, manage and monitor construction phase in liaison with contractor.
- Prepare, develop and implement a written plan and site rules. (Initial plan completed before the construction phase begins.)
- Give contractors relevant parts of the plan.
- Make sure suitable welfare facilities are provided from the start and maintained throughout the construction phase.
- Check competence of all appointees.
- Ensure all workers have site inductions and any further information and training needed for the work.
- Consult with the workers.
- Liaise with CDM coordinator regarding ongoing design.
- Secure the site.

Contractors

All construction projects (Part 2 of the Regulations)
- Check client is aware of their duties.
- Plan, manage and monitor own work and that of workers.
- Check competence of all their appointees and workers.
- Train own employees.
- Provide information to their workers.
- Comply with the specific requirements in Part 4 of the CDM Regulations.
- Ensure there are adequate welfare facilities for their workers.

Additional duties for notifiable projects (Part 3 of the Regulations)
- Check a CDM coordinator and a principal contractor have been appointed and HSE notified before starting work.
- Cooperate with principal contractor in planning and managing work, including reasonable directions and site rules.
- Provide details to the principal contractor of any contractor whom he engages in connection with carrying out the work.
- Provide any information needed for the Health and Safety File.
- Inform principal contractor of problems with the plan.
- Inform principal contractor of reportable accidents, diseases and dangerous occurrences.

Everyone

- Check own competence.
- Cooperate with others and coordinate work so as to ensure the health and safety of construction workers and others who may be affected by the work.
- Report obvious risks.
- Comply with requirements in Schedule 3 and Part 4 of the CDM Regulations for any work under their control.
- Take account of and apply the general principles of prevention when carrying out duties.

1/SM5: Inspecting the site

Proper inspections and surveys of sites and existing buildings are essential at Stage 1. Rough preliminary surveys are not good enough and are an inadequate basis on which to judge feasibility. Ill-founded recommendations at this stage can lead to serious problems later.

When considering survey action, try to establish:

- the kind of survey needed and precisely what is to be surveyed
- who will carry out the survey – the practice's own staff, external land or building surveyors, or other specialists
- who will pay for the survey and where liability will rest in the event of errors.

Identify the boundaries of the site to be surveyed or the limits of the building. Confirm with the client that access will be available and obtain keys if necessary. Notify persons on site as appropriate.

Do not overlook statutory obligations arising, particularly those concerning occupiers' liability, and health and safety. Always heed the RIBA Safety Code for occupied building sites and unoccupied buildings and sites (see Figure 1/2).

Information about immediate area

Check:

- general context and character, outstanding visual features
- local development plan, action area plans, construction work currently under way
- evidence of social and economic patterns
- traffic movement patterns, noise, pollution
- derelict areas, nearby black spots, visually detracting features.

Visual inspection of site

Check:

- aspect, orientation, shelter, overshadowing from adjacent buildings or trees
- hedges, ditches, ponds, wet/soft patches, underground streams
- benchmarks, contours and slope of site
- paths, gates, stiles which might indicate rights of way
- overhead cables, pylons and poles
- possible health and safety hazards, e.g. flooding, exposure, unsafe trees
- properties adjoining the site, their condition, usage, evidence of subsidence, fire risks, party walls, etc.
- possible health and safety hazards, such as radon or other gases, pollutants and contamination from previous use, filled basements

- adjacent waterways, railways, busy roads
- possible restrictions on site access, delivery or site working
- possible restrictions due to sensitive building uses adjacent, e.g. hospital, nursery school, law court.

Site survey information

If the site survey is to be undertaken by a surveying firm, ensure that it is agreed with the client that this will not form part of the architect's services and will be billed directly.

Confirm:

- by whom the surveyors are to be engaged
- how the surveying fees are to be paid
- who is doing which part of the work
- how the results are to be presented
- arrangements for access, security, protection and insurance.

If appropriate, arrange for a survey of tree species and condition and an analysis of topsoil.

The information presented in the survey plans and reports might be expected to include the following:

Plans, showing:

- existing and proposed boundaries
- outline of existing buildings and roads
- boundary fences, access ways, garden and adjacent walls, their height, profile, material, ownership and condition
- ditches, ponds, waterways above or below ground
- wet or bad patches (discover seasonal variations from local sources)
- rock outcrops and other geological features, their type and size
- position of trial holes
- rights of way/access (check with client's solicitors, local authority).

Sections, drawn on separate sheets taken along the full length of section lines on the key drawings, to the same scale as the plan.

Levels, showing:

- position and level of benchmarks or basis of datum
- calculated levels in true relationship to an ordnance datum level
- spot levels on a 10 metre grid related to Ordnance Survey grid, or closer where local variations occur, e.g. at changes of level, hillocks.

Spot levels, indicating:

- the base of all trees
- all services covers, etc.
- pavement kerbs and road crowns where they enter the site.

Indicate contours, intervals (in metres) and position of section lines (on grid lines where possible).

Indicate all services above and below ground adjacent to, connecting into or crossing the site with relevant levels, falls, heights, access points, manholes (show cover levels and inverts). Also:

- pylons, posts (show headroom)
- soil and surface water drains
- water mains
- electricity cables
- telecommunication cables
- gas mains
- any other services.

Indicate trees, hedges and large shrubs, their height and position, spread of branches and diameter of trunk 1 metre above ground level.

Soil investigations

On a domestic project or one which involves a relatively small and light structure, it might well be sufficient for the architect to instruct the digging of trial pits. These should be set out with regard to the siting of the proposed building. On anything larger, investigation by boreholes may be necessary to obtain information and data for the design and construction of foundations, underground structures, roadworks, earthworks, etc. On sites containing contaminated land or unstable landfill, specialist advice will be needed on the surveying techniques to be used.

The structural engineer may be able to give preliminary advice by examining available information about the geology and history of the site, e.g. maps and memos produced by the British Geological Survey, Ordnance Survey maps, engineering data from earlier works in the area or aerial photographs.

The structural engineer should recommend the type and extent of investigations to be carried out, including the number of trial holes necessary to obtain an accurate assessment of the subsoil and water table conditions.

The investigating firm must allow for carrying out the work in accordance with any special requirements of the existing owners or occupiers of the site. They and/or their subcontractor specialists should be made responsible for all security, protection and related insurance during execution of the work.

The field work should be supervised by the structural engineer, and daily liaison should be maintained so that any variations indicated by the borehole findings can be made. Daily site records of boreholes should be sent to the structural engineer stating:

- borehole numbers and location
- date and times of boring
- type of plant and method of boring
- diameter of boring casing and core
- description of strata and depth of base of each stratum
- level at bottom of casing when sample taken, or in situ test carried out on each core drilled
- depths at which each sample was taken and in situ tests made
- water levels.

On completing the site work, the contractor should submit to the structural engineer preliminary borehole logs together with a list of samples so that instructions can be given for laboratory testing.

The final site investigation should be submitted as a draft (for approval of its form, not content). Unless otherwise specified it should contain:

- description of work carried out (i.e. site and laboratory work)
- borehole logs
- laboratory test results, including geological classification, index properties, acidity, sulphate content, etc.
- records of water levels in standpipes and/or piezometers installed in boreholes, with notes of any variations
- results of strength tests
- diagrammatic cross-section through site showing trial holes related to a datum and assumed connecting geological structure, water table, etc.
- plan showing position of trial holes, incorporated with main survey plan if appropriate.

Surveys of existing buildings

It is essential that the architect personally walks through every room in the building to be surveyed, regardless of whether the survey is being done by in-house personnel or by a surveying firm. It is important to perceive the architectural character of a building and the way it has been constructed.

The measured survey drawings might show:

- plans, sections, elevations
- elevational features, e.g. plinths, string courses, openings
- precise levels at floors, datum, thickness and construction
- levels of external ground

- details of decoration, profiles, false columns, etc.
- finishes and colours
- loose equipment, landlord's fittings, etc.

A written report might include information that cannot be shown graphically, such as:

- structural and other defects and their causes
- dry rot, damp penetration, condensation
- infestation by rodents, beetles and other insects
- recent repairs and decoration
- settlement cracks, misshapen openings, gaps at skirtings and windows
- walls that are misaligned or have bulges
- sagging roofs, defective roof coverings
- deflection of beams or lintels, cracks at beam bearings.

The architects/surveyors should state whether or not they were able to see inside the structure of the building and how much they were able to see. It is important not to infer the state of the whole building from sight of one part of it. A statement on the following lines should appear at the end of the relevant part of the report (as stipulated in most PI insurance policies):

> *It has not been possible to make a detailed examination of the floor or roof construction except at the positions described because material damage would have been caused in gaining access. It is therefore impossible to make any statement about the condition of the unexamined structure.*

Where appropriate, the client should be advised to call in specialists in particular areas, e.g. mechanical, electrical, timber treatment.

1/SM6: Project Execution Plan

A Project Execution Plan should be created. The plan might contain the following information:

Project description

- the client's design requirements
- a synopsis of brief and priorities
- an intended lifespan of building overall and of components
- constraints which arise from legislation or other sources.

Project organisation

- the identity of the client and representatives
- agreed procedures for consultations/approvals
- project team members and their defined responsibilities and contact details (this can be set out as a Contractual Tree)
- the Design Responsibility Matrix
- project timetable/programmes
- management, procedures for administration, including coordination.

Control procedures

- Information Exchanges
- Project Programme
- Communication Strategy
- brief development control and reviews
- design input control, design management and development, and patterns of design review
- design and information output control
- project specification basis and development
- project administration and document control procedures
- procurement, and procedures for appointment of the project construction team
- contract administration procedures
- monitoring of contractors' quality management
- CAD/BIM protocols (if appropriate)
- sustainability targets.

Change control

- agreed procedures for modifications or changes to approved brief
- agreed procedures for modifications or changes to approved designs
- records of modifications or changes
- identification of documents subjected to revision, and withdrawal to prevent unintended use.

Tests

- programme for inspections and tests, and personnel involved
- procedures and check sheets or reports to be used
- corrective action in the event of non-conforming work
- programme for audits, personnel involved and audit reports.

Particular instructions

- those items in the practice's quality system to be expressly excluded in the case of this particular project
- items not covered by the practice's quality system to be specifically included in the case of this particular project.

Records

- end of project reviews
- experience feedback studies and reports
- operating and maintenance manuals
- 'As-constructed' Information
- job records and files.

To summarise, a Project Execution Plan will be in the form most appropriate for the particular project. It should be a document which:

- defines activities and how they are to be carried out
- should be adequate for submission to a client for acceptance and review
- is reviewed regularly as the project progresses, with amendments and revisions, as necessary, submitted for acceptance before implementation.

For BIM-enabled projects the following are of particular importance:

Technology Strategy

Agreement of the Technology Strategy for a project is an essential first step because different parties involved in a project team are likely to use different software packages. It is important to ensure that each member of the project team is capable of working successfully with other members, and that the implications of hardware and software are considered and agreed prior to appointments being made and design work commencing.

Communication Strategy

The Communication Strategy is closely related to the Technology Strategy. Its purpose is to set out when the project team will meet, how they will communicate effectively and the protocols for issuing information between the various parties, both informally and at Information Exchanges.

BIM manual

The BIM manual sets out file- and drawing-naming conventions and other processes in relation to BIM. A CAD manual is typically a single-party document, whereas the BIM manual, which sets out project-wide conventions and processes, needs to be considered and agreed by the collaborative project team. Agreement of the BIM manual is a core requirement in the development of a collaborative project team.

1/SM7: Financial appraisal

The financial appraisal is usually prepared by the cost consultant. The cost consultant is the expert on costs, and can call on the Royal Institution of Chartered Surveyors (RICS) or other information service, as well as their own knowledge and expertise. Such an appraisal could be a document to be developed as the design progresses and form a basis for effective cost planning.

However, on a small project where no cost consultant is appointed the architect may have to write an appraisal for inclusion in the feasibility report. This is likely to be little more than an estimate to test the viability of the client's budget figure. A proper cost plan will need to be developed later.

Where the architect undertakes to prepare this appraisal, the approach should be as follows.

Define status

Define the status of the appraisal and set out the assumptions on which estimates are made. List any items of important information which were not available, and any items for which no allowance has been made.

State basis for estimates

State the basis for estimates (e.g. cost indices, £ per square metre, etc.) on current or predicted rates (if projected, to what date).

Estimate capital cost

When estimating the capital cost of the building project, consider:

- location (e.g. whether remote) and access (e.g. a difficult, tight site)
- site investigation and abnormal site works
- demolition or preliminary contracts for enabling works
- programme and phasing
- building substructure and superstructure (e.g. systems, cladding)
- finishes (e.g. expensive or standard)
- engineering services installations
- designers' and contractors' contingencies
- fitting out and furnishings
- landscape treatment – both hard and soft, including planting.

Other costs

Other costs to be taken into account might include:

- fees for statutory approvals
- fees and expenses for the design team
- fees and expenses for the CDM coordinator.

An estimate should also clarify the VAT position and the possible effects of inflation, and warn that fluctuations are possible after the start of the building contract, even in the case of a lump sum contract. It might also be helpful to suggest the phasing of payments so that the client can begin to consider how best to manage their cash flow. VAT in relation to construction projects is a complex area and the client should be guided to take appropriate professional advice on the interpretation of VAT charges.

In addition to the estimate of the capital cost of the building project, the client will need to take into account the cost of the site, legal and other fees, finance costs, the risk and profit element, and an assessment of in-use costs for the building.

Figure 1/1

Specimen agenda for initial design team meeting

Job no: Job title:

Specimen agenda for initial design team meeting

1. Project team and reports

   Appointments, personnel
   Roles and responsibilities
   Lines of communication for
   policy/day-to-day matters
   Pattern and reporting procedures
   for future meetings
   Project Programme
   Team members' programmes and progress

2. Brief

   Client's requirements
   Development of brief
   Changes to brief, implications
   and control procedures
   Pattern and procedures for reporting to client
   Preparation of stage reports to client

3. Site

   Information from client about
   site, foreseeable hazards
   Assessment of risks
   Development constraints,
   physical and statutory
   Surveys and consents

4. Approvals

   Private individuals/bodies
   Funders, insurers
   Town and country planning
   Building Regulations
   Fire officer
   Legal (e.g. adjoining owners)

5. Health and safety

   Risk assessment
   Pre-construction information
   Health and Safety File

6. Design and cost control
   – concepts
   – feasibility assessment
   – development of the brief

   Coordination of design team
   – general design
   – structures
   – services

   Drawings
   – agreed methods, scales,
     software, referencing
   – cost control
   – development of cost plan
   – variations

7. Contract

   Priorities and phasing
   Programming
   Procurement
   Tendering procedures and documents,
   Health and Safety Plan
   – main contract
   – subcontracts

8. Any other business

9. Date of next meeting

Figure 1/2

Visits to sites and unoccupied buildings

Health and Safety

Health and Safety legislation lays clear obligations on clients, designers, and principal contractors. The following code is complementary advice to all architects engaged in visits to buildings and sites.

Visits to building sites, unoccupied buildings and construction operations can be potentially dangerous. Consider the likely hazards. Follow the safety code.

1 Occupied building sites

The Contractor or occupier has a responsibility for the safety of persons lawfully on site. Do not enter sites or buildings without permission, and immediately report to the person in charge. Comply with all requests from the contractor, his representative or other supervisory staff. See the contractor when you arrive, and when you leave the site.

Wear suitable clothing, in particular protective headgear (a hard hat) and stout shoes or boots. Do not wear thin-soled or slippery shoes. Avoid loose clothes which might catch on an obstruction.

Check that ladders are securely fixed and that planks are secure. Beware of overhead projections, scaffolding and plant, and proceed with caution. Particular care is necessary in windy, cold, wet or muddy conditions. Keep clear of excavations and beware of openings in floors etc. Do not lean on guard rails, scaffoldings etc. Do not interfere with any temporary barriers, guard rails or lights. Beware of ladders on which the rungs may have rusted or rotted, and never climb a ladder which is not securely fixed at the top.

Do not touch any plant or equipment. Keep clear of machinery and stacked materials. Watch out for temporary cables, pumps, hoses and electric fittings.

Do not walk and look around at the same time. Keep one hand free at all times when moving. Make sure that you are in a safe and balanced position whenever making notes or taking photographs.

Report to the contractor anything that comes to your notice on the site as being unsafe.

2 Unoccupied buildings and sites

As a general rule do not visit an empty building or unoccupied site on your own. Make sure someone knows where you are, and at what time you expect to return.

Do not take chances. Do not visit an empty building if you think it unsafe. Do not visit an unoccupied site if you think it dangerous. Anticipate hazards.

Common dangers include:

– the possibility of partial or total structural collapse
– rotten or insecure floors and stairs
– hidden pits, ducts, openings etc, fragile construction, eg asbestos or plastic sheets on roofs
– space which has not been used or ventilated for some time
– live services
– contamination by chemicals or asbestos
– intruders who may still be around
– contamination by vermin or birds, or poisonous substances put down to control them.

Plan the visit and make sure that you take with you appropriate equipment and protective clothing. Apart from stout shoes and a hard hat, remember that unoccupied buildings can be dirty, damp, cold and dark; so go prepared.

Look for defects in the floors ahead, eg wet areas, holes, materials that might be covering up holes.

Familiarise yourself beforehand with the plan of the building, particularly the exit routes. Make sure that security devices on exits will allow you to reach safety quickly.

Walk over the structural members (eg joists, beams, etc) whenever possible - do not rely on floorboards alone.

Do not walk and look around at the same time. Keep one hand free at all times when moving. Do not walk and try to take notes at the same time. Make sure that you are in a safe and balanced position when taking photographs or stretching out to take measurements.

Check on protection when approaching stairwells, lift shafts, roof perimeters, etc.

Do not assume that services (eg cables, sockets, pipes, etc) are safe or have been isolated.

If you suspect the presence of gas, inflammable liquids, dangerous chemicals or free asbestos fibre leave the building immediately.

If you sustain cuts, penetration by nails or other serious injury, seek immediate medical advice.

Always heed these three golden rules:

– do not rush
– if uncertain do not proceed – seek advice or assistance
– do not smoke or use naked flame.

Concept Design

CONTENTS

Plan of Work and Stage Activities

Supplementary Material

Figures

RIBA
Plan of
Work
2013

Excerpt from the RIBA Plan of Work 2013

RIBA
Plan of
Work
2013

Stage 2

Concept Design

Task Bar	Tasks
Core Objectives	Prepare **Concept Design**, including outline proposals for structural design, building services systems, outline specifications and preliminary **Cost Information** along with relevant **Project Strategies** in accordance with **Design Programme**. Agree alterations to brief and issue **Final Project Brief**.
Procurement Variable task bar	*The Procurement activities during this stage will depend on the procurement route determined during Stage 1.*
Programme Variable task bar	Review **Project Programme**.
(Town) Planning Variable task bar	*The RIBA Plan of Work 2013 enables planning applications to be submitted at the end of Stage 2. However, this is not the anticipated norm, but rather an option to be exercised only in response to a specific client's needs and with due regard to the associated risks.*
Suggested Key Support Tasks	Prepare **Sustainability Strategy**, **Maintenance** and **Operational Strategy** and review **Handover Strategy** and **Risk Assessments**. Undertake third party consultations as required and any **Research and Development** aspects. Review and update **Project Execution Plan**. Consider **Construction Strategy**, including offsite fabrication, and develop **Health and Safety Strategy**. *During this stage a number of strategies that complement the design are prepared. These strategies consider post-occupancy and operational issues along with the consideration of buildability. Third party consultations are also essential.*
Sustainability Checkpoints	• *Confirm that formal sustainability pre-assessment and identification of key areas of design focus have been undertaken and that any deviation from the* **Sustainability Aspirations** *has been reported and agreed.* • *Has the initial Building Regulations Part L assessment been carried out?* • *Have 'plain English' descriptions of internal environmental conditions and seasonal control strategies and systems been prepared?* • *Has the environmental impact of key materials and the* **Construction Strategy** *been checked?* • *Has resilience to future changes in climate been considered?*
Information Exchanges (at stage completion)	**Concept Design** including outline structural and building services design, associated **Project Strategies**, preliminary **Cost Information** and **Final Project Brief**.
UK Government Information Exchanges	Required.

Summary

During Stage 2, the initial Concept Design is produced in line with the requirements of the **Initial Project Brief**.

The project team also develops, in parallel with the Concept Design, a number of **Project Strategies**. Their importance at this stage will depend on how they are to influence the Concept Design. For example, the **Sustainability Strategy** is likely to be a fundamental component of the Concept Design, whereas a security strategy may have minimal or no impact and can therefore be developed during a later stage.

It is essential to revisit the brief during this stage and it should be updated and issued as the **Final Project Brief** as part of the Information Exchange at the end of Stage 2.

In parallel with design activity, a number of other related tasks need to be progressed in response to the emerging design, including a review of the **Cost Information**, the development of a **Construction Strategy**, a **Maintenance and Operational Strategy** and a **Health and Safety Strategy** and updating of the **Project Execution Plan**.

Mapping to RIBA Outline Plan of Work 2007

Stage 2 maps exactly to the former Stage C.

2.1	Core Objectives

During Stage 2, the preferred option from the Stage 1 Feasibility Studies is developed into the Concept Design in line with the requirements of the Initial Project Brief. The project team also develops the various Project Strategies, which might include matters such as fire engineering, maintenance and operation of the building and sustainability. These strategies are prepared in outline at Stage 2 and in detail at Stage 3. Strategies that have little effect on the Concept Design, for example on security, are likely to be developed at a later stage.

The brief is reviewed and developed into the Final Project Brief by the end of the stage.

2.2	Procurement

2.2.1   Review the procurement strategy and the Construction Strategy.

Review with the client the options for procurement and note any matters which could affect the choice of procurement route. In particular it is important to identify at an early stage who will be carrying out all specialist areas of design, for example whether they will be handled by the design team or by specialist subcontractors. This has implications for the consultant's terms of appointment, liability and warranty arrangements as well as affecting the procurement route to be adopted.

NOTE

If procurement is through design and build:

- *for an employer client: confirm with the client the extent of information to be included in the Employer's Requirements*

- *for a contractor client: check the Employer's Requirements issued for tendering purposes, and advise the client on any apparent omissions or inconsistencies. Confirm with the client the extent of information to be provided for inclusion in the Contractor's Proposals.*

2.3	Programme

2.3.1	Regularly check progress against the timetable for services.

2.4	(Town) Planning

2.4.1	Hold discussions as appropriate with the planning officer.
2.4.2	Discuss with the client the potential benefits in obtaining outline or full planning approval, if appropriate.
2.4.3	Prepare an application for outline or full planning permission if appropriate and not yet obtained, and submit the application if instructed by the client. Advise the client if this application relates to a listed building or building in a conservation area, and action accordingly.
2.4.4	Explain to the client the benefits of submitting a pre-application submission and, if this strategy is agreed, prepare and submit the necessary drawings and other information. Refer to the RIBA Good Practice Guide *Negotiating the Planning Maze* (2009) for detailed advice on the planning process, and also to the UK Government website www.planningportal.gov.uk.

| 2.5 | **Suggested Key Support Tasks** |

| 2.5.1 | Information required |

2.5.1.1 Check that all information necessary during Stage 2 is available, which might include the following:

- brief developed to Initial Project Brief stage, including cost and time targets and any proposals accepted by the client, noting any agreed amendments

- further information as requested, supplied by the client

- notes, sketches and details made on further visits to site and/or existing buildings

- published material, technical press articles as appropriate

- technical information (e.g. planning or design guides, British Standards, codes of practice), manufacturers' trade literature

- results of surveys and tests conducted during Stage 1

- relevant legislation, circulars or guides to assist in statutory compliance

- contributions, information and recommendations from consultants and specialists

- consider any feedback received from the client and other stakeholders on the Stage 1 design

- BIM protocols.

If procurement is through design and build: 2/SM1

- *for an employer client: information as above for development into the Employer's Requirements*

- *for a contractor client: the Employer's Requirements as issued to tenderers.*

2.5.2	Brief

| 2.5.2.1 | Review the Initial Project Brief and develop it into the Final Project Brief as part of the Information Exchanges at the end of the stage.

Evaluate the content of the brief to establish that:

- the client's stated objectives are reflected

- an adequate basis for design is provided

- the time and cost parameters are reasonable

- all the information the client should provide before design commences is provided.

NOTE *If changes to the brief are necessary, make sure that these are subject to the Change Control Procedures established, for example in the Project Execution Plan.* |
|---|---|

2.5.2.2	Advise the client of the results of the evaluation and seek instructions regarding any further information needed.

2.5.2.3	Obtain project-specific information from potential subcontractors and suppliers.

2.5.2.4	Coordinate and integrate information from the cost consultant and other consultants and specialists.

2.5.3	Appointment

| 2.5.3.1 | If coming new to the project at this stage in the Plan of Work:

- ascertain that previous stage checks have been carried out

- allow for familiarisation and reviewing of all usable material when agreeing fees and timetable with the client

- confirm the role of the architect in relation to the rest of the design team if appointed, i.e. whether appointed as project lead, lead designer or design team member, or whether a project manager has been appointed – direct access to the client, particularly during the design stages, is highly desirable |
|---|---|

- ensure that you have adequate professional indemnity (PI) insurance cover in accordance with ARB and RIBA requirements.

2.5.3.2 Establish the scope, content and context for Stage 2 activities.

NOTE *Put this information into context, particularly if previous stages have been undertaken by others or if material produced is likely to be acted upon by others taking over subsequent stages.*

2.5.3.3 Check that the client's instruction to proceed has been given and confirmed in writing.

2.5.3.4 Check appointing documents with respect to services and fees.

- If the services, cost or time targets are different from those agreed with the client, agree a formal variation by letter or deed as appropriate. Fees based on percentage of anticipated building costs or a lump sum may have to be reassessed and agreed based on the updated Initial Project Brief budget.

- If the extent of professional services for Stage 2 is not settled, agree with the client and confirm in writing. If the methods and levels of charging for Stage 2 are not settled, agree with the client and confirm in writing.

NOTE *Enquire whether additional services will be wanted which are not included under the agreement. These might extend to special studies, community surveys and participation exercises with a user client, attendance at meetings, presentation materials, etc.*

2.5.3.5 Assess the office resources needed for Stage 2 and ensure that they are available and adequate.

2.5.3.6 Carry out checks for compliance with in-house quality management procedures, including updated Project Execution Plan.

2.5.3.7 Review the application of practice procedures to the project.

2.5.4 Client

2.5.4.1 Alert the client to any matters raised during preliminary discussions with statutory or other bodies which seem likely to affect the brief or design proposals.

| 2.5.4.2 | Advise the client on the need to appoint further consultants and specialists. Decisions may be needed for the Concept Design which require specialist advice on structure, services, environmental and other matters. |

| 2.5.4.3 | Advise the client on health and safety matters. Remind the client about the need to appoint or retain a CDM coordinator to coordinate matters connected with the pre-construction information at this design stage. |

| 2.5.4.4 | Make specific requests to the client for further necessary information if that provided is not adequate. |

2.5.5   Project team

| 2.5.5.1 | Agree input to the stage by design team members. |

Remind design team members contributing at Stage 2 to identify current legislation (e.g. Building Regulations, health and safety legislation) with which the project must conform. Discuss with design team members the performance standards, environmental provisions and budget allocation required to comply with the brief, and the presentation of material in a way which can be readily integrated into the overall design concept.

| 2.5.5.2 | Coordinate consultant inputs into the planning application. |

| 2.5.5.3 | Establish or review project quality management procedures together with relevant procedures of all design team members. |

| 2.5.5.4 | Check the scope of professional services agreed with other consultants as they are appointed. |

| 2.5.5.5 | Confirm the Stage 2 timetable for services and note its relationship to the project timetable as agreed with the client. The timetable should show critical points by which information from the client and design team members will be required. |

| 2.5.5.6 | Confirm arrangements for communication between the client, CDM coordinator, project manager and lead designer. |

2.5.5.7	Cooperate with the CDM coordinator and all other designers in carrying out risk assessments and in drafting the pre-construction information.
2.5.5.8	Confirm the programme and pattern for design team meetings.

2.5.5.9 If appointed as information manager:

- organise a BIM pre-start meeting

- organise initial model sharing with the design team for strategic analysis and options appraisal

- identify key model elements such as prefabricated components and create concept level parametric objects for all major elements

- enable design team access to BIM data

- agree extent of performance specified work

- assist members of the design team to develop the design using the BIM model, ensuring that data sharing protocols are followed

- check and sign off the model at agreed stages

- issue or assist in the issue of design data at agreed times throughout the development of the design

- assist in the development of data relative to the agreed levels of detail

- assist in the integration of contractor's, subcontractors' and suppliers' data into the BIM model

For further advice on working with BIM, refer to the RIBA publication *BIM Demystified* (2012).

BIM data can be used for environmental performance and area analysis at this stage.

2.5.6	General matters
2.5.6.1	Check that the client has signed off or approved the Initial Project Brief.
2.5.6.2	Check that the client has settled all accounts to date.
2.5.6.3	Undertake a design review as appropriate.
2.5.6.4	Prepare the Concept Design, including outline proposals for structural design, services systems, landscape, outline specifications and preliminary Cost Information along with relevant Project Strategies.
NOTE	*Innovation in design, specification or selection of materials and methods can involve risk. Take care that risks are assessed before proposals are finalised. Check and test against known criteria.*
2.5.6.5	Review the Maintenance and Operational Strategy and the Health and Safety Strategy and update the Project Execution Plan.
2.5.6.6	Continue resource control procedures for the job: • check expenditure against the office job cost allocation for Stage 2 • monitor fee income against projected fee income.
2.5.6.7	Report regularly to the client on fees and expenses incurred, and submit accounts at agreed intervals.
2.5.6.8	Check that the client settles all accounts promptly.
	Refer to the *Architect's Handbook for Practice Management* (2010), Chapter 7 'Financial Management' and to the RIBA Good Practice Guide *Fee Management* (2012).

2.5.6.9 Keep careful records of all conversations, consultations and design team meetings. File all notes and sketches prepared during the design process. Keep all manufacturers' or trade literature to which reference was made. It might be needed later as proof of the 'state of the art' at the time.

> NOTE *Always check with your PI insurers if any aspects of the Concept Design are considered to be innovative.*

2.5.7 Inspections/tests

2.5.7.1 Make further visits to the site and/or existing buildings as authorised.

2.5.7.2 Carry out a visual inspection of the extent of existing buildings, site boundaries, etc. before completing outline design or proposals. If necessary, ask the client to ascertain the exact details of site boundaries, covenants, easements, etc. In the case of design and build particularly, the employer client may carry total responsibility for accuracy.

2.5.7.3 Carry out or supervise further survey work if appropriate and if instructed by the client.

2.5.7.4 Consider the need for tests using physical or computer models to obtain and analyse information about environmental performance, air circulation, temperature distribution, etc.

Prepare models for testing, and record and analyse results if instructed by the client.

> NOTE *Preparation of special models does not form part of the Services under the RIBA Standard Agreement 2010 (2012 revision) unless identified under Part 3 'Other Services'.*

2.5.8	Consultations, approvals and consents

2.5.8.1	Hold informal discussions with authorities as appropriate before making formal submission for permission, approval or consent.
NOTE	*Consultation with statutory authorities is not included in the RIBA Standard Agreement 2010 (2012 revision) until Stage 3, although it appears from Stage 0 in the RIBA Plan of Work 2013. In practice, to establish feasibility of proposals, consultations are likely to be necessary at Stages 0 and 1.*
2.5.8.2	Establish with the local authority building control department: • whether the project is one which will require approval under Building Regulations • whether it would be more beneficial to submit Building Regulations applications to the local authority or an approved inspector, and report to the client • whether a dispensation would be likely where the legal requirements of Building Regulations could be particularly onerous and damaging to the architectural integrity of a historic building.
2.5.8.3	Check whether there is any local legislation, or legislation particular to the proposed development or building type, which should be complied with.
2.5.8.4	Check whether bodies such as the Environment Agency could have their interests affected by the proposed development. If this seems possible, they should be consulted.
2.5.8.5	Check with relevant authorities concerning highways, drainage, water, gas and electricity, etc. and note requirements for plant and meter housings, substations, etc.
2.5.8.6	Agree with the client the need and/or arrangements for discussions with authorised users of the building in developing the Final Project Brief and the Concept Design. Consult with user clients if authorised to do so.

2

NOTE *Failure to agree party wall awards can lead to delays to the start of work on site. Establish at an early stage whether notices under the Party Wall etc. Act 1996 will be needed.*

NOTE *Consultations with users or some third parties do not form part of the Services under the RIBA Standard Agreement 2010 (2012 revision) unless identified under Part 3 'Other Services'. Services in connection with party wall matters form part of the Services under the conditions of the RIBA Standard Agreement 2010 (2012 revision).*

NOTE *Outline planning submission and pre-application planning consultation (item 10) as well as submissions to and negotiations with landlords, freeholders, etc. form part of the Services under the RIBA Standard Agreement 2010 (2012 revision). If further services are required when applying for outline planning permission, these must be identified under Part 3 'Other Services'.*

2.5.8.7 Submit applications for necessary approvals or consents required from third parties if instructed by the client.

NOTE *Applications for outline planning permission and approval of landlords, funders, etc. do not form part of the Services under the RIBA Standard Agreement 2010 (2012 revision) unless identified under Part 3 'Other Services'.*

2.5.9 Cost planning

2.5.9.1 Review the Cost Information.

FIG. Provide information to the cost consultant for the initial cost plan and cash flow projection (or prepare an approximation of construction cost if appointed to do so).   **Fig. 2/1**

2.5.9.2 Compare the initial cost plan and cash flow forecast with the latest approved cost.

2.5.9.3 Discuss with the design team and the client the effect of major design decisions on the allocations within the cost plan before they are taken.

NOTE *An increase in cost of one element, e.g. for a sophisticated external wall cladding system, may require corresponding savings in other areas, such as the mechanical services installation. Changes in the initial cost plan may require adjustment of the budget and fees, and these changes should be agreed with the client.*

| 2.5.9.4 | Report to the client on cost matters at agreed intervals. |

NOTE *If procurement is through design and build for a contractor client, provide information to the contractor's estimators for costing out design proposals.*

2.6   Sustainability Checkpoints

Sustainability Checkpoint 2

NOTE *During Stage 2 the Sustainability Strategy is developed along with other core strategies as the design progresses. The Sustainability Aspirations may also be reviewed and included in the Final Project Brief.*

Sustainability aims

To develop a Concept Design that embodies the underpinning Sustainability Aspirations of the project with sufficient detail and analysis to be confident that key strategies can be delivered in practice.

Checkpoints

- Confirm that formal sustainability pre-assessment and identification of key areas of design focus have been undertaken and that any deviation from the Sustainability Aspirations has been reported and agreed.

- Has the initial Building Regulations Part L assessment been carried out?

- Have 'plain English' descriptions of internal environmental conditions and seasonal control strategies and systems been prepared?

- Has the environmental impact of key materials and the Construction Strategy been checked?

- Has resilience to future changes in climate been considered?

Key actions

- Undertake formal sustainability pre-assessment and identification of key areas of design focus.

- Report on deviation from aspirations.

- Undertake initial Approved Document L assessment.

- Prepare a 'plain English' description of internal environmental conditions, seasonal control strategy and systems.

2

- Check the environmental impact of key materials and the Construction Strategy.

- Consider resilience to future changes in climate.

- Set out the site-scale environmental design criteria (e.g. solar orientation, overshadowing, SuDS, waste).

- Consider the design of the space between buildings as well as the buildings themselves.

- Consider the need for and scale of private, semi-private and public external space.

- Establish maximum plan depths to achieve desired levels of natural ventilation, daylight and view.

- Design for buildability, usability and manageability.

- Consider the impact of complexity of form on thermal performance, airtightness and inefficient or wasteful use of materials.

- Establish an appropriate glazing proportion and shading strategy for each orientation to provide good levels of daylight while avoiding excessive glare, solar gain or heat loss.

- Establish appropriate element thicknesses to achieve the U-values required by the energy strategy.

- Check that materials and the construction approach will provide a level of thermal mass that is appropriate to the environmental design strategy.

- Refine and review design decisions to minimise the quantity of materials used and to minimise construction waste (for guidance, see www.wrap.org.uk/designingoutwaste).

- Review the embodied impacts of the materials and the construction approach in the context of the building's lifespan.

- Avoid design solutions that inhibit adaptation and alternative use of the building or its components and materials.

- Take particular care to avoid short- and long-term damage to retained traditional building fabric from ill-considered upgrade interventions.

- Ensure that the design implications of any components essential to the success of the Sustainability Strategy (e.g. space for fuel deliveries and waste handling, roof collector area and orientation, location and size of rainwater harvesting tanks, SuDS attenuation, etc.) are understood by all members of the project team.

- Refine the energy and servicing strategy, incorporating energy-efficient services design and design techniques.

- Carry out sufficient compliance or advanced modelling to prove the design concept before freezing the design (e.g. SBEM/SAP/PHPP (Passivhaus Planning Package) or dynamic modelling).

- Audit the emerging design against the project's Sustainability Strategy and Project Outcomes.

- Set up a programme of intermediate evaluations and reality checks involving stakeholders and key users as well as the design team.

2.7　Information Exchanges

2.7.1　Check that all the agreed outputs have been produced before the conclusion of Stage 2. Outputs might include the following:

- fully developed Final Project Brief

- Concept Design (including outline structural and mechanical services design by others) – this should show the design sufficiently developed for the client to comprehend, comment on and approve the proposals. A diagrammatic analysis of requirements, use of site, solutions to functional and circulation problems, relationship of spaces, massing, construction and environmental methods may be included

- the necessary Project Strategies

- preliminary Cost Information – an estimate of the construction cost sufficient to allow a cost plan to be prepared (see Figure 2/1).

If procurement is through design and build:

- *for an employer client: outline proposals for the Employer's Requirements*

- *for a contractor client: outline drawings for the Contractor's Proposals.*

2.8　UK Government Information Exchanges

2.8.1　Information Exchanges are required.

Supplementary Material

2/SM1: Design and build documentation

Employer's Requirements

The amount of information to be included in the Employer's Requirements can vary enormously. A straightforward project requiring a relatively simple design solution which can be left largely to the contractor may need little more than basic details of site and accommodation. With a more complex problem, or a design which needs sensitivity of detail, the Employer's Requirements might extend to a full scheme design.

The number and detail of documents which make up the Employer's Requirements will be influenced by considerations such as:

- how much design control the employer wishes to retain, for example in the interests of maintenance programmes or because of functional requirements
- whether the employer regards the process as more of a develop and construct operation, where only constructional details are left in the hands of the contractor
- whether contractor's standard unit types will form the basis of the scheme
- whether the employer will require design continuity via novation or a 'consultant switch'
- whether the employer has appointed a planning supervisor and whether a pre-tender Health and Safety Plan exists.

Generally the Requirements will always need to include basic information, such as the following:

- site information and requirements (e.g. boundaries, topography, known subsoil conditions, existing services)
- site constraints (e.g. limitations of access, storage) and relevant easements or restrictive covenants
- topographical surveys
- geotechnical reports
- planning permission obtained or conditions known (contractors will not usually tender until outline planning permission has been obtained)
- reports on other statutory consultations
- existing Health and Safety Files, client's health and safety policy documents
- functional nature of the building(s) (e.g. kind and number of units) and accommodation requirements

- schematic layout of the building (or more developed design as appropriate)
- specific requirements as to forms of construction, materials, services, finishes, equipment, etc.
- specification information, probably including performance specifications
- room data sheets
- equipment and fitting schedules
- details of special programming requirements (e.g. phased completion)
- contract data or special requirements (e.g. named subcontractors, 'As-constructed' Information)
- requirements concerning contractor's design liability, insurance cover, design team, requirement to use employer's designers, etc.
- clear statement of the extent of information and detail to be included in the Contractor's Proposals
- content and form of the contract sum analysis.

It is generally accepted that too specific an approach to design and constructional matters, or the specifying of proprietary systems and materials, may reduce the contractor's design liability in the event of a failure.

Contractor's Proposals

These will be in direct response to the Employer's Requirements. Architects acting as consultants to a contractor client will first need to check the information provided to establish whether it is adequate. A query list is often necessary to obtain clarification on matters of conflict or omission.

Submissions sometimes take the form of an A3 brochure, and typically include the following:

- design drawings (e.g. site layout, floor plans, elevations, principal sections, some detailed drawings, landscaping)
- structural details (e.g. foundation and structure general arrangement drawings)
- mechanical services (e.g. layouts of ducts, pipe runs, schematic indications for all systems)
- electrical services (e.g. floor layouts showing lighting, power, alarms)
- specifications (e.g. particular for trades prescription and performance, general specification for workmanship, materials, finishes)
- programme (e.g. bar chart)
- method statements (e.g. general organisational matters and, in particular, Health and Safety Plan proposals).

The tender figure will usually be required to be made separately. With it will be the contract sum analysis.

The structure of the contract sum analysis will be in accordance with the Employer's Requirements. A typical breakdown could be:

- Design work
- Preliminaries
- Health and safety provisions
- Demolition
- Excavation
- Concrete
- Brickwork and blockwork
- Roofing and cladding
- Woodwork
- Structural steelwork
- Metalwork
- Mechanical and plumbing services
- Electrical services
- Glazing
- Painting and decorating
- Drainage and external works.

2/SM2: Design team roles

Cost consultant

The cost consultant can assist the design team in reviewing financial aspects of the Concept Design and monitoring costs against the budget. They should be involved continuously and should report regularly at consultant team meetings.

The cost consultant will evaluate the Strategic Brief and advise on the cost implications of design and energy options. They will prepare an initial cost plan and cash flow forecast, relying on input from other consultant team members.

Structural engineer

The structural engineer can work with the architect to develop structural concepts which are integral with the overall design in the Concept Design. They will visit the site and advise on the structural constraints it imposes and on any surveys needed, for example where there are special conditions such as contaminated land. The structural engineer can advise on environmental issues such as excavation and landfill. They should also liaise with services engineers to ensure integrated design. Priorities should be established and conflicts resolved at design team meetings.

Building services engineer

At Concept Design stage, the architect will take into account orientation, climatic and other environmental factors. There will also be a need to establish performance, installation and costs in use. The building services engineer can play an important role in contributing to an integrated design approach, including consideration of sustainability issues. They will identify surveys required and initiate preliminary consultations with statutory authorities. They should contribute regularly to design team meetings.

Health and safety

All design team members should cooperate with the CDM coordinator in carrying out risk assessments and starting to prepare material for inclusion in the Health and Safety File and the pre-construction information.

2/SM3: Final Project Brief checklist

By the end of Stage 2 the brief should be finalised and signed off by the client. The Final Project Brief should normally address the following:

(a)   the aim of the design, including:
   • prioritised Project Objectives
   • accommodation requirements, including disabled access policy
   • space standards
   • environmental policy, including energy
   • environmental performance requirements
   • image and quality
   • flexibility to accommodate future reorganisation
   • allowance for future expansion or extension
   • lifespan for structure, elements and installations
   • operational and maintenance requirements
   • special considerations (e.g. security)

(b)   the site, including details of accessibility and planning
   • site constraints (physical and legal)
   • legislative constraints

(c)   the functions and activities of the client
   • schedule of functions or processes
   • activities
   • spatial relationships
   • schedule of installations

(d)   the structure of the client organisation
(e)   the size and configuration of the facilities
(f)   options for environmental delivery and control
(g)   servicing options and specification implications, e.g. security, deliveries, access, workplace
(h)   outline specifications of general and specific areas
(i)   a budget for all elements
(j)   the procurement process
(k)   the Project Execution Plan
(l)   key targets for quality, time and cost, including milestones for decisions
(m)   method for assessing and managing risks and validating design proposals.

Figure 2/1

Budget estimate

Job no: _____   Job title: _____

Cost plan / budget estimate

		Cost of elements	Cost per m² gross floor area	Element shown as % of whole
Substructure				
Superstructure	Frame			
	Upper floors			
	Roof			
	Stairs			
	External cladding			
	Windows and external doors			
	Internal partitions			
	Internal doors and windows			
Internal finishes	Ceiling finishes			
	Wall finishes			
	Floor finishes			
Fittings	Furniture and fittings			
Services	Sanitary installation			
	Mechanical installation			
	Electrical installation			
	Special installations			
	Elevators and hoists			
	Builder's work			
	Builder's profit and attendance			
Building work	Sub-total			
Additional	Site works			
	Drainage			
	External services			
	Extra temporary works (phasing)			
	Inflation at 3%			
	Preliminaries at 5%			
Total	Excluding VAT and contingencies			

STAGE 3

Developed Design

CONTENTS

Plan of Work and Stage Activities

Supplementary Material

Figures

RIBA
Plan of
Work
2013

Excerpt from the RIBA Plan of Work 2013

RIBA
Plan of
Work
2013

Stage 3

Developed Design

Task Bar	Tasks
Core Objectives	Prepare **Developed Design**, including coordinated and updated proposals for structural design, building services systems, outline specifications, **Cost Information** and **Project Strategies** in accordance with **Design Programme**.
Procurement Variable task bar	*The Procurement activities during this stage will depend on the procurement route determined during Stage 1.*
Programme Variable task bar	*The RIBA Plan of Work 2013 enables this stage to overlap with a number of other stages depending on the selected procurement route.*
(Town) Planning Variable task bar	*It is recommended that planning applications are submitted at the end of this stage.*
Suggested Key Support Tasks	Review and update **Sustainability**, **Maintenance and Operational** and **Handover Strategies** and **Risk Assessments**. Undertake third party consultations as required and conclude **Research and Development** aspects. Review and update **Project Execution Plan**, including **Change Control Procedures**. Review and update **Construction** and **Health and Safety Strategies**. *During this stage it is essential to review the **Project Strategies** previously generated.*
Sustainability Checkpoints	• *Has a full formal sustainability assessment been carried out?* • *Have an interim Building Regulations Part L assessment and a design stage carbon/energy declaration been undertaken?* • *Has the design been reviewed to identify opportunities to reduce resource use and waste and the results recorded in the Site Waste Management Plan?*
Information Exchanges (at stage completion)	**Developed Design**, including the coordinated architectural, structural and building services design and updated **Cost Information**.
UK Government Information Exchanges	Required.

Summary

During this stage, the Concept Design is further developed and, crucially, the design work of the core designers is progressed until the spatial coordination exercises have been completed. This process may require a number of iterations of the design and different tools may be used, including design workshops.

By the end of Stage 3, the architectural, building services and structural engineering designs will all have been developed, and will have been checked by the lead designer, with the stage design coordinated and the **Cost Information** aligned to the **Project Budget**.

Project Strategies that were prepared during Stage 2 should be developed further and in sufficient detail to allow the client to sign them off once the lead designer has checked each strategy and verified that the **Cost Information** incorporates adequate allowances.

Change Control Procedures should be implemented to ensure that any changes to the Concept Design are properly considered and signed off, regardless of how they are instigated.

While specialist subcontractors will undertake their design work at Stage 4, they may provide information and guidance at Stage 3 in order to facilitate a more robust developed design.

Mapping to RIBA Outline Plan of Work 2007

Stage 3 maps broadly to the former Stage D and part of Stage E. The strategic difference is that in the RIBA Plan of Work 2013 the Developed Design will be coordinated and aligned with the **Cost Information** by the end of Stage 3. This may not increase the amount of design work required, but extra time will be needed to review information and implement any changes that arise from comments made before all the outputs are coordinated prior to the **Information Exchange** at the end of Stage 3.

3.1   Core Objectives

At Stage 3 the Concept Design approved by the client is developed and the Final Project Brief is completed. The work of the core designers is progressed until the spatial coordination exercises have been completed. As lead designer, the architect will need to be satisfied that there are no insurmountable problems ahead concerning the integration of the consultants' proposals into the overall design concept. By the end of the stage the architectural, building services and structural engineering designs will all have been developed, and will have been checked by the lead designer, with the stage design coordinated and the Cost Information aligned with the Project Budget. As 'designer', within the meaning of that term in the CDM Regulations, the architect will also have to be sure that all health and safety implications have been properly considered at this stage.

Project Strategies that were prepared during Stage 2 should be developed further and in sufficient detail to allow the client to sign them off once the lead designer has checked each strategy and verified that the Cost Information contains adequate allowances.

Change Control Procedures should be implemented to ensure that any changes to the Concept Design are properly considered and signed off, regardless of how they are instigated.

With design and build, where the architect is acting for an employer client, Stage 3 might cover design formulation to the extent necessary for inclusion as part of the Employer's Requirements. If the project has been tendered at an early stage in the development of the design, Stage 3 may involve the architect in assessing the contractor's design proposals and reporting to the employer client.

With a contractor client, the architect may be involved in the development of the design information already included as part of the Contractor's Proposals. The development of the Technical Design will probably not take place until there is confirmation that the contractor's bid has been approved, or a second-stage tender is invited.

Where management procurement is followed, there will still need to be an overall design scheme even though it is anticipated that the detailed development will be phased. Thought should be given to how the works packages will be broken down, as this in turn might influence some design decisions.

NOTE *'Management procurement' is the term used in this book to cover any form of procurement using management methods, such as 'management contracts' and 'construction management'. With management contracts, a management contractor is appointed through a tender and interview process and paid on the basis of the scheduled services, prime costs and a management fee. Its role is to manage the execution of the work, but it is not usually directly involved in carrying out any of the construction work, which will be done in 'packages' undertaken by works contractors, usually appointed by the management contractor.*

With construction management agreements there is usually a lead designer and a construction manager responsible for managing and coordinating the work, with the client entering into all trades contracts.

 For detailed advice on this refer to Which Contract? *(2007).*

3.2   Procurement

3.2.1	Review and update the Project Execution Plan, including the Change Control Procedures.
3.2.2	Review and update the Construction Strategy and the Health and Safety Strategy.
3.2.3	Confirm in writing with the client the procurement method and the form of contract to be adopted.
3.2.4	Discuss with the client and the design team whether any preliminary tender action for specialist subcontractors and suppliers will be required.

3

3.2.5	Discuss with the client and the consultant team whether any action will be needed on advance orders (noting the risk involved in placing orders in advance of planning permission being granted).
3.2.6	Identify works packages where applicable.
3.2.7	Identify any performance-specified work or contractor's designed portion items.
3.2.8	Discuss with the client any particular requirements for phased or sectional completion.

3.3   Programme

3.3.1	Confirm the stage timetable for services, and note its relationship to the project timetable as agreed with the client. The timetable should show critical points by which information from the client and design team members will be required.

3.4   (Town) Planning

NOTE	*Although it is set out as a 'variable' task in the RIBA Plan of Work 2013, it is usual for the planning application to be submitted at this stage.*	**3/SM1**
3.4.1	Prepare and submit application for approval of reserved matters following an outline planning permission if appropriate.	
3.4.2 BIM	Export data as appropriate from the BIM model to enable preparation and submission of the application for full planning permission, listed building consent and conservation area consent as relevant and if instructed by the client. Ensure that all applications are accompanied by relevant documents, including payment by the client of the appropriate fee.	**1/SM3**

3.4.3	Discuss with the planning officer any difficulties or conditions arising from an outline planning permission, and any problems likely to occur with a full planning application. Check whether the authority operates particular planning policies, issues its own supplementary guidance notes, etc.
3.4.4	Enquire whether the planning authority requires information additional to that of the usual form of application for full planning permission, and whether additional copies could speed up the consultation process.
3.4.5	Enquire whether it is possible to have representation at the planning committee at which the application is considered, should this be thought desirable.

3.5	**Suggested Key Support Tasks**

3.5.1	Information required

3.5.1.1	Check that all the information necessary during Stage 3 is available, which might include the following: • Final Project Brief • Stage 2 Concept Design as accepted by the client in written confirmation, incorporating any agreed design changes • further information as requested by the architect and supplied by the client • notes, sketches and details made on visits to other projects • relevant published material, technical information, etc. • results of tests conducted during Stage 2 • relevant legislation, circulars or guides • further contributions, information and recommendations from consultants and specialists • initial cost plan prepared by the cost consultant.

3.5.1.2   Obtain codes, standards, digests, etc. relevant to the project.

 When designing to meet legislative standards or codes of practice, always check that the current versions are being used.

3.5.1.3   Obtain project-specific information from potential subcontractors and suppliers.

 When adopting proprietary systems or components for a design, take care that proposals will satisfy British and European Standards or other technical standards prescribed and not contain deleterious materials. Manufacturers' published test results might relate to tests carried out under circumstances quite unlike those which might apply to a particular project. Check that products specified are suitable for the purpose and location, and obtain verification, certificates and warranties, as appropriate, before making a design commitment.

 Refer to the British Council for Offices (BCO) guide Good Practice in the Selection of Construction Materials 2011.

3.5.2   Brief

3.5.2.1   Check that the brief, as presently developed, still meets the client's stated objectives.

 The client must have been advised at the end of Stage 2 that the Final Project Brief has been finalised and that any modifications thereafter could mean abortive work. Changes to the Final Project Brief at this stage are likely to have an effect on the Project Programme and Project Budget. If changes are necessary they should be subject to the Change Control Procedures and only undertaken once written agreement has been issued by the client's representative.

3.5.3   Appointment

3.5.3.1   Establish scope, content and context for Stage 3 activities.

 Put this information into context, particularly if previous stages were undertaken by others. If possible, establish whether material produced now is likely to be acted upon by others taking over subsequent stages.

3.5.3.2	If coming new to the project at this stage in the Plan of Work:

- ascertain that relevant Concept Design stage and earlier stage checks have been carried out

- allow for familiarisation and reviewing of all usable material when agreeing fees and timetable with the client

- confirm the role of the architect in relation to the rest of the design team

- ensure that you have adequate professional indemnity (PI) insurance cover in accordance with ARB and RIBA requirements.

3.5.3.3	Check that the client's instruction to proceed has been given and confirmed in writing.

3.5.3.4	Check that the client has settled all accounts submitted to date.

3.5.3.5	Check appointing documents with respect to services and fees.

- If the extent of professional services for Stage 3 is not yet settled, agree with the client and confirm in writing.

- If the methods and levels of charging for Stage 3 are not yet settled, agree with the client and confirm in writing.

3.5.3.6	Assess the office resources needed for Stage 3 and ensure that they are available and adequate.

3.5.3.7	Carry out checks for compliance with in-house quality management procedures, including the updated Project Execution Plan.

3.5.3.8	Review the application of practice procedures to the project.

3.5.4	Client

3.5.4.1	Check whether the client has confirmed in writing acceptance of the Concept Design submitted at Stage 2. Establish points to be discussed and developed during Stage 3.

3

3.5.4.2	Advise the client on the need to appoint further consultants and specialists.
3.5.4.3	Alert the client about any matters raised during discussions with statutory or other bodies which might affect the proposals. Explain the implications and discuss what actions should be taken.
3.5.4.4	Alert the client to the design implications arising out of health and safety legislation (e.g. circulation, design of workstations, environmental comfort) and implications for future maintenance, repair and replacement.
3.5.4.5	Check that all information requested from the client concerning the site or existing buildings has been supplied.
3.5.4.6	Ask the client for information and requirements concerning processes, plant and other installations, room layouts and equipment, etc. and record this information appropriately, if not already included in the Final Project Brief. Check on particular requirements concerning the life expectancy of components, fittings and installations, and performance requirements for environmental and services aspects, etc.
3.5.4.7	Check whether the client wishes the project to be planned to allow for phasing of completion or completion to a particular sequence. This might have design implications.
3.5.4.8	Check whether the client has decided the method of procurement, and confirm any decision in writing. If no decision is reached, explain the importance of reaching a decision before the detailed design is developed. This procurement method could affect the amount and type of design information needed at this stage.
3.5.4.9	Advise the client on the need for a party wall surveyor, if appropriate. If the architect is to be appointed as party wall surveyor, this appointment must form a separate agreement.

3.5.5	Project team
3.5.5.1	If appointed as information manager: • assist members of the design team to develop the design using the BIM model, ensuring that data-sharing protocols are followed • check and sign off the BIM model at agreed stages • issue or assist in the issue of design data at agreed times throughout the development of the design • assist in the development of data relative to the agreed levels of detail • assist in the integration of contractors', subcontractors' and suppliers' data into the BIM model. For further advice on working with BIM, refer to the RIBA publication *BIM Demystified* (2012).
3.5.5.2	Establish or review project quality management procedures together with relevant procedures of all design team members.
3.5.5.3	Check the scope of professional services agreed with other consultants as they are appointed.
3.5.5.4	Agree input to the stage by design team members.
3.5.5.5	Confirm the programme and pattern for design team meetings.
3.5.5.6	Appraise input from specialist firms, including potential subcontractors and suppliers.
3.5.5.7	Confirm arrangements for communication between the client, CDM coordinator, project manager and lead designer.

3.5.5.8   Monitor, coordinate and integrate input from design team members and specialists.

Maintain close collaboration with consultants and specialists. The architect might not be responsible for their individual performance, but will be responsible for the coordination and integration of their work into the overall design.

3.5.5.9   Check the designers' cooperation with the CDM coordinator with respect to the pre-construction information.

As project lead or lead designer, the architect has an obligation to check that every designer pays due regard to the CDM Regulations and avoids foreseeable risks, or takes steps to combat them at source when designing.

3.5.5.10   *During this stage the structural engineer should collaborate in developing the design, and advise on structural options and preferred solutions. The architect is responsible for coordination and integration into the overall design concept. This will include checking that structural proposals are compatible with the space and access requirements of the services installations.*

The structural engineer should produce the initial structural design, prescribe profiles, basic specifications and building tolerances, define basic rules for voids and holes which might need to be provided and which might affect the structure, and take steps as necessary to establish compliance with statutory requirements. They will provide information for the elemental and firm cost plan, and should contribute information and advice for inclusion in the Stage 3 report to the client.

3.5.6   General matters

3.5.6.1   Prepare the Developed Design, including coordinated and updated proposals for structural design, services systems, landscape, outline specifications, Cost Information and Project Strategies.

During this stage it is wise to draft preliminary specification notes, and to collate information as it comes to hand. Specification writing is part of the design process and should be undertaken by the designer.

3.5.6.2   Review and update the Sustainability Strategy (including interim Approved Document L assessment), the Maintenance and Operational Strategy and the Handover Strategy.

3.5.6.3	Advise the client about any proposals to introduce innovative design or construction ideas or the specifying of relatively new materials, and ask the client to confirm awareness of these in writing.
3.5.6.4	Undertake design review workshops at regular intervals as required.
3.5.6.5	Finalise the Developed Design. The presentation to the client of Stage 3 proposals is particularly important. Establish early how this is to be effected, and prepare the material accordingly. It will usually entail a written report and visual material and may require an oral presentation.
NOTE	*At the conclusion of Stage 3, get the satisfied client to 'sign off' the Developed Design. Clearly, beyond this point any changes which are client-originated might mean abortive work and additional expense.*
3.5.6.6	Prepare the stage report and submit to the client.
3.5.6.7	Check progress against the timetable for services regularly.
3.5.6.8	Continue resource control procedures for the job: • check expenditure against the office job cost allocation for Stage 3 • monitor fee income against projected fee income.
3.5.6.9	Report regularly to the client on fees and expenses incurred, and submit accounts at agreed intervals.
3.5.6.10	Check that the client settles all accounts promptly.
3.5.6.11 BIM	Share and integrate data for design coordination and detailed analysis of the design, including data links between models.
3.5.6.12 BIM	Develop and integrate generic and bespoke design components. *BIM data can be used for environmental performance and area analysis.*

3.5.6.13 Share data for design coordination, technical analysis and addition of specification data.

BiM

3.5.6.14 Assess 4D and/or 5D data as appropriate.

BiM

3.5.7   Inspections/tests

3.5.7.1 Make further site/building visits as authorised.

3.5.7.2 Early on in the stage, arrange to inspect similar projects elsewhere if appropriate, perhaps accompanied by the client. Appraise and analyse the schemes. It would be wise to check first that expenditure is authorised by the client.

3.5.7.3 Arrange for testing and record and analyse results if instructed by the client. These tests might include production prototypes, mock-ups, sample components and panels to be tested under specified conditions and to stipulated methods as appropriate, for example testing for structural performance, durability, consistency, etc. of components, fittings and finishes.

NOTE   *Surveys, inspections or specialist investigations and preparation form part of the Services under the RIBA Standard Agreement 2010 (2012 revision) (item 5). However, where special models are required, services for this do not form part of the Services under of the RIBA Standard Agreement 2010 (2012 revision) unless identified under Part 3 'Other Services'.*

NOTE   *The Services under the RIBA Standard Agreement 2010 (2012 revision) includes outline planning submission and pre-application planning consultation (item 10) as well as submissions to and negotiations with landlords, freeholders, etc. If further services other than those mentioned above are required when applying for outline planning permission, these would need to be identified under Part 3 'Other Services'.*

3.5.8	Consultations, approvals and consents
3.5.8.1	Hold further meetings with statutory bodies as necessary.
3.5.8.2	Continue discussions with the building control and fire authorities over matters where overall design could be fundamentally affected, such as compartmentation, atrium design, fire resistance of elements, escape routes, smoke lobbies and active systems, e.g. sprinklers.
3.5.8.3	Consult insurers, as appropriate, regarding the application of codes of practice or design guides relating to fire safety which might have design implications, such as compartmentation, atrium design, fire resistance of elements, and active systems, e.g. sprinklers.
3.5.8.4	Check health and safety legislation requirements likely to affect detailed planning. Continue to cooperate with the CDM coordinator and other designers over design implications of the pre-construction information required under the CDM Regulations.
3.5.8.5	Continue checks with relevant authorities for highways, drainage, water, gas, electricity supplies, etc.
3.5.8.6	Consult further with user clients, third parties and adjoining owners, if authorised. If instructed, issue party wall notices as soon as the proposals are sufficiently finalised, on behalf of the client. NOTE *Consultations with users or third parties, and for party wall matters, do not form part of the Services under the RIBA Standard Agreement 2010 (2012 revision) unless identified under Part 3 'Other Services,' but note items 8 and 12.*
3.5.8.7	Check whether necessary third party consents are being obtained.

3

| 3.5.8.8 | Prepare and submit application for express consent to display an advertisement, application or notification to fell or lop trees covered by a Tree Preservation Order or in a conservation area, as relevant. |

| 3.5.8.9 | Conclude any Research and Development activities related to the project. |

3.5.9 Cost planning

| 3.5.9.1 NOTE | *The cost consultant should collaborate with the architect and other consultants to develop and refine the full cost plan as the design is developed and outline specification notes are prepared.* |

During this stage the cost consultant will prepare an elemental cost plan followed by a firm cost plan and cash flow forecast, relying on input from other design team members, and will advise on cost effects of compliance with statutory requirements. The cost consultant should contribute information and advice for inclusion in the Stage 3 report to the client.

| 3.5.9.2 | Discuss with the design team and the client the effect of major design decisions on the allocations within the cost plan before they are taken. |

| NOTE | *There must be regular two-way exchange of information if designers are to keep within cost targets or limits.* |

| 3.5.9.3 | Provide the cost consultant with information on the cost plan and cash flow projection (or prepare a cost estimate if appointed to do so). |

| 3.5.9.4 | Report to the client on cost matters at agreed intervals. |

| NOTE | *If procurement is through design and build for a contractor client, provide information to other consultants and the contractor's estimators to cost detailed proposals.* |

3.6   Sustainability Checkpoints

Sustainability Checkpoint 3

Sustainability aims

To ensure that the Developed Design reflects the underpinning Sustainability Strategy.

Checkpoints

- Has a full formal sustainability assessment been carried out?

- Have an interim Building Regulations Part L assessment and a design stage carbon/energy declaration been undertaken?

- Has the design been reviewed to identify opportunities to reduce resource use and waste and the results recorded in the Site Waste Management Plan?

Key actions

- The Sustainability Strategy is reviewed and the level of detail for any supporting strategies is developed including those that impact on any statutory legislation.

- Produce a full formal sustainability assessment.

- Produce an interim Approved Document L assessment and design stage carbon/energy declaration (e.g. Carbon Buzz).

- Review the design to identify opportunities to reduce resource use and waste and recorded in the Site Waste Management Plan.

- Refine and distil the project's Sustainability Strategy, checking against brief and targets.

- Update energy modelling as the design develops and check against targets.

- Refine the climate adaptation strategy and make provision for future adaptation interventions.

- Incorporate environmental and sustainability issues in the Planning Application Design and Access Statement, including a development of the Stage 2 'plain English' description of internal environmental conditions, seasonal control strategy and systems. Provide a supplementary detailed report if appropriate.

- Consider peer reviews of environmental control strategies and also involve stakeholders and users.

- Instigate initial involvement of and advice to contractors and specialist subcontractors where specialist products or systems are proposed.

- Audit the Developed Design to ensure integration and compliance with the project's sustainability targets.

3.7   Information Exchanges

3.7.1   Check that all agreed outputs have been produced before the conclusion of Stage 3, which might include the following:

- the Developed Design, including the coordinated architectural, structural and mechanical services design

- updated Cost Information

- drawings showing coordinated design intentions, site layout, planning and spatial arrangements, elevational treatment, construction and environmental systems and buildability

- prototypes, mock-ups, models, sample panels, etc.

- proposals developed sufficiently to allow an application for full planning permission, listed building consent, conservation area consent, etc. as applicable.

NOTE

If procurement is through design and build:

- *for an employer client: detailed proposals for incorporation into the Employer's Requirements*

- *for a contractor client: further notes, sketches, details and drawings as necessary to develop the scheme included in the Contractor's Proposals.*

3.8   UK Government Information Exchanges

3.8.1   Information Exchanges are required.

3

Supplementary Material

3/SM1: The planning application

Make preparations:

- prepare all documentation on the assumption that it might serve as supporting evidence in an appeal
- confirm by letter all meetings, phone calls, etc. with the planning authority
- make sure that the client's representative also attends all critical meetings with the planning authority
- at an early stage consider project presentations to attract the interest and support of neighbourhood and parish groups, appropriate lobbies and news media.

Check the following:

- dates and procedures of planning meetings
- probable date by which decision is to be given
- number and types of drawings required
- procedures, e.g. notices in the press, site notices
- processes for public consultation and response to any objections.

When making a planning application, check that:

- forms are carefully completed – identify or list submitted drawings on forms or in a covering letter
- an accurate site plan identifies the land concerned, clearly defined in red
- a covering letter accompanies the application, explaining features of the scheme
- an Ownership Certificate A (or B, C, D as appropriate) is served
- payment from the client for the appropriate sum is submitted at the same time (having checked the correct amount with the planning authority, as it usually increases year on year)
- the application is date-stamped by the planning authority (this defines the start of the period for determination)
- a copy of the written report by the planning officer to the planning committee is obtained
- if permitted and appropriate, oral representation is made to the planning committee.

The planning meeting

If appropriate, attend critical meetings with the client's representative. Keep a written note of what is discussed. If planning permission is refused and an appeal is contemplated, send your account of proceedings to the chief executive of the authority. If not dissented from, your account may have the status of 'agreed notes'. Examine the agenda and record of the meeting; these may constitute the basis for an appeal.

For more detailed advice on the planning process refer to the RIBA Good Practice Guide *Negotiating the Planning Maze* (2009).

Figure 3/1

Specimen design change notice and record

Job no: Job title:

Design change notice and record

To:

_____   _____
_____   _____

_____   _____

Enclosures: Please find enclosed the documents listed below.
                     Please enter comments, photocopy, and return original notice by

_____   (Date)

_____
_____
_____
_____
_____
_____

                     Issued by _____   Date: _____

Comments:
_____
_____
_____
_____
_____
_____
_____
_____
_____
_____
_____
_____
_____
_____
_____
_____

                     Signed _____   Date: _____

Implementation record   Change adopted YES/NO   Included in contract YES/NO

                     Covered by Contract
                     Administrator's Instruction   No.   issued   (date)

Drawings or other documents indicating proposed design changes should be circulated under cover of a change notice, which invites comments from recipients. These forms should be filed and the action taken recorded. Following the adoption of design changes, amendments might be needed to the entries in the register of drawings.

RIBA
Plan of
Work
2013

Excerpt from the RIBA Plan of Work 2013

RIBA
Plan of
Work
2013

Stage 4

Technical Design

Task Bar	Tasks
Core Objectives	Prepare **Technical Design** in accordance with **Design Responsibility Matrix** and **Project Strategies** to include all architectural, structural and building services information, specialist subcontractor design and specifications, in accordance with **Design Programme**.
Procurement Variable task bar	*The Procurement activities during this stage will depend on the procurement route determined during Stage 1.*
Programme Variable task bar	*The RIBA Plan of Work 2013 enables this stage to overlap with a number of other stages depending on the selected procurement route.*
(Town) Planning Variable task bar	*The RIBA Plan of Work 2013 suggests that any conditions attached to a planning consent are addressed during this stage, prior to work starting on site during Stage 5.*
Suggested Key Support Tasks	Review and update **Sustainability, Maintenance and Operational** and **Handover Strategies** and **Risk Assessments**. Prepare and submit Building Regulations submission and any other third party submissions requiring consent. Review and update **Project Execution Plan**. Review **Construction Strategy**, including sequencing, and update **Health and Safety Strategy**. *A further review of the **Project Strategies** and documentation previously generated is required during this stage.*
Sustainability Checkpoints	• *Is the formal sustainability assessment substantially complete?* • *Have details been audited for airtightness and continuity of insulation?* • *Has the Building Regulations Part L submission been made and the design stage carbon/energy declaration been updated and the future climate impact assessment prepared?* • *Has a non-technical user guide been drafted and have the format and content of the Part L log book been agreed?* • *Has all outstanding design stage sustainability assessment information been submitted?* • *Are building **Handover Strategy** and monitoring technologies specified?* • *Have the implications of changes to the specification or design been reviewed against agreed sustainability criteria?* • *Has compliance of agreed sustainability criteria for contributions by specialist subcontractors been demonstrated?*
Information Exchanges (at stage completion)	Completed **Technical Design** of the project.
UK Government Information Exchanges	Not required.

Summary

The architectural, building services and structural engineering designs are now further refined to provide technical definition of the project and the design work of specialist subcontractors is developed and concluded. The level of detail produced by each designer will depend on whether the construction on site will be built in accordance with the information produced by the design team or based on information developed by a specialist subcontractor. The **Design Responsibility Matrix** sets out how these key design interfaces will be managed.

Using the design coordinated during the previous stage, the designers should now be able to develop their Technical Designs independently, with a degree of autonomy. The lead designer will provide input to certain aspects, including a review of each designer's work.

Once the work of the design team has been progressed to the appropriate level of detail, as defined in the **Design Responsibility Matrix** and the **Design Programme**, specialist subcontractors and/or suppliers undertaking design work will be able to progress their design work. The lead designer and other designers, where required as part of their **Schedule of Services**, may have duties to review this design information and to ensure that specialist subcontractor design work is integrated with the coordinated design.

By the end of this stage, all aspects of the design will be completed, apart from minor queries arising from the site during the construction stage. In many projects, Stage 4 and 5 work occurs concurrently, particularly the specialist subcontractor design aspects.

Mapping to RIBA Outline Plan of Work 2007

Stage 4 comprises the residual technical work of the core design team members. At the end of Stage 4, the design work of these designers will be completed, although they may have to respond to **Design Queries** that arise from work undertaken on site during Stage 5. This stage also includes and recognises the importance of design work undertaken by specialist subcontractors and/or suppliers employed by the contractor (Performance Specified Work in JCT contracts) and the need to define this work early in the process in the **Design Responsibility Matrix**.

4.1	Core Objectives

In Stage 4 the design team further develops the Stage 3 Developed Design in sufficient detail for tendering and construction/assembly activities on site. If design activities are to be undertaken by specialists or subcontractors then the design will need to be developed to a level that allows for this and the design team may have obligations to check this information or respond to Design Queries as set out in the Design Responsibility Matrix. The lead designer and other designers may have duties to review this design information and to ensure that the design work is integrated with the coordinated design. By the end of the stage all aspects of the design will have been completed, apart from minor queries arising from site during the construction stage. The Design Responsibility Matrix will set out how the key design interfaces will be managed.

Using the design coordinated during Stage 3, the designers should now be able to work with a degree of autonomy. The lead designer will provide input to certain aspects, including the review of each designer's work.

The Technical Design will include the required construction details, choice of materials and standards of workmanship. The client may be expected to contribute information or comments on finishes, furnishings and equipment. Design work by consultants and specialists must be coordinated, and relevant information passed to the CDM coordinator for inclusion in the pre-construction information and the Health and Safety Plan.

Generally at Stage 4 the Developed Design is translated into precise technical instructions sufficient to allow for pricing and for construction of the proposed works. This information will normally be conveyed by means of written descriptions, drawings and schedules.

Design and build procurement

In design and build procurement with an employer client, the design will be developed to the level of detail previously agreed. It is unusual for the employer client to require Technical Design services as part of the Employer's Requirements. However, some exploratory detail design is often necessary before the Employer's Requirements can be finished.

Responsibility for Technical Design in design and build procurement will depend on the particular circumstances. It would be very unusual for an employer client to arrange for Technical Design directly, although they might retain a consultant team to monitor Technical Design prepared and submitted by the contractor. Alternatively, the employer client might require the continued use of their team by the successful contractor through a consultant switch or 'novation'. The contractor client will require Technical Design to be undertaken. An architect engaged in this context should establish exactly how much work, how many drawings, etc. will be required before agreeing a programme or fee. The contractor might wish to impose conditions in respect of the method of structuring and supply of Technical Design, preferred technical solutions, materials, etc.

Management procurement

With the management procurement approach a significant proportion of Technical Design will depend on the input of the specialists involved with the works packages under Stage 5 and the two stages will run concurrently. With management contracting much will remain to be resolved after the contract and works packages have been let. Great reliance has to be placed on the management contractor or construction manager, and an early appointment will help the Technical Design development. Close attention should be given to the appropriate number of packages and control maintained to minimise the risk of overlap or duplication. Monitoring of detail design will continue well into the construction phase, and the Construction Phase Plan might require regular adjustment.

The amount of Technical Design available at the commencement of the project will be limited to the extent that much detail information will be supplied by the works contractors by way of shop or installation drawings. Nevertheless, the general Technical Design will originate from the design team, and the process of coordinating and integrating information will continue throughout the construction of the project.

4

4.2	Procurement

4.2.1 For matters related to tendering that are typically dealt with at this stage, refer to the chapter 'Contractor Engagement' at page 313.

4.2.2 If acting as project lead, review any proposals for work by subcontractors or suppliers.

> **NOTE** *In projects where there are to be many specialist subcontractors, particularly where these are undertaking some design obligations, it may be necessary to initiate some tender action for subcontractors at an early stage. This will enable design proposals to be integrated into the overall design and quotations to be checked against the cost plan. This information may be needed before the main contract tender documentation can be finalised.*

4.2.3 Review/update standing lists or register of specialist tenderers and check you have written confirmation from the client for their inclusion. Check willingness and availability of firms included as listed subcontractors and, if necessary, decide on additional names.

4.2.4 Initiate tender action for quotations from specialist subcontractors and suppliers if appropriate.

Check tender invitation documents for sending to specialists.

Invite further tenders as appropriate.

> **NOTE** *When inviting tenders for specialist subcontract work that includes a design element, make certain that the client consents in writing, and that their interests are properly protected by warranty.*

4.2.5 Inspect tenders and information submitted by specialist subcontractors and suppliers.

Refer specialist tenders to the CDM coordinator and relevant consultants for comment.

Refer all tenders to the cost consultant for cost checking.

Approve specialist tenders and notify all tenderers of this decision.

NOTE	*Follow meticulously the procedures stated in the main contract to be used for the appointment of specialist subcontractors.*
NOTE	*Only place advance orders with specialist subcontractors or suppliers as provided for in the subcontract documentation, and only if authorised in writing by the client, as advised by the CDM coordinator.*

4.2.6	Discuss the list of potential main contractors (or construction managers if appropriate) with the client and the design team. Check whether the client holds a general list of approved contractors from which tenderers must be selected. Make preliminary enquiries with contractors if appropriate.
NOTE	*Tender lists should only include firms well known to the architect, or firms which have been satisfactorily investigated.*

4.2.7	Discuss with the client the tender procedures, including:	
	• whether firms which wish to be considered as tenderers should complete a tendering questionnaire	P/SM3
	• whether the client will require tenderers to complete a non-collusion or other similar certificate.	P/SM5

4.2.8	Discuss with the client and the CDM coordinator the tendering period and procedures to be followed in opening tenders, and notify the results.

4.2.9	Continue discussion with the client on the inclusion of any special clauses or amendments to the Building Contract. Remind the client of the need to take legal advice before amending standard forms of contract. Discuss with the client the implications of any advice obtained.

4.2.10	Review the position with respect to advance orders for design, materials and fabrication by specialist subcontractors and suppliers, including named subcontractors. If authorised, take further necessary action.
NOTE	*Always obtain authorisation before taking action on advance orders.*

4.2.11	Confirm with the client the details of any preliminary contracts for enabling works and, if authorised, take the necessary action.

4

4.3	**Programme**

4.3.1	Check progress against the timetable for services regularly.

4.3.2	Confirm the stage timetable for services, and note its relationship to the project timetable as agreed with the client.

4.4	**(Town) Planning**

4.4.1	Review with the design team implications of any conditions attached to full planning permission.

4.4.2	Discuss with the planning officer the implications arising from any planning permission conditions. If permission was refused, discuss the reasons for the refusal and prepare, for the client, recommendations as to the best course of action.

NOTE	*Revision of documents to comply with planning or other statutory authority requirements does not form part of the Services under the RIBA Standard Agreement 2010 (2012 revision) unless identified under Part 3 'Other Services'.*

4.4.3	In the event of a refusal of planning permission, amend the scheme and re-submit the application as appropriate.

4.5	**Suggested Key Support Tasks**

4.5.1	Information required

4.5.1.1	Check that all information necessary during Stage 4 is available, which might include the following:

- Developed Design as accepted by the client in written confirmation, incorporating any agreed amendments

- cost plan prepared by the cost consultant

- published material and technical information, including samples relevant to the project

- results of tests conducted during Stage 3

- relevant legislation

- further contributions, information and recommendations from consultants and specialists, including possible subcontractors and suppliers

- technical information from manufacturers and recommendations or test results relevant to the particular use intended, context and location

- any amendments recommended by local building control and fire authorities during consultations, particularly relating to construction details and fire prevention, including finishes.

 Under the Regulatory Reform (Fire Safety) Order 2005, the law does not require fire certificates but makes it the duty of the person responsible for (non-domestic) premises, employers or building constructors with a degree of control over premises to have a suitable and sufficient fire risk assessment in place.

 The recommended guidance is contained in HSG 168 Fire Safety in Construction (2010), *available from the Health and Safety Executive website: www.hse.gov.uk.*

4.5.2   Brief

4.5.2.1 *Any changes to the Final Project Brief at this stage are likely to have an effect on programme and cost. If changes are necessary they should be subject to the Change Control Procedure and only undertaken once written agreement has been issued by the client's representative.*

4.5.3	Appointment

4.5.3.1	Establish the scope, content and context for Stage 4 activities.

 Put this information into context, particularly if previous stages have been undertaken by others. If possible, establish whether material produced now is likely to be acted upon by others taking over subsequent stages.

4.5.3.2	If coming new to the project at this stage in the Plan of Work:

- ascertain that relevant earlier stage checks have been carried out

- agree fees and timetable with the client

- allow for familiarisation and reviewing of all usable material from Stages 1 to 3 when agreeing fees and timetable with the client

- confirm the role of the architect in relation to the rest of the design team

- ensure that you have adequate professional indemnity (PI) insurance cover in accordance with ARB and RIBA requirements

- request a copy of the project-specific pre-construction health and safety information and review it

- advise the client of their responsibilities under the CDM Regulations and ensure that a CDM coordinator has been appointed.

 Where a project is notifiable, the Regulations require that the client appoints a CDM coordinator as soon as is practicable after initial design work or other preparation for construction work has begun. This would generally be at Stage 2.

4.5.3.3	Check that the client's instruction to proceed has been given and confirmed in writing.

4.5.3.4	Check that the client has settled all accounts submitted to date.

4.5.3.5	Check appointing documents with respect to services and fees.
	• If the services, cost or time targets are different from those agreed with the client, agree a formal variation by letter or deed, as appropriate.
	• If the extent of professional services for Stage 4 is not settled, agree with the client and confirm in writing.
	• If the methods and levels of charging for Stage 4 are not yet settled, agree with the client and confirm in writing.
4.5.3.6	Assess the office resources needed for Stage 4 and ensure that they are available and adequate.
4.5.3.7	Carry out checks for compliance with in-house quality management procedures, including updated Project Execution Plan.
4.5.3.8	Review the application of practice procedures to the project.

4.5.4	Client

NOTE	*If procurement is through design and build:*
	• for an employer client: check whether the client has confirmed in writing acceptance of proposals and information supplied so far to form part of the Employer's Requirements
	• for a contractor client: check whether the client has confirmed in writing acceptance of design proposals to form part of the Contractor's Proposals.

4.5.4.1	Check whether the client has confirmed in writing acceptance of the Developed Design submitted at Stage 3. Establish points to be discussed and developed during Stage 4.
4.5.4.2	It is important to remind the client that any changes to the approved Developed Design which are client-originated might mean abortive work, additional fees and expenses and delays.

| 4.5.4.3 | Continue discussion with the client on more detailed aspects of procurement, and confirm decisions in writing. The decisions will affect the finalisation of the design during this stage, the amount and type of design information needed at this stage and the role of the consultants. |

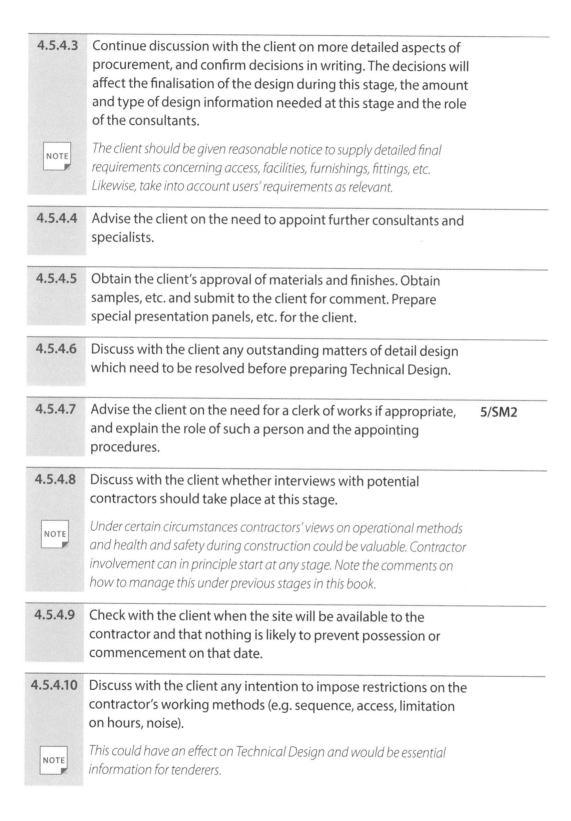

> NOTE
>
> *The client should be given reasonable notice to supply detailed final requirements concerning access, facilities, furnishings, fittings, etc. Likewise, take into account users' requirements as relevant.*

| 4.5.4.4 | Advise the client on the need to appoint further consultants and specialists. |

| 4.5.4.5 | Obtain the client's approval of materials and finishes. Obtain samples, etc. and submit to the client for comment. Prepare special presentation panels, etc. for the client. |

| 4.5.4.6 | Discuss with the client any outstanding matters of detail design which need to be resolved before preparing Technical Design. |

| 4.5.4.7 | Advise the client on the need for a clerk of works if appropriate, and explain the role of such a person and the appointing procedures. | **5/SM2** |

| 4.5.4.8 | Discuss with the client whether interviews with potential contractors should take place at this stage. |

> NOTE
>
> *Under certain circumstances contractors' views on operational methods and health and safety during construction could be valuable. Contractor involvement can in principle start at any stage. Note the comments on how to manage this under previous stages in this book.*

| 4.5.4.9 | Check with the client when the site will be available to the contractor and that nothing is likely to prevent possession or commencement on that date. |

| 4.5.4.10 | Discuss with the client any intention to impose restrictions on the contractor's working methods (e.g. sequence, access, limitation on hours, noise). |

> NOTE
>
> *This could have an effect on Technical Design and would be essential information for tenderers.*

4.5.4.11	Discuss with the client essential information for completing contract documents (e.g. appendix) and which will need to be referred to in preliminaries (or project management sections) of specifications or schedules of work.
4.5.4.12	Check with the client any special or optional contract provisions.
4.5.4.13	Check with the client and advisers on insurance for works, etc.
4.5.4.14	Report regularly to the client on fees and expenses incurred, and submit accounts at agreed intervals.
4.5.4.15	Check that the client settles all accounts promptly.

4.5.5   Project team

4.5.5.1	If appointed as information manager:
	• assist members of the design team to develop the design using the BIM model, ensuring that data-sharing protocols are followed
	• check and sign off the model at agreed stages
	• issue or assist in the issue of design data at agreed times throughout the development of the design
	• assist in the development of data relative to the agreed levels of detail
	• assist in the integration of contractor's, subcontractors' and suppliers' data into the BIM model.
	For further advice on working with BIM, refer to the RIBA publication *BIM Demystified* (2012).
4.5.5.2	Establish or review project quality management procedures together with relevant procedures of all design team members.

4

4.5.5.3   Check the scope of professional services agreed with other consultants as they are appointed.

4.5.5.4   Agree input to the stage by design team members.

NOTE *Remember that the procurement method chosen will greatly affect the amount of detail design information necessary at this stage.*

4.5.5.5   Confirm arrangements for communication between the client, CDM coordinator, project manager and lead designer and between design team members.

NOTE *Cooperation can be encouraged by:*

- *setting up an integrated team involving designers, principal contractor and other relevant contractors (once appointed)*

- *the appointment of a lead designer*

- *agreeing a common approach to risk reduction during design*

- *regular meetings of the whole design team, including the CDM coordinator, with the contractor and others (once appointed)*

- *regular reviews of the evolving design*

- *site visits, through which designers can gain a direct insight into how the risks are to be managed in practice.*

4.5.5.6   Establish the information flow schedule and delivery programme.

4.5.5.7   Have an agreed policy for coordinating information on drawings and between documents.

NOTE *Coordinated Project Information should be introduced at the earliest* **4/SM3** *possible stage in information preparation.*

NOTE *There must be an organised flow of information between the architect and other consultants, particularly with the cost consultant.*

4.5.5.8   Confirm the programme and pattern for design team meetings.

4.5.5.9	Monitor, coordinate and integrate input from design team members and specialists. Appraise input from specialist firms, including potential subcontractors and suppliers. The architect needs to bring both design and management skills to Stage 4. Collaboration with other design team members and coordination of their contributions is often difficult to achieve in practice.
NOTE	*The lead designer is responsible for facilitating the coordination of all information and its integration into the general scheme.*

4.5.5.10	Check the designers' cooperation with the CDM coordinator with respect to the pre-construction information.

4.5.5.11	Check that any design changes now instructed are recorded and subject to the Change Control Procedures.
NOTE	*No design team members should attempt to make decisions unilaterally.*

4.5.5.12	Review with the design team the client's response to Stage 3 Developed Design and decide what action is necessary.

4.5.5.13	Coordinate and integrate information from design team members.

4.5.5.14	Confirm the stage timetable for services and note its relationship to the project timetable as agreed with the client.
NOTE	*Establish a cut-off point for information to be passed to the cost consultant. This will become information for tenderers. Any subsequent changes are then to be treated formally as contract variations at the appropriate time.*

4.5.5.15	Adopt a formal approach to 'question and answer' procedures with the cost consultant as soon as possible.

4.5.5.16	Ask the cost consultant to state priorities for receiving information for billing purposes.

4.5.5.17	At an early stage, request that all consultant team members use the CPI system for Technical Design if this is practicable	4/SM2 4/SM3

4

4.5.5.18	• Continue to cooperate with the CDM coordinator.
	• When carrying out design work, avoid foreseeable risks to those involved in the construction, future use, cleaning and maintenance of the building and in so doing eliminate hazards, as far as reasonably practicable, and reduce risk associated with those hazards that remain.
	• Provide adequate information about any uncommon and significant risks associated with the design.
	• Coordinate your work with others in order to improve the way that risks are managed and controlled.
	• Provide information that other team members are likely to need to identify and manage the remaining risks.
	• Cooperate with the client and other designers, including those designing temporary works, to ensure that incompatibilities between designs are identified and resolved.
	• Discuss with the CDM coordinator any outstanding matters of designers' contributions to the pre-construction health and safety information.

 Remember that the pre-construction health and safety information, as prepared by the CDM coordinator, will need to be issued in the tender documents.

4.5.5.19	Confirm with design team members the arrangements for inviting specialist tenders.
4.5.5.20	Appraise input from specialist firms, including potential subcontractors and suppliers.

4.5.6   General matters

4.5.6.1	Continue resource control procedures for the job:
	• check expenditure against the office job cost allocation for Stage 4
	• monitor fee income against projected fee income.
4.5.6.2	Review and update the Sustainability Strategy, Maintenance and Operational Strategy and the Handover Strategy.

4.5.6.3	Review the Construction Strategy, including sequencing and programme, and update the Health and Safety Strategy.

4.5.6.4	Review and update the Project Execution Plan.

4.5.6.5 BIM	Carry out detailed modelling, integration and analysis using the BIM model.

4.5.6.6 BIM	Create Technical Design level parametric objects for all major elements (where appropriate and information exists this may be based on Tier 2 suppliers' information).

4.5.6.7   Developing the Technical Design:

- Prepare the Technical Design in accordance with the Design Responsibility Matrix and Project Strategies.

- Include all architectural, structural and mechanical services information and specifications.

- The lead designer reviews and signs-off all information.

Drawings: 4/SM2

- Prepare a schedule of drawings and other information needed.

- Draw up a programme for the preparation and delivery of the drawings and the other stage outputs and assess the resource required to complete it in line with the programme.

- Confirm a system for recording and distributing information and revisions.

NOTE   *Use standard title panels for all drawings and try to limit the number of different sizes of drawings; A1 is generally the preferred size for hard copy drawing output.*

Compile specification notes as relevant during the production of drawn information.

Specifications/schedules/bills of quantities:

- Agree with the design team a strategy, including a programme, for the production of appropriate documents (e.g. specifications/schedules/bills of quantities).

- Assemble specification notes made during Stage 3.

- Prepare a checklist to show which headings or subheadings might be relevant for the particular project.

- Allocate responsibilities for writing particular parts of the specification.

- Select specification sections and clauses from a standard specification library (NBS Create is recommended).

- Mark up a library of clauses and produce a draft copy of the specification.

- Identify sections or items that are not covered adequately for the particular project and which will require supplementary information. Establish which parts will be by prescription and which by performance requirements.

- If specifying by reference to documents, e.g. British Standards, obtain the documents and carefully read the relevant parts.

- Review the selection of materials, descriptions of workmanship, etc. and check with the cost plan.

- Decide on the presentation of the specification.

- Check the final copy for errors, omissions and possible inconsistencies, either within parts of the document or between the specification and other Technical Design.

- Establish the number of copies required and distribute as appropriate.

To assist the cost consultant during preparation of the bills, the architect might be expected to supply the following:

• specification or specification notes for incorporation in work sections

• information for inclusion in preliminaries (or project management sections) such as:

– form of contract, supplements, option clauses, amended clauses, etc.

– content and use of contract documentation

– method statements required

– pre-tender health and safety information

– work to be done by the employer direct

    – *requirements concerning sequence, time limitations, etc.*

    – *provisional sums to be included*

    – *provision for named subcontractors/suppliers*

• *diagrams for inclusion in the bills (e.g. extent of retaining structures, cornice profiles, multi-coloured paintwork).*

General Rule 5.3 of the Standard Method of Measurement of Building Works (SMM) *(seventh edition) refers to the use of dimensioned diagrams in place of a dimensioned description. Drawn information to accompany the bills:*

• *location drawings (i.e. block plan, site plan, floor plans, sections and elevations)*

• *component drawings (i.e. showing information necessary for manufacture and assembly)*

• *drawn schedules*

• *dimensions, which will normally appear on the drawings listed above.*

In particular, the cost consultant will require overall dimensions, and internal dimensions of all rooms and spaces. General Rules 5.1, 5.2 and 5.4 of SMM (seventh edition) refer to drawn information. These might be expected to apply to most of the work sections listed above. In many cases it will simply show the scope and location of the work.

NOTE *The cost consultant will almost certainly expect a rapid response to the query sheets directed at the architect during bill preparations. It will also assist the cost consultant if information is dispatched to suit the taking-off process; that will ensure that the right information is received in the right sequence.*

The SMM contains a full set of the general rules. The SMM Measurement Code, published in conjunction with CPI, includes a commentary on particular rules and contains illustrative material likely to be of assistance to the architect.

Refer also to 4/SM3
                                                      4/SM3

4.5.6.8   Embed the specification into the BIM model.

4.5.6.9 Complete the information with respect to prescriptive/ performance items in bills, etc.

NOTE *Take care when including a provisional sum that the figure is adequate, and that wherever possible it is for defined work.*

4.5.6.10 Draft preliminaries (or project management sections) together with work sections – specifications for materials and workmanship (or systems, products and execution).

NOTE *Use specification clauses which are clear and precise. It should be normal practice to use the appropriate version of NBS Create. It is important that the specification, in addition to bill of quantities, is incorporated so that it forms part of the contract documentation.*

4.5.6.11 Prepare and submit the Building Regulations submission and any other third party submissions requiring consent.

BIM Export data from the BIM model for analysis by local authority building control.

4.5.6.12 Provide information as agreed to the cost consultant for preparation of tender pricing documents (or prepare pricing documents if appointed to do so).

4.5.6.13 *If procurement is through design and build:*

NOTE • *for an employer client: check whether the client has confirmed in writing acceptance of proposals and information supplied so far which are to form part of the Employer's Requirements*

• *for a contractor client: review any client's comments on the detail design or development and note any adjustments which may be unavoidable owing to modifications introduced lately by component manufacturers or specialist subcontractors.*

NOTE *Detail design amendments might also be necessary, for example, because of substitutions forced by long delivery times.*

Check what action is to be taken as a result.

4.5.6.14 Undertake a final review and sign off of the BIM model.

4.5.6.15 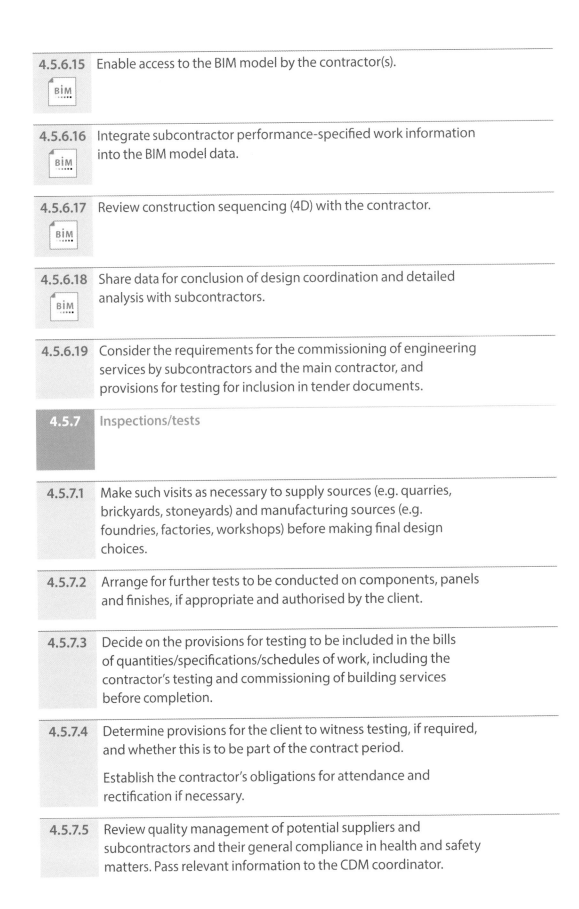	Enable access to the BIM model by the contractor(s).
4.5.6.16	Integrate subcontractor performance-specified work information into the BIM model data.
4.5.6.17	Review construction sequencing (4D) with the contractor.
4.5.6.18	Share data for conclusion of design coordination and detailed analysis with subcontractors.
4.5.6.19	Consider the requirements for the commissioning of engineering services by subcontractors and the main contractor, and provisions for testing for inclusion in tender documents.
4.5.7	**Inspections/tests**
4.5.7.1	Make such visits as necessary to supply sources (e.g. quarries, brickyards, stoneyards) and manufacturing sources (e.g. foundries, factories, workshops) before making final design choices.
4.5.7.2	Arrange for further tests to be conducted on components, panels and finishes, if appropriate and authorised by the client.
4.5.7.3	Decide on the provisions for testing to be included in the bills of quantities/specifications/schedules of work, including the contractor's testing and commissioning of building services before completion.
4.5.7.4	Determine provisions for the client to witness testing, if required, and whether this is to be part of the contract period. Establish the contractor's obligations for attendance and rectification if necessary.
4.5.7.5	Review quality management of potential suppliers and subcontractors and their general compliance in health and safety matters. Pass relevant information to the CDM coordinator.

4

4.5.8	Consultations, approvals and consents

| 4.5.8.1 | Continue discussions with the building control and fire authorities. Prepare a building notice for submission under the Building Regulations, or prepare an application for approval by deposit of full plans. Prepare a submission to an approved inspector for issue of an initial notice for acceptance by the local authority, if this is the chosen option. | 4/SM5 |

NOTE *It is advisable to submit for all necessary approvals at the earliest possible date. However, the stage at which a submission can be made will depend on how much detail the authority requires – there is an increasing tendency to ask for a high level of detail so submission may not be possible until Stage 4 or 5.*

| 4.5.8.2 | Review the adequacy of information on building services from statutory undertakers for detail design. |

| 4.5.8.3 | Continue discussions with relevant authorities for highways, drainage, water, gas, electricity supplies, etc. on matters concerning detail design. Check adequacy of information on building services from statutory undertakers for detail design. |

| 4.5.8.4 | Consult insurers as appropriate regarding the application of codes of practice or design guides relating to construction, materials, standards and finishes in detail design, and their requirements for fire prevention during site operations which might have design implications. |

| 4.5.8.5 | Consult user client/third parties, if authorised. |

| 4.5.8.6 | If instructed, issue party wall notices on behalf of the client. |

If notices are being issued by others, check that all party wall and foundation notices have been served.

NOTE *Consultations with users or third parties and party wall matters do not form part of the Services under the Conditions of the RIBA Standard Agreement 2010 (2012 revision) unless identified under Part 3 'Other Services'.*

4.5.8.7	Check whether minor amendments to the Technical Design at this stage go beyond the scope of the planning permission granted. If so, it may be necessary to deposit amended drawings.	
4.5.8.8	Prepare material for submission to the client's insurers if necessary and if instructed by the client.	
4.5.8.9	Check that all necessary information has been obtained with respect to building control approval. Hold further discussions with authorities as necessary to resolve outstanding points.	4/SM5
4.5.8.10	If appropriate, continue discussions with the highways authority on matters such as access to site, waiting or off-loading restrictions, siting and design of temporary fencing, hoardings, etc.	
4.5.8.11	If appropriate, discuss with the relevant body (e.g. English Heritage) protective measures for existing works during site operations.	
4.5.8.12	Submit the building notice or application for approval by deposit of full plans, if not already submitted, together with relevant documents, including payment from the client for the appropriate fee.	
NOTE	*Compliance can be certified either by the local authority or by an approved inspector. A list of approved inspectors can be obtained from the Construction Industry Council: www.cic.org.uk.*	4/SM5

4.5.9   Cost planning

| 4.5.9.1 | Discuss with the design team and the client the effect of detailed design decisions on the allocations within the cost plan before implementation. |
| 4.5.9.2 | Provide information to the cost consultant for revision of the cost estimate and cash flow projection (or revise the cost estimate if appointed to do so). |

4.5.9.3	Report to the client on cost matters at agreed intervals.

 If procurement is through design and build for a contractor client:

- *provide any further necessary information to the contractor's estimators*

- *review estimates received from specialist firms, either direct or through consultants, for inclusion in the tender documents or as basis for provisional sums.*

4.5.9.4	Provide information for the cost consultant to review the cost plan and monitor cost implications of decisions during the preparation of Technical Design (or revise the cost estimate if appointed to do so).

4.5.9.5	If procurement is through design and build:

- for an employer client: provide revised information if relevant for corrected cost estimates

- for a contractor client: provide revised information if relevant to contractor's estimators

4.5.9.6	*Cost consultant (or architect if appointed to do so) to review quotations received from specialist firms and check against provisional sums or budget figures.*

4.6   Sustainability Checkpoints

Sustainability Checkpoint 4

 During this stage the crucial activity is checking the constituent parts of the Sustainability Strategy against the developing Technical Design and that the work of specialist subcontractors does not impact on the Sustainability Strategy.

Sustainability aims

To ensure that the final design work prepared by the design team and the follow-on design work by specialist subcontractors reflects the technical requirements of the underpinning Sustainability Strategy.

Checkpoints

- Is the formal sustainability assessment substantially complete?

- Have details been audited for airtightness and continuity of insulation?

- Has the Building Regulations Part L submission been made and the design stage carbon/energy declaration been updated and the future climate impact assessment prepared?

- Has a non-technical user guide been drafted and have the format and content of the Part L log book been agreed?

- Has all outstanding design stage sustainability assessment information been submitted?

- Are building Handover Strategy and monitoring technologies specified?

- Have the implications of changes to the specification or design been reviewed against agreed sustainability criteria?

- Has compliance of agreed sustainability criteria for contributions by specialist subcontractors been demonstrated?

Key actions

- Make Approved Document L submission, design stage carbon/energy declaration update and future climate impact assessment.

4

- Draft the non-technical user guide and agree the format and content of the Approved Document L log book.

- Submit all outstanding design stage sustainability assessment information.

- Assess the compliance of contributions by specialist consultants and contractors with agreed sustainability criteria demonstrated.

- Specify the building handover process and monitoring technologies.

- Agree technical requirements to support the monitoring strategy.

- Ensure that artificial lighting and daylighting strategies and controls are mutually supportive in delivering low energy consumption.

- Involve facilities management and users in reviewing the environmental control systems and manual and automatic controls to ensure that they are appropriately simple and intuitive, and that there is a match between expectations and the design.

- Make sure that the project team is aware of the technical consequences of strategic sustainability decisions.

- Specify sustainable materials and products, balancing life-cycle assessment, maintenance regime, durability and cost.

- Complete consultation with subcontractors and suppliers with regard to Technical Design issues and review information packages to check that they are coordinated, complementary and support all components of the Sustainability Strategy.

- Agree responsibilities and routines for data recording to monitor performance.

- Review the potential knock-on implications of value engineering on performance and sustainability targets.

- Review the final details, including subcontractors' packages, for airtightness and continuity of insulation.

- Review the information required to demonstrate compliance with sustainability requirements (e.g. materials certification).

4.7   Information Exchanges

4.7.1   Check that all the agreed outputs have been produced before   **4/SM3**
the conclusion of Stage 4. These outputs will comprise the
Technical Design for consultant elements of the design and
must be in sufficient detail to enable Fabrication Design or
Construction to commence. The outputs may include:

- updated Cost Information

- detail design drawings

- specification notes (prescriptive and performance) on materials
  and workmanship (or systems, products and execution), etc.

- notes for draft preliminaries (or project management sections)
  for specifications or schedules of work

- further detailed information on proposals for existing, perhaps
  historic, buildings

- information for preparation of full plans submission for
  approval under the Building Regulations

- non-technical information for use in dealings with third parties,
  landlords, tenants, funders, etc. (e.g. in connection with leases,
  boundaries, party walls)

- Technical Design coordinated documents – probably including
  location, component and assembly drawings, drawn schedules,
  bills of quantities/specifications/schedules of work

- information prepared specially for use in self-build or semi-
  skilled operations

- information for issue to specialist subcontractors and suppliers
  in connection with tender invitations

- information for inclusion in pre-construction health and safety
  information to be passed to the CDM coordinator

- information which is not necessarily part of the tender package
  for use in dealings with third parties, landlords, tenants,
  funders, etc. (e.g. in connection with leases, boundaries, party
  walls).

4

NOTE	*If procurement is through design and build:*
	• *for an employer client: detail design information for incorporation into Employer's Requirements*
	• *for a contractor client: further design development drawings and design team members' work on scheme submitted in the Contractor's Proposals and general arrangement drawings, interface details, performance.*
NOTE	*The bill of quantities will normally be produced by the cost consultant.* **4/SM4**

4.7.2	Prepare the stage report and submit to the client.

4.8 UK Government Information Exchanges

4.8.1	There are no Information Exchanges at this stage.

Supplementary Material

4/SM1: Design information – implications of procurement method

The production of information, its amount, type and timing, are likely to be directly affected by the procurement method chosen, and ultimately by the type of contract selected.

For example, the extent to which there is to be contractual reliance on drawings might determine their form and detail. Whether bills of quantities or schedules of work will be needed will depend on the form of contract and the nature of the work.

It is important to identify at detail design stage who will have responsibility for producing what information – architect, other consultants, contractor, specialist firms, etc.

The more complex the pattern of information required, the greater the risk of omissions, errors and inconsistencies between documents. Greater, too, is the need for collaboration in order to bring about integration and coordination of design information.

Ideally all information necessary for the construction of the project should be completed before construction work begins. In practice this ideal is rarely, if ever, achieved, but if a great deal is left to be prepared during the construction stage, then very high levels of management skill will be needed from all those involved.

Even in traditional procurement it is rarely possible to bring a lump sum project to a fully designed state pre-tender. Most building contracts accept the need for further information to be issued during progress of the works.

With design and build, or management contracts, it is recognised that a substantial amount of detail design work will take place after the main contract has been let.

In an attempt to control the amount and flow of information, and recognising that everything will not always be available at the start of a contract, a schedule of information still to be provided is sometimes agreed beforehand by the architect and the contractor. This has now been embodied in many JCT standard form contracts as an optional Information Release Schedule.

Sometimes the successful tenderer is required to inspect the documentation and provide the client with verification that it will be sufficient to carry out and complete the project. Then, should it be necessary to produce further drawings or calculations, this will be the contractor's risk. However, the architect will then be involved in checking the contractor's submissions to ensure that detail design is not compromised.

Design information flow: traditional procurement

1.   Origination

Design information can originate from:

- the architect
- design team members
- specialist subcontractors and suppliers
- the main contractor (to the extent provided for in the Building Contract).

2.   Coordination and integration

Responsibility for coordinating and integrating such information into the overall design rests with the architect as project lead or lead designer.

3.   Avoidance of conflict and overlap

Design information originating from various sources should be coordinated, to eliminate any conflicts or duplication. It is normally the task of the lead designer to check design coordination. A key example is the coordination required between structure and services, to make sure that different services are not competing for the same duct spaces, or that holes are not expected at critical structural points. Design integrity and quality should not need to be sacrificed because of the requirements of other design team members, but achieving acceptable compromise and satisfactory integration can be a demanding process.

Smaller projects which might need only a dozen or so drawings, and very limited input from consultants, are unlikely to present real problems in terms of integration and coordination.

Larger and more complex projects will need a more formalised set of procedures. The design concept is likely to be founded on a totally integrated approach. There should be an agreed strategy for the coordination of information between the architect and other design team members.

Design information flow: design and build procurement

1. Origination

Design information can originate from:

- the employer client (through Employer's Requirements with input from their design team)
- the contractor client (through Contractor's Proposals and subsequent development of these, with input from their design team).

2. Coordination and integration

If acting as project lead or lead designer appointed by either the employer client or the contractor client, responsibility for coordinating and integrating the relevant design information may rest with the architect, always depending on the terms of appointment.

3. Employer client's design in Employer's Requirements

Where an employer client includes a scheme devised by their own design team as part of the Employer's Requirements, some Stage 4 detail work might be relevant. The extent of the commitment should be agreed with the client before work is undertaken. In the event that novation is envisaged, particular care might be needed to establish design liability. The point of changeover for design liability from one client to the other must be carefully defined.

4. Contractor client's design in Contractor's Proposals

Where a contractor client is expected to offer a scheme design as part of the Contractor's Proposals, this may involve only a fairly limited design exercise, or require a more developed design approach, particularly in the case of two-stage tendering. Either way, some exploratory detail design work is necessary to establish the viability of the proposal. The extent of the commitment should be agreed with the client before work is started.

Contractor's Proposals sometimes entail the preparation of a considerable number of architectural drawings – general arrangement, plans, sections and elevations, sectional and elevational details and landscape proposals. There may also be full structural details and a substantial number of services drawings. Obviously effective coordination and integration of the information is very important.

5. Detail design work

Stage 4, insofar as it might be relevant for a contractor client, could continue intermittently throughout the early stages of construction. Detail design might be subject to fairly liberal interpretation, with last minute amendments, revisions or substitutions by the contractor client. The client might also have a particular preference for detail design solutions which are familiar, will wish to use materials or components which are available to suit the programme, and will wish to keep in line with the estimator's calculations.

Stage 4, insofar as it might be relevant for an employer client, will probably apply mainly to the development of the Employer's Requirements. Once the Building Contract has been let, any changes in these are likely to be costly and weighted heavily in the contractor's favour.

6.   Avoidance of conflict

Once the contract is under way, should any conflict between the Employer's Requirements and the Contractor's Proposals emerge, then depending on the wording of the Building Contract, the latter is likely to take precedence. Careful scrutiny at Stage 4 is therefore advisable, whether the architect is acting for the employer client or the contractor client.

Design information flow: management procurement

Management procurement is likely to be particularly suitable where the project is fairly large or complex, where there is need for early completion, or where the requirements of the client might change or perhaps only be formalised in detail during work on site. Design is still in the hands of the design team. The management contractor is appointed early enough to advise the team on buildability but carries no responsibility for the design. As project lead or lead designer, responsibility for coordinating and integrating information into the overall design rests with the architect, although considerable design input will normally come from the specialist works contractors.

1.   Origination

Design information can originate from:

- the architect
- design team members
- specialist works contractors.

2.   Detail design work

Two general lines of the design will be shown in the project drawings and project specification produced by the design team. Some Stage 4 design is an essential precursor to information issued when inviting tenders for works packages.

Further detail design work will arise when the works contractors are appointed. Each discrete work package must be placed in the context of the overall design. The information flow can produce management problems if not effectively controlled. Risk of frustrated design work and perhaps abortive fabrication can occur unless agreed procedures are adopted by the management contractor and the design team.

3.   Coordination and integration

The management contractor can expect to be closely involved in the appointment of works contractors. This might be on the basis of developed detail drawings, specifications and perhaps bills of quantities. Drawings prepared by the works contractors will be mainly installation or shop drawings, and should be passed to the architect by the management contractor for inspection with regard to their integration and incorporation into the overall design.

4/SM2: Technical Design drawings

Coordinated Project Information

Many problems and delays on site are due to inaccurate or incomplete information, and it is essential that the tender drawings, specifications, etc., and any subsequent Technical Design produced, is complete and fully coordinated.

The use of Coordinated Project Information (CPI) is recommended for all projects regardless of procurement method. The Construction Project Information Committee (CPIC), a body made up of representatives of the RIBA, RICS, ICE, CIBSE and the Construction Confederation, has been responsible for providing best practice guidance on the content, form and preparation of construction Technical Design and making sure this best practice is disseminated throughout the UK construction industry. The CPIC publication *Production Information: A Code of Procedure for the Construction Industry* provides best practice advice for this aspect of the procurement process – it can be found on the CPIC website: www.cpic.org.uk.

The importance of non-adversarial team working has long been recognised. Current IT technology facilitates such tools as the single project model, which rely on an integrated team structure and so good information is essential in maintaining a non-adversarial environment and a successful project.

Structure of drawings

P/SM1 sets out how Technical Design drawings should comprise location drawings, component drawings and dimensioned diagrams in accordance with SMM.

Drawings from the structural engineer and the building services engineer should be structured in a compatible manner despite the fact that, in their cases, information is likely to come from a number of sources, including specialist subcontractors and suppliers.

Purpose of drawings

Drawings at this stage are produced for three main reasons:

- because they must accompany a bill of quantities or other tendering documentation and generally as stipulated by SMM
- because they will later become contract documents
- because they may need to be developed or issued as other 'necessary information' under the building contract to the main contractor when work on site commences.

The number of drawings required is likely to be influenced by the size of the project, the procurement method to be adopted (i.e. who actually produces the drawings) and the relative significance of drawn information in relation to other contract documents.

Whatever drawings are produced it is important to be clear about their intended purpose and the needs of the user of the drawing. Any drawing should provide such information as shape or profile, dimensions (notional or finished), position, composition and relation to other parts, including tolerances, fixing methods, etc. On a simple project, where only a small number of drawings is necessary, these might embrace the needs of all trades and suppliers and be annotated to the extent that no other supporting document is required.

Conversely, more complex projects will require a considerable number of drawings and schedules, each devised with a particular trade or element in mind. Cross-referencing to other drawings will be required, which must be carried out with great care.

A checklist of the parts of a building that may need to be covered in a Technical Design drawing and schedule programme is given in Figure 4/1.

Schedules

Some information is more clearly and conveniently conveyed in schedule form. Schedules commonly include:

- ironmongery (with location and fixings)
- doors
- windows (to include glazing)
- finishes (floor, walls, ceilings)
- precast lintels and sills
- inspection chambers and manhole covers
- colours.

Any elements or components which are repetitive or can be grouped may be suitable for scheduling. The exercise is a good coverage check for compilers, but information should not be repeated on the drawings as this might lead to confusion and inconsistencies.

It is quite common for suppliers to provide schedules on the architect's behalf, but these should be thoroughly checked.

4/SM3: Specification and schedules of work

CPI procedures

The introduction of Coordinated Project Information (CPI) procedures has created an efficient way of achieving integrated architectural and engineering drawings, specifications and bills of quantities. The Common Arrangement of Work Sections for building works (CAWS) has been adopted throughout the documents. CAWS is the result of detailed analysis of UK subcontracting practice and is compiled at the level of 'minimum subcontract package', termed 'work sections'. There should never be a need for further granulation, but it is normal to aggregate a number of work sections when letting actual subcontract packages. The National Building Specification (NBS), National Engineering Specification (NES) and the Standard Method of Measurement (SMM) all use this arrangement. The architect and the cost consultant will find it easier to prepare and interpret a specification where it shares a common arrangement with the method of measurement used in preparing the bills, which also facilitates better understanding of the documents by contractors and specialists.

In 2012, RICS published volume 2 of its New Rules of Measurement (NRM) suite. It advises that NRM2 has 'guidance note' status for RICS members, with an effective commencement date of 1 January 2013. RICS advises that while it is for each surveyor to decide on the appropriate procedure to follow in any professional task, where members do not comply with the practice recommended in a guidance note, they should do so only for a good reason. References have been included for NRM2 as its use is likely to be favoured by quantity surveyors, for example, although it is not mandatory for non-RICS members, nor is it aligned with CAWS.

The need for change of CPI procedures has been steadily growing and a working group was established to deal with this. In 2011, the Construction Project Information Committee endorsed NBS proposals for a new work section classification – Uniclass Table J – which will replace CAWS. The classification system provides the framework for NBS Create, a new version of the standard specification library.

The specification

It is vital to understand that long before a specification evolves into a written document it is a process completely integrated with design. It eventually becomes a written document which may describe the materials or products to be used, standards of workmanship required, performance requirements and the conditions under which the work will be carried out. It should be clearly and economically worded, with the objective of transferring information from designers to constructors with accuracy and certainty.

A specification can be prescriptive, in that there is precise description of the materials, workmanship, etc. which leaves no area of choice to the tendering contractor. It can also be written as performance requirements, either for the building components or for engineering services, in which case there will remain an area of choice on the part of the contractor as to how the stated performance will be achieved. If performance specification is to be used, great care needs to be taken in ensuring that the contractual terms recognise this additional responsibility of the contractor. In reality, most modern specification sections use a combination of performance and prescription.

Some architects' practices might use a system of specification clauses developed for use with particular types of work (e.g. housing refurbishment). Care must be taken to keep such clauses relevant and up to date, and it is generally safer and more convenient to adopt a well-developed system such as NBS. This allows for consistent description of materials and workmanship (or systems, products and execution) with full reference to British Standards and other codes and standards. NBS also enables performance specifications to be developed.

NBS is available in electronic form as NBS Building and NBS Create (refer to www.thenbs.com). These easy-to-use software packages enable the development of specifications on screen, referring to guidance and other technical information, such as British Standards. Some clauses require additional information that can be typed in or completed by using drop-down 'value' lists of suggested solutions.

Under CPI the specification is the core document to which the other Technical Design information refers. The description of materials and workmanship (or systems, products and execution) contained in the specification should therefore not be repeated on the drawing or in the bills – these documents should refer to clause numbers in the specification. A specification will therefore be needed even when there is a separate bill of quantities.

Where there is no bill of quantities, it may be wise to append a schedule of work to the specification for pricing purposes, possibly supported by a schedule of rates, or to require the tendering contractor to provide a priced activity schedule. If the specification has been prepared using the CAWS system then a breakdown according to work sections may not be very helpful when it comes to valuing variations or certificates.

The architect as designer is responsible for the method of specification selected and the content. Specification notes will normally be compiled during the design process. The specification is a key document and will provide information to:

- the cost consultant when preparing bills of quantities
- the contractor's estimator when preparing a tender
- the contractor during construction work.

Members of the design team might prepare the specification for those parts of the work which require specialist knowledge, but the architect as lead designer should coordinate overall content.

Schedules of work

Schedules of work comprise lists of the various items of work to be carried out, usually on a room-by-room basis. It is customary to introduce a number or area alongside each item to encourage systematic pricing by tenderers. Items in respect of each room are usually listed under headings such as doors, ceilings, wall finishes, floor finishes, fittings, etc. Schedules of work should not contain quantities, for they are not exact documents by nature. A contractor, when pricing, should be expected to include everything necessary to complete the works.

A schedule of work might be a contract document where there is no bill of quantities. They are sometimes regarded as an alternative to a specification, particularly when used for housing refurbishment or alteration work. However, CPI would recommend that the specification is used, and that the items in the schedule of work refer to the detailed descriptions in the specification.

4/SM4: Bill of quantities

Pricing a bill of quantities is the traditional method of obtaining comparable tenders for projects where the design has been fully detailed beforehand. Where an accurate or full bill of quantities becomes part of the contract documentation, it usually means that quality and quantity included in the price will be as stated in the contract bills. It is therefore important to ensure that the bill accurately reflects the intentions of the architect and does not conflict with information shown on the drawings.

Notional bill or approximate quantities

Where it is not possible to present the cost consultant with a completely detailed design and specification, it may be possible to invite tenders on the basis of a notional bill or approximate quantities. These should be reasonably accurate as to description and items, with only the amounts left subject to measurement after completion.

Work which cannot be quantified with certainty, even in an accurate bill of quantities, may be covered by the introduction of provisional sums (for either defined or undefined work), prime cost sums (where an accurate figure can be placed on a subcontract or supply item) or an approximate quantity (where the item is certain but the quantity is not).

The inclusion of a contingency sum is nothing more than a provisional figure for undefined work of an unforeseeable nature. All such items require later instructions from the architect before the contractor can act on them.

Standard Method of Measurement

A uniform basis of measuring work for inclusion in a bill of quantities may be found in the *Standard Method of Measurement of Building Works* (SMM), currently in a seventh edition. For building work this is most likely to be using the Common Arrangement and in accordance with SMM. The contents of a bill prepared in this way are likely to include the following:

Preliminaries/general conditions

- Items which are not specific to work sections but which have an identifiable cost (e.g. site facilities, insurances).
- Items for fixed and time-related costs (e.g. plant, temporary works).

Work sections (also incorporating cross-references to drawings and specification)

C   Demolition/alteration/renovation
D   Groundwork
E   In situ concrete/large precast concrete
F   Masonry – brick, block, stonework, etc.
G   Structural/carcassing – metal and timber
H   Cladding/covering – patent glazing, plastics, etc.
J   Waterproofing
K   Linings/dry partitions
L   Windows/doors/stairs
M   Surface finishes – screeds, tiling, decorating, etc.
P   Building fabric sundries – trims, ironmongery, etc.
Q   Paving/planting/fencing/outdoor furniture
R   Disposal systems – pipework gutters, drainage
Y   Mechanical and electrical services

Refer to Figure 4/1 for a comprehensive schedule of drawings required.

4/SM5: Building control approval

Preparing an application for Building Regulations approval is normally one of the services provided by the architect. In many cases, although informal consultations may well have taken place earlier, the drawings and calculations necessary to support a formal submission will not be sufficiently developed until well into Technical Design and Fabrication Design.

The UK Government website www.planningportal.gov.uk provides a clear explanation of all the current regulations and the procedures for making applications for approval. This site includes sections on such matters as water efficiency, the Code for Sustainable Homes, the legislation that governs the Building Regulations, technical guidance on all the Approved Documents, the approval process, determination and appeals, a list of useful contacts and links to related internet sites.

Another useful website is www.communities.gov.uk. This contains information on energy performance certificates, fire safety legislation and many other relevant matters.

Over recent years there have been significant changes to Approved Document L: Conservation of Fuel and Power. In particular, it is important to note the requirement to submit an energy performance certificate on completion of construction work, which must be issued by an energy assessor who is accredited to produce energy performance certificates for the category of building to which the certificate relates.

Regard should also be had to the Equalities Act 2010, a copy of which can be found at www.legislation.gov.uk

Figure 4/1

Checklist of necessary drawn information

Refer to the notes on 'level of detail' on page 7.

Job no: _____   Job title: _____

Drawn information checklist

Summary		Site layouts	
		General arrangements	
		drawings	

| Substructure | | Excavation | Foundations |
| | | Floors beds | Pile foundations |

Structure	**Primary**	External walls	Stairs and ramps
		Internal walls	Roofs
		Floors and galleries	Frames
	Secondary	External wall openings	Balustrades
		Internal wall openings	Suspended ceilings
		Floor openings	Roof openings
	Finishes	External wall finishes	Stair finishes
		Internal wall finishes	Ceiling finishes
		Floor finishes	Roof finishes

Services	**Piped and ducted**	Refuse disposal	Refrigeration
		Drainage	Space heating
		Hot and cold water	Ventilation and air conditioning
		Gases	
	Electrical	Power	Transport
		Lighting	Security
		Communications	

Fittings	**Fixtures**	Circulation	Sanitary
		General room	Cleaning
		Culinary	Storage
	Loose equipment	Circulation	Sanitary
		General room	Cleaning
		Culinary	Storage

External		Substructure	Services
		Structure	Fittings
		Finishes	

Figure 4/2

Drawing registers

Register of drawings

Most practices will already have a standard register of drawings, which might record, among other things:

• job number and title
• drawing number, title, date, revisions (A, B, etc.)
• scale of drawing, size of drawing (A3, A4, etc.)
• number of copies sent, distribution, and date sent.

Where recipients are to be charged for copies, the register might also allow entries indicating the charge made and by whom payable. Great care must be taken to keep the register updated.

Schedules of drawings

Drawing schedules can be a convenient record for several purposes:

• for listing at the start of Stage 4 what drawings or drawn schedules need to be prepared
• for listing drawings or drawn schedules issued for tender purposes
• for listing necessary information still to be prepared by the architect and/or the contractor during progress of the works
• for listing drawings or drawn schedules supplied to the client on completion – either for record purposes or for incorporation in the Health and Safety File.

Drawings issued

Drawings should never normally be issued simply under cover of a compliments slip. It is better practice to use a drawing issue sheet which indicates the purpose of the action and allows a proper record to be kept (see page 219).

Where drawings are issued electronically they should be issued in a locked, uneditable format. They should be accompanied with a disclaimer that identifies the locked data as the formal issue and any editable data for information only. The editable information is used by the recipient entirely at their risk.

Drawings received

A practice should also have its standard record of drawings received. All incoming drawn or scheduled information should be entered, and the sheets might record, among other things:

- job number and title
- drawing number, title, date, revision
- name of originator
- date received
- whether a response is required and, if so, by when
- response made and date achieved.

4

Figure 4/2 (continued)

Architect's drawing issue sheet

Job no: Job title:

Architect's drawing issue sheet

Please find enclosed the drawings listed below.
Any errors or omissions should be notified immediatlely.

Distribution   No. copies

Purpose of issue   For information ☐   For comment ☐

                        For approval ☐   For cost check ☐

Drawing no.	Revision	Drawing title

Signed: Date:

CONTENTS

RIBA
Plan of
Work
2013

Excerpt from the RIBA Plan of Work 2013

RIBA
Plan of
Work
2013

Stage 5

Construction

Task Bar	Tasks
Core Objectives	Offsite manufacturing and onsite **Construction** in accordance with the **Construction Programme** and resolution of **Design Queries** from site as they arise.
Procurement Variable task bar	Administration of **Building Contract**, including regular site inspections and review of progress.
Programme Variable task bar	*The RIBA Plan of Work 2013 enables this stage to overlap with a number of other stages depending on the selected procurement route.*
(Town) Planning Variable task bar	*There are no specific activities in the RIBA Plan of Work 2013, however the contractor will need to comply with any construction-specific planning conditions, such as monitoring of noise levels.*
Suggested Key Support Tasks	Review and update **Sustainability Strategy** and implement **Handover Strategy**, including agreement of information required for commissioning, training, handover, asset management, future monitoring and maintenance and ongoing compilation of **'As-constructed' Information**. Update **Construction** and **Health and Safety Strategies**. *Support tasks are now focused on health and safety on site and ensuring that the project handover and post-occupancy activities, determined earlier, are properly facilitated.*
Sustainability Checkpoints	• *Has the design stage sustainability assessment been certified?* • *Have sustainability procedures been developed with the contractor and included in the* **Construction Strategy**? • *Has the detailed commissioning and* **Handover Strategy** *programme been reviewed?* • *Confirm that the contractor's interim testing and monitoring of construction has been reviewed and observed, particularly in relation to airtightness and continuity of insulation.* • *Is the non-technical user guide complete and the aftercare service set up?* • *Has the* **'As-constructed' Information** *been issued for post-construction sustainability certification?*
Information Exchanges (at stage completion)	**'As-constructed' Information**.
UK Government Information Exchanges	Not required.

5

Summary

During this stage, the building is constructed on site in accordance with the **Construction Programme**. Construction includes the erection of components that have been fabricated off site.

The procurement strategy and/or the designer's specific **Schedule of Services** will have set out the designer's duties to respond to **Design Queries** from site generated in relation to the design, to carry out site inspections and to produce quality reports.

The output of this stage is the **'As-constructed' Information**.

Mapping to RIBA Outline Plan of Work 2007

Stage 5 maps to the former Stage K – Construction to Practical Completion – but also includes Stage J – Mobilisation.

5.1   Core Objectives

Stage 5 comprises contractor mobilisation and construction activities. It also encompasses offsite manufacturing.

In the strict sense of the term, mobilisation is likely to be mainly the responsibility of the appointed contractor. However, an architect acting as the project lead can do much at this stage to see that the contract is properly set up from the outset.

Contract documents have to be prepared and the Building Contract should be signed before work on site commences. There will need to be an exchange of information between the architect and the contractor, and confirmed agreement on procedures to be followed.

The client will enter into the Building Contract as the employer, and the site given into the possession of the contractor so that work may proceed as programmed. The employer, contractor and relevant consultants will need to be advised on their respective responsibilities under the Building Contract.

The contractor must have reasonable time to mobilise resources. Employer and contractor insurances for the construction period will need to be put in place and checked. Site inspectorate will need to be appointed and briefed. Arrangements should be made for the formal initial project team meeting, sometimes also referred to as the pre-start or pre-contract meeting.

The architect may be nominated as the contract administrator. The terms of the Building Contract bind only the parties themselves, i.e. the employer and the contractor; they do not place contractual obligations on the architect. Nevertheless, should the architect as contract administrator fail in the procedural duties set out, for example not issuing a certificate as required, this could constitute a breach of contract on the part of the employer against whom the contractor may be able to claim losses. It is therefore important that the architect's contract for professional services reflects accurately their role under the Building Contract.

With traditional procurement, the contractor normally undertakes to carry out and complete the works in accordance with the Building Contract, to proceed regularly and diligently, to complete by the agreed completion date and to comply with instructions empowered by the Building Contract.

The employer normally undertakes to give the contractor possession in order to carry out the work, ensure that all necessary information is made available to the contractor, appoint a contract administrator and pay all amounts properly certified or due under the Building Contract.

With traditional procurement, the role of the contract administrator will vary considerably depending on the particular form used, but the contract administrator would normally issue necessary information to the contractor, issue instructions empowered or required by the Building Contract and issue certificates as required by the Building Contract, and would be required to act in a fair and reasonable manner where impartial judgement is required by the Building Contract.

 Activities in Stage 5 to be undertaken by the architect as contract   **CA**
administrator are annotated 'CA' in the margin.

Design and build procurement

There is normally no role for an impartial contract administrator with design and build procurement. The architect will therefore have no direct involvement in contract administration. Where acting for an employer client, consultancy advice might be needed, or an architect might be appointed as the employer's agent. Where acting for a contractor client, any involvement will not go beyond giving consultancy advice. The authority of the employer's agent comes from the employer, not the construction contract, and the employer's agent has no duties under the Building Contract.

Management procurement

With management procurement there is usually the need for an independent contract administrator whose duties will normally include the issue of necessary information and instructions and the issue of certificates. The obligations of the contractor will differ from those under traditional procurement and will be fully described in the Building Contract.

5

5.2	Procurement

5.2.1	Review the post-tender situation. In the event of an omission or a substitution necessitating revisions to detail design, take appropriate action if authorised by the client. Alert the client to any additional costs, fees or alterations to the Project Programme.	CA
NOTE	*Post-tender cost-reduction exercises usually mean additional work. Allow time for this.*	

5.2.2	Prepare Building Contract documents for signature. Send by registered/recorded post or deliver by hand. It is customary to send these first to the contractor and then to the employer.	5/SM1 P/SM1 CA
NOTE	*When preparing Building Contract documents for signature or completion as a deed, check meticulously that entries are correct and relate to the tender documents. If there is more than one copy, check that they are identical.*	

5.2.3	Check that parties have properly signed the Building Contract documents and that any agreed alterations are initialled.	CA

5.2.4	Check that all unsuccessful tenderers have been properly notified.	CA

5.2.5	Check that additional copies of drawings and other documents are handed to the main contractor as required by the Building Contract. If an Information Release Schedule does not form part of the Building Contract, agree with the contractor a schedule for further necessary information.	CA

5.2.6	Provide the contractor with copies of contract documents as required under the Building Contract.	CA

5.2.7	Remind the client of their responsibility for the building in terms of insurance, security and maintenance in good time.	CA

5.3	**Programme**

5.3.1	If acting as contract administrator, check that the contractor is working according to the Construction Programme and report to the employer on this. The contractor will be expected to review progress against the Construction Programme and annotate the programme accordingly.	**CA**

5.4	**(Town) Planning**

5.4.1	Monitor the contractor's compliance with planning conditions.

5.5	**Suggested Key Support Tasks**

5.5.1	Information required

5.5.1.1	Check that all information necessary during Stage 5 is available, which might include the following:	**CA**

- form of Building Contract, with all necessary entries and supplements, ready for completion by the parties

- contract documents, including drawings and bills of quantities/ specifications/schedules of work, incorporating any necessary adjustments, ready for issue

- completed tender documents from the successful tenderer

- written records of any post-tender changes to the contracted project

- administration forms published for use in contract administration, suitable for the particular form of Building Contract to be used

- contractor's preliminary programme and required method statements

5

- coordinated Technical and Fabrication Design: drawings, drawn schedules, priced bills of quantities/specifications/schedules of work

- contractor's rates or contract sum analysis if appropriate, and/or priced bills of quantities/specifications/schedules of work

- specialists' tenders and 'numbered documents' ready for nomination instructions to be issued

- contractor's master programme

- copies of the construction phase Health and Safety Plan developed by the contractor and certified by the CDM coordinator

- copies of method statements prepared by the contractor as required in the Building Contract conditions

- Information Release Schedule, or

- schedule agreed with the contractor indicating what further information is needed from the architect and by when, or

- verification by the contractor, if applicable, that all necessary information has been supplied, and accepting that any further drawings will be their own responsibility.

5.5.2   Brief

| 5.5.2.1 | *Any changes to the brief should be strenuously avoided at this stage as there will be significant cost and time consequences. Any changes that are made must be done following the Change Control Procedures.* |

5.5.3   Appointment

5.5.3.1   Establish the scope, content and context for Stage 5 activities.

NOTE

Put this information into context, particularly if previous stages were undertaken by others. If possible, establish whether material produced now is likely to be acted upon by others taking over subsequent stages.

If the appointment includes Soft Landings activities under Stage 6, the architect must:

- discuss with the contractor the initial occupation provisions specified in the Building Contract

- review design information from the contractor or specialists for compliance with occupation and facilities management strategies

- review and monitor the contractor's building readiness programme

- prepare the building's user guide and contribute to periodic reports.

If the appointment includes Post-occupancy Evaluation activities under Stage 6, the architect must:

- discuss with the contractor the specified review provisions

- identify any changes to targets, and their causes, and contribute to periodic reports.

5.5.3.2   If coming new to the project at this stage in the Plan of Work:

- ascertain that all earlier stage checks have been carried out

- agree fees and timetable with the client

NOTE *Allow for familiarisation and reviewing of all usable material when agreeing fees and timetable with the client.*

- confirm the role of the architect in relation to the rest of the design team

- ensure you have the necessary competency and resources to undertake the work and address the health and safety issues likely to be involved in it

- request a copy of the project-specific pre-construction health and safety information and review it

- re-advise the client in writing of their responsibilities under the CDM Regulations and ensure that a CDM coordinator has been appointed

NOTE *Where a project is notifiable, the Regulations require that the client appoints a CDM coordinator as soon as is practicable after initial design work or other preparation for construction work has begun. This would generally be at Stage 2.*

- ensure that you have adequate professional indemnity (PI) insurance cover

- confirm the scope and frequency of site meetings, visits and issuing of interim certificates.

| 5.5.3.3 | Check that the client's instruction to proceed has been given and confirmed in writing. |

| 5.5.3.4 | Check that the client has settled all accounts submitted to date. |

| 5.5.3.5 | Check appointing documents with respect to services and fees: |

- if the services, cost or time targets are different from those agreed with the client, agree a formal variation by letter or deed as appropriate

- if the extent of professional services for Stage 5 is not yet settled, agree with the client and confirm in writing

- if the methods and levels of charging for Stage 5 are not yet settled, agree with the client and confirm in writing.

NOTE
Remember that the agreed services must reflect the role of the architect under the form of building contract selected. Inform the client in advance if more frequent visits are required than those allowed for in the agreement and which would incur additional expenditure.

| 5.5.3.6 | Assess the office resources needed for Stage 5 and ensure that they are available and adequate. |

| 5.5.3.7 | Confirm contract administration and site inspection services and frequency and procedures for site visits for Stage 5. |

| **5.5.4** | **Client** |

| 5.5.4.1 | If a clerk of works or site inspector is to be appointed, check whether the client has confirmed the appointment. | CA |

| 5.5.4.2 | Remind the client that any insurances for which they have accepted responsibility should have been taken out. Policies should be kept available for inspection by the contractor at all reasonable times. | 5/SM4 CA |

| 5.5.4.3 | Discuss with the client the main contractor's master programme. Draw to the client's attention significant dates by which any further decisions or information will be needed, and by which any persons directly employed are programmed to start and finish. | CA |

5.5.4.4	Confirm to the client their responsibilities and obligations under the Building Contract as employer. Confirm the architect's role and duties as agent and contract administrator.	**CA**
5.5.4.5	Remind the client of the obligation to honour monetary certificates within the periods stated in the Building Contract and of the procedure should any deduction be anticipated, for example in respect of liquidated damages.	**CA**
NOTE	*Explain the certificates' provisions in detail. If any deduction is intended from amounts certified, it will be essential to issue notices as required by the Building Contract.*	
5.5.4.6	Remind the client that empowered instructions to the contractor can only be issued by way of a contract administrator's instruction, and advise the client of the employer's obligations under the Building Contract and of the role and duties of the architect in administering the Building Contract.	**CA**
5.5.4.7	Check with the client that the Building Contract documents have been completed and signed as a simple contract or a deed as applicable.	**CA**
5.5.4.8	Check that the site or existing buildings have been given into the possession of the appointed contractor for the duration of the works.	**CA**
5.5.4.9	Remind the client of relevant statutory obligations under the CDM Regulations relating to the role of the CDM coordinator and the competence of the principal contractor and other contractor's performance in health and safety matters.	**CA**
5.5.4.10	Explain to the client the implications of Practical Completion. Should partial possession be desired, advise the client, about the contractual implications and procedures.	**CA**
5.5.4.11	Discuss with the client the need to appoint maintenance staff in time to attend the commissioning of the project, and to enter into maintenance agreements if relevant.	
5.5.4.12	Discuss with the client the requirements for 'As-constructed' Information and operation and maintenance manuals.	
5.5.4.13	Remind the client of the requirement for a Health and Safety File to be deposited in a safe place at the completion of the project.	

| 5.5.4.14 | If procurement is through design and build for an employer client, check whether the client has confirmed the appointment of an employer's agent. The authority of this person should be clearly stated in writing, and the contractor should be informed. | |

| **5.5.5** | **Project team** | |

| 5.5.5.1 | If appointed as information manager, for any residual detailed design activities occurring at this stage: | |

- assist members of the design team to develop the design using the BIM model, ensuring that data-sharing protocols are followed

- check and sign off the model at agreed stages

- issue or assist in the issue of design data at agreed times throughout the development of the design

- assist in the development of data relative to the agreed levels of detail

- assist in the integration of contractor's, subcontractors' and suppliers' data into the BIM model.

For further advice on working with BIM, refer to the RIBA publication *BIM Demystified* (2012).

| 5.5.5.2 | Check the scope of professional services agreed with the client for continued presence of the design team members as members of the project team. | **CA** |

| 5.5.5.3 | Agree the scope and timetable for any amendments needed to Building Contract documents as a result of post-tender negotiations. | **CA** |

| 5.5.5.4 | Agree with the cost consultant a timetable for the preparation of a bill of reductions or similar document setting out agreed adjustments to the tender figure, if relevant. | **CA** |

| 5.5.5.5 | Brief the site inspectorate. | **CA** |

NOTE *Site inspectorate who are under the direction of the architect should be thoroughly briefed. If one has been appointed, give the clerk of works clear instructions on procedures and reporting.* **5/SM2**

5.5.5.6	Confirm dates for the construction phase with the client and CDM coordinator.	CA
5.5.5.7	Convene and chair site progress meetings or attend progress meetings chaired by the contractor.	5/SM6 CA
NOTE	*Methodically keep accurate minutes of meetings, and record discussions, progress statements and decisions. In assessing subsequent claims or allegations, these records may prove invaluable and more than justify the effort needed to maintain them.*	
5.5.5.8	Confirm that all instructions concerning specialist subcontractors or suppliers are to be channelled through the architect. If acceptable, they will be included under a contract administrator's instruction issued to the main contractor.	CA
5.5.5.9	Confirm that consultants are to supply relevant information for the preparation of operating instructions, maintenance manuals, record drawings of installation, etc.	CA
5.5.5.10	Check the designers' cooperation with the CDM coordinator.	CA
5.5.5.11	Confirm that consultants are to pass relevant information to the CDM coordinator for inclusion in the Health and Safety File.	CA
5.5.5.12	Confirm that consultants are to carry out detailed inspection of specialist work and report to the architect. If authorised, consultants should also attend commissioning, testing and witnessing and report.	CA
5.5.5.13	Confirm with the client and cost consultant the procedures for valuation and certification.	CA
5.5.5.14	Confirm arrangements for reporting regularly to the client, and for providing regular financial reports.	CA
5.5.5.15	Agree the timing and scope of Soft Landings activities.	
5.5.5.16 BIM	Coordinate and release 'end of construction' BIM record model data.	

5

5.5.6	General matters

5.5.6.1	Review and update the Sustainability Strategy.

5.5.6.2	Review implementation of the Handover Strategy, including agreement of information required for commissioning, training, handover, asset management, future monitoring and maintenance and ongoing compilation of 'As-constructed' Information.

5.5.6.3	Update the Health and Safety Strategy.

5.5.6.4	Regularly check progress against the timetable for services.

5.5.6.5	Continue resource control procedures for the job (usually monthly): • check expenditure against the office job cost allocation for Stage 5 • monitor fee income against projected fee income.

5.5.6.6	Report regularly to the client on fees and expenses incurred, and submit accounts at agreed intervals (usually monthly). NOTE *Check that the client settles all accounts promptly.*

5.5.6.7	Set up procedures for ensuring that drawings and other information are prepared and provided to the contractor as required, or as set out in the Building Contract.

5.5.6.8	Set up accounts procedures for invoicing the appointed main contractor monthly for the cost of copies of drawings and documents additional to those stated in the Building Contract, whether these involve prints or software.

5.5.6.9	Compile a directory of all parties involved in the construction stage.

5.5.6.10	Set up procedures to issue fee accounts regularly.	
5.5.6.11	Confirm dates for commencement and completion.	**CA**
5.5.6.12	Clarify any queries from the contractor.	**CA**
5.5.6.13	Establish and inspect the contractor's programmes and confirm information schedules.	**CA**
5.5.6.14	Call for all the contractor's insurance policies. Pass on to the employer for checking by their brokers or insurance advisers. NOTE *Check original documents carefully for cover and renewal dates. Do not accept assurances.*	**5/SM4** **CA**
5.5.6.15	Check bonds and warranties required from the contractor. NOTE *These should be obtained before the Building Contract is signed – it may be impossible to obtain them later.*	**CA**
5.5.6.16	Check that the CDM coordinator has expressed satisfaction with the contractor's construction phase Health and Safety Plan, and that this is confirmed in writing.	**CA**
5.5.6.17	Carefully inspect the contractor's preliminary programme, particularly if it indicates dates by which critical information is required. Comment as appropriate, but do not approve it.	**CA**
5.5.6.18	Check that the contractor has prepared a Health and Safety Plan which is acceptable to the CDM coordinator. NOTE *Under no circumstances can work start on site without a Health and Safety Plan in place which conforms with the principles of the CDM Regulations.*	**CA**
5.5.6.19	Check quality management proposals and procedures with the contractor.	**CA**
5.5.6.20	Check proposed site planning and accommodation with the contractor.	**CA**

5

5.5.6.21	Hold a pre-contract meeting with the employer, main contractor, consultants, cost consultant and clerk of works. Chair the initial project meeting, if appropriate, and issue minutes.	**5/SM3** **CA**

NOTE

When chairing the initial project team meeting, be fair, firm and pleasant. This is an opportunity to make relevant introductions and establish clear procedures.

5.5.6.22	Arrange for the handover of site and/or existing buildings, allowing the contractor exclusive possession or to the extent previously agreed.	**CA**

5.5.6.23	Meet the contractor on site to note setting out, including boundaries, fencing and hoardings, site huts, amenities and welfare arrangements, protective measures, spoil heaps, etc. to establish compliance with the contractor's method statements and the requirements of the Building Contract.	**CA**

NOTE

Administer the Building Contract in accordance with the procedural rules and the conditions, acting fairly and impartially between the parties.

It is essential to acquire a good knowledge and understanding of all the Building Contract documents. Keep a copy to hand at all times.

BIM

Where possible use 4D/5D BIM data for contract administration purposes.

NOTE

Issue contract administrator's instructions, discretionary or obligatory, as empowered under the Building Contract and in accordance with the contract provisions:

- *all instructions to the contractor should be in writing: it is good practice to issue them on a contract administrator's instruction form (not via correspondence or site meeting minutes)*

- *only empowered instructions should be issued: keep the wording concise and unambiguous*

- *confirm oral instructions as soon as necessary to avoid difficulties and to ensure that cost appraisals are realistic.*

| 5.5.6.24 | Provide information as set out on the Information Release Schedule, or provide additional necessary information to the contractor as required under the provisions of the Building Contract. | CA |

NOTE *It is important to ensure that there is no reasonably necessary information outstanding, general or specific. Watch the contractor's programme and progress for indicated dates and signs.*

NOTE *Deal with claims as empowered under the terms of the Building Contract.* **5/SM9** *Variations should be pre-priced if possible, otherwise the likely full implications should be estimated and agreed before action is taken.*

It may be that negotiation is the best way forward, but do not exceed your authority. Do not be overawed by the volume of documents sometimes presented by claims consultants – quantity does not equate with the validity of a case.

Beware of claims regarding matters not dealt with under the express terms of the Building Contract because the architect has no power to settle these; they must be dealt with between the parties.

NOTE *Issue instructions with respect to provisional sums and the appointment* **5/SM8** *of specialist subcontractors, etc.*

If possible, named subcontractors should be appointed at the commencement of the Building Contract, always strictly in accordance with stipulated procedures. Note the subcontract dates for compatibility with the main contractor's programme.

| 5.5.6.25 | Issue certificates as empowered and required in accordance with the Building Contract procedures. Request vouchers from the contractor as empowered under the contract. | CA |

NOTE *Be punctilious about valuations and certificates for payment. Notify the* **5/SM10** *cost consultant in writing of any work not properly carried out, so that such work is not included in any valuation. Alert the client to any rights to make a deduction from the amount certified, and the procedures involved.*

NOTE *Review the Health and Safety File information at regular intervals.*

NOTE *Maintain 'As-constructed' Information, as required under the Building Contract provisions, and pass relevant information to the CDM coordinator for possible incorporation in the Health and Safety File.*

NOTE *Check that the project team maintain adequate records and pass relevant information to the CDM coordinator for possible incorporation in the Health and Safety File.*

5.5.6.26	Obtain the contractor's forecast date for Practical Completion and advise the client of the procedures.	5/SM11 CA

5.5.6.27	Initiate pre-completion checks on the works and make records of outstanding items.	CA

NOTE
Any lists are for the benefit of the design team and the client, and not normally for issue to the contractor. Under JCT traditional forms, quality control on site, snagging, etc. is entirely the responsibility of the contractor.

5.5.6.28	When completion is near, make sure that the contractor is fully aware that commissioning must be completed and operating manuals available before the building is handed over.	CA

5.5.6.29	Identify responsibility for commissioning, testing and witnessing of engineering services and ensure they are carried out according to the provisions of the Building Contract.	

5.5.6.30	Check that information relating to the Health and Safety File and operating and maintenance manuals is complete and ready for handing over to the CDM coordinator.	CA

5.5.6.31	Make sure that operating manuals have been properly checked and are ready by the time of handover.	CA

5.5.6.32	Cooperate with the CDM coordinator, who will want to make sure that the Health and Safety File has been compiled and is ready at the time of handover.	CA

5.5.6.33	Issue the certificate of Practical Completion in accordance with the provisions of the Building Contract.	CA

NOTE
Certify Practical Completion only when, in your opinion, this state has been attained. Be very wary of pressure from the contractor or client to certify Practical Completion early – the consequences can be serious for all concerned.

5.5.6.34	Hold a formal handover meeting, if the terms of appointment or Building Contract require it.	CA

5.5.7	Inspections/tests	
5.5.7.1	Confirm the programme and procedures for the architect's site visits.	5/SM7
5.5.7.2	Brief site inspection staff about their duties and the procedures to be followed.	5/SM2 5/SM3 5/SM7 CA
	NOTE *Visit the site as provided for in the agreement with the client, whether for periodic checks, predictive checks or spot checks, to observe and comment on the contractor's site supervision and examples of work.*	
5.5.7.3	Prepare an inspection plan which identifies when visits should be made, and when checks can be made on tests which the contractor is obliged to make under the Building Contract, including visits by building control.	CA
5.5.7.4	FIG. Keep methodical records of all site visits and results of all tests witnessed or reported.	Fig. 5/4
	NOTE *Allow adequate time on site to carry out checks properly. Make careful notes and compile a systematic record of visits. It helps to prepare checklists relating to the stage of the work. Check that work is being executed generally in accordance with the provisions of the Building Contract, in a proper and workmanlike manner and in accordance with the Health and Safety Plan.*	CA
5.5.7.5	Inspect the contractor's progress measured against the Construction Programme, and generally inspect goods and materials delivered to the site.	CA
5.5.7.6	Check the contractor's quality management performance measured against the plan submitted in the contractor's method statement.	CA

5

5.5.8 Consultations, approvals and consents

5.5.8.1 Check that any necessary approvals and consents have been obtained and are on file. If any are still outstanding, explain to the client the consequences of starting on site prematurely.

> **NOTE** *It is wise to draw up an approvals and conditions tracker that identifies when and how each is discharged.*

5.5.8.2 Check that all notices granting planning permission and approval under Building Regulations are to hand. Check that statutory approvals are still valid within time limits.

5.5.8.3 Check that the Health and Safety Executive (HSE) has been given particulars required by law under the CDM Regulations.

5.5.8.4 Check with the client that all necessary party wall awards are in place. **CA**

5.5.9 Cost planning

5.5.9.1 Check with the cost consultant, if appointed, the contractor's schedule of rates and the contract sum analysis where relevant. **CA**

5.5.9.2 Liaise with the cost consultant to monitor costs arising from contract administrator's instructions, and for forecasting monthly reports. **CA**

5.5.9.3 Provide the client with estimates of costs arising from contract administrator's instructions, including variations. **CA**

5.5.9.4 Notify the cost consultant of any work against which monies must be withheld or where 'an appropriate deduction' is to be made from the contract sum. **CA**

5.5.9.5 Liaise generally with the cost consultant over remeasurement, valuations and the issue of monetary certificates, and applications for direct loss and/or expense. **CA**

| 5.5.9.6 | Deal with applications for reimbursement of direct loss and/or expense fairly and promptly. | CA |
| 5.5.9.7 | Report to the client on cost matters at agreed intervals. | CA |

5.6   Sustainability Checkpoints

Sustainability Checkpoint 5

NOTE

With the design work complete the majority of activities at this stage are in relation to ensuring that the commissioning and handover activities agreed during Stage 1 are properly implemented.

Sustainability aims

To ensure that the Sustainability Strategy underpinning the design is carried through into construction and to manage the handover in a way that will ensure that the client can operate the building as intended on occupation.

Checkpoints

- Has the design stage sustainability assessment been certified?

- Have sustainability procedures been developed with the contractor and included in the Construction Strategy?

- Has the detailed commissioning and Handover Strategy programme been reviewed?

- Confirm that the contractor's interim testing and monitoring of construction has been reviewed and observed, particularly in relation to airtightness and continuity of insulation.

- Is the non-technical user guide complete and the aftercare service set up?

- Has the 'As-constructed' Information been issued for post-construction sustainability certification?

Key actions

- Pass the Site Waste Management Plan to the contractor.

- Design stage sustainability assessment to be certified.

- Develop construction sustainability procedures with the contractor.

- Review the commissioning and handover programme.

- Review and observe the contractor's interim testing and monitoring of construction, particularly airtightness and continuity of insulation.

- Review the implications of changes to the specification or design against agreed sustainability criteria.

- Complete the non-technical user guide and aftercare service set-up.

- Assist with collating as-built information for post-construction sustainability certification.

- Collaborate with the contractor to maximise construction phase potential to meet sustainability criteria as economically as possible.

- Submit final information for statutory approval and certification, including Building Regulations Part L submission and energy performance certificates (EPC).

- Visit the site to check that quality, installation, etc. is in line with sustainability targets.

- Review the content of the operating and maintenance manual with the facilities manager, who should sign it off when it is complete and acceptable.

- Stress the importance of design elements that are essential to meeting sustainability targets and how to monitor whether they are operating correctly.

- Work with the client's facilities managers to ensure a smooth handover, with all records finalised and coordinated and with adequately trained operating and maintenance staff in place in advance of completion.

- Check that adequate maintenance contracts are in place and that they will commence immediately after handover.

- Confirm responsibilities and routines for data recording to monitor performance and assist in fine tuning.

- Identify aftercare representative(s) and when they will be available on site.

5.7 Information Exchanges

5.7.1 Check that all the agreed outputs for Stage 6 have been produced.

The outputs following mobilisation might include the following:

- bill of reductions or similar document setting out agreed adjustments to the tender figure, if relevant, to arrive at an acceptable contract figure

- Building Contract documents duly signed and initialled as appropriate by the employer and contractor as parties to the contract

- requisite sets of drawings, schedules and other documents for **CA** issue to the main contractor

- approved tenders and numbered documents in respect of specialist subcontractors for issue to the main contractor

- construction phase Health and Safety Plan and HSE notification by the principal contractor

- requisite forms and documents for issue to the clerk of works if appropriate.

The outputs from construction might include the following:

- 'As-constructed' Information

- information (drawn and written), decisions and instructions (obligatory or discretionary), as necessary for the contractor to perform their obligations under the Contract Building, issued during the progress of the works

- valuations (on minor works) and certificates (monetary and **CA** otherwise), issued in accordance with the Building Contract, during the progress of the works

5

- records of all correspondence, instructions and certificates, and   **CA**
  'state of the art' documents, whether from manufacturers or
  other sources, which should be retained in case there are later
  disputes

- manuals or other maintenance information required under the
  Building Contract

- Health and Safety File information, as required under the CDM
  Regulations

- programmes for maintenance, if required.

5.8	UK Government Information Exchanges

5.8.1   There are no Information Exchanges at this Stage.

5

Supplementary Material

5/SM1:   Dealing with Building Contract documents (actions for the contract administrator)

Notifying all tenderers

A letter should be sent to the selected tenderer confirming the decision to accept the tender. This may be subject to agreed modifications to the contracted works, usually to fit within the cost plan. This letter might state that a contract will not exist until the documents have been prepared and signed by the parties. If this is so, it is important to make sure that the signing of the Building Contract takes place before the date agreed for possession, to avoid possible allegations of frustration.

Once the tender has been accepted, a list of compliant tender prices and tenderers should be sent to all tenderers within a reasonable period of time.

The formalities of the Building Contract agreement should always be completed before work starts on site. You are strongly advised that construction work should not commence without a signed contract and that letters of intent can leave consultants exposed to significant liabilities.

NOTE

Refer to the recent Technology and Construction Court decision in Ampleforth Abbey Trust v Turner & Townsend Project Management Limited *(2012), which acts as a warning to contract administrators on the scope of their standard of care, and to construction professionals in general of the risk of 'unreasonable' limitation of liability clauses within their standard terms and conditions being held as unenforceable.*

Under no circumstances should construction work be started before the contractor has prepared a Health and Safety Plan which complies with the CDM Regulations.

Completing the Building Contract documents

Both parties should enter into a contract on the basis of a complete set of documents, each of which has been completed as necessary (see P/SM1 for a list of contract documents).

The agreement between the employer and the contractor should be dated and should reflect the correct titles and addresses of the parties. Normally the addresses will be those to which notices, instructions, certificates, etc. are to be sent. If either party wishes to have all contractual communications sent to a different address, this should be recorded in the Building Contract documents.

Signing the Building Contract

The form of Building Contract containing the Articles of Agreement is normally sent first to the contractor, accompanied by the drawings listed in the Recitals and the other contract documents as appropriate. Indicate where the contractor is to sign (usually in the lower set of spaces). Documents returned by the contractor should be examined carefully to see that they have been completed properly, as requested in the covering letter.

The documents should then be passed to the employer, with a covering letter asking the employer to date the Articles. Documents returned from the employer should be examined carefully to see that they have been completed properly.

Signing confirmed

Instead of signing separately, the parties may agree to meet at some convenient place and complete the execution of the Building Contract in each other's presence.

If the Building Contract is to be executed as a simple contract, only the signatures of both parties are necessary. The signatures of witnesses – desirable, although not a legal necessity – confirm the existence of the agreement.

If the Building Contract is to be executed as a deed then appropriate wording should be used for the attestation clause. Special wording may be required depending on the memorandum or standing orders of an authority or corporate body.

The manner of execution of the main contract does not necessarily mean that subcontracts or collateral agreements have to be similarly executed. However, thought should be given to this matter so as to avoid confusion and unnecessary complications and costs.

It is sometimes stated in the contract conditions who is to have custody of the original contract documents – usually the employer. The documents should be kept in a secure fireproof place. Copies of the contract documents should be suitably endorsed, for example: 'This is a certified copy of the Agreement dated . . . between . . . and . . .' and signed by the architect. A set is given to the contractor; the architect would be wise to keep another complete set safe in the office.

5/SM2:   Site inspectorate appointment and briefing (actions for the contract administrator)

On large works, full-time resident consultants (e.g. architects, engineers) or a clerk of works might be needed to monitor conformity of materials, construction and quality, and also to liaise on the many activities upon which the full standards of the building's performance will depend.

On most large projects, a clerk of works is a full-time and valuable presence. The clerk of works must appreciate the extent of their powers and duties, which are generally to observe, inspect, check and report. With JCT contracts, the clerk of works operates under the direction of the contract administrator and must be thoroughly conversant with the form of building contract employed.

The *Clerk of Works and Site Inspector Handbook* (2006) is a useful source of information. It sets out standard terms of appointment, defines duties and responsibilities, lists the documents which the clerk of works should maintain and offers a range of forms which might assist both the clerk of works and the architect.

The duties of a clerk of works are to observe, inspect, check and report. A site diary is for recording day-to-day events. There is also a need to provide the architect with periodic reports to record progress on site, usually on a weekly basis. Printed forms will be provided for the clerk of works to complete and sign. The Institute of Clerks of Works publishes a Project Report Form which will be suitable for most situations.

5/SM3: Pre-contract meeting (actions for the contract administrator)

This meeting, sometimes referred to as the pre-start meeting, is crucial.

The site inspectorate may have already been briefed at separate meetings, or the briefing could form part of the initial project team meeting. At the meeting, all personnel will be introduced, and lines of communication can be unequivocally identified and defined. This is the first opportunity for all the project team members to meet and for effective working arrangements to be established.

It is essential for the person identified as the contract administrator to know the full range of contractual requirements of the project, and to be alert to potentially difficult areas. As chairman of the meeting, this person must establish mutual confidence and see that different viewpoints are aired and accommodated before the project gets under way.

The business of the meeting is likely to cover a wide range of topics and it is important to start with a clear agenda and stick to it. For a specimen agenda, see Figure 5/1.

Agenda items at pre-contract meeting

Introductions

- Introduce the representatives who will regularly attend progress meetings and clarify their roles and responsibilities. The client, the contractor and the design team may wish to introduce themselves.
- Briefly describe the project and its priorities and objectives, and any separate contract which may be relevant (e.g. preliminary, client's own contractors).
- Indicate any specialists appointed by the client (e.g. for quality control, for commissioning) for this contract.

Contract

- Describe the present position with regard to preparation and signature of contract documents.
- Hand over any outstanding Technical Design and variation instructions. Review the situation for issuing other important information.
- Request that insurance documents be available for inspection immediately; remind the contractor to check specialist subcontractors' indemnities. Check whether further instructions are needed for special cover.
- Confirm the existence, status and use of the Information Release Schedule, if used. Establish the procedure for agreeing adjustments to the schedule should they be necessary.

- Confirm the contractor's status and role as competent constructor under the CDM Regulations.

Contractor's matters

- Check that the contractor's master programme is in the form required and that it satisfactorily accommodates the specialist subcontractors. It must:
  - contain adequate separate work elements to measure their progress and integration with services installations
  - allocate specific dates for specialist subcontract works, including supply of information, site operations, testing and commissioning
  - accommodate public utilities, etc.
- Agree a procedure for the contractor to inform the architect of information required in addition to any shown on the Information Release Schedule. This is likely to involve a contractor's schedule of information required, which must relate to their works programme and must be kept up to date and regularly reviewed. It should include information, data, drawings, etc. to be supplied by the contractor/specialist subcontractors to the architect/design team.
- Review in detail the particular provisions in the Building Contract concerning site access, organisation, facilities, restrictions, services, etc. to ensure that no queries remain outstanding.
- Quality control is the contractor's responsibility. Remind the contractor of the contractual duties to supervise, of your duties to inspect, and the site inspectorate's duties in connection with the works. Clarify what standards, quality of work and management are required during the execution of the works.
- Numerous other matters may need special coverage, e.g.:
  - check whether immediate action may be needed by the contractor over specialist subcontractors and suppliers
  - emphasise that drawings, data, etc. received from the contractor or specialist subcontractors will be inspected by the architect/design team (not approved), and will remain the responsibility of the originator
  - review outstanding requirements for information to or from the contractor in connection with specialist works
  - clarify that the contractor is responsible for coordinating the performance of specialist works and for their workmanship and materials, for providing specialists with working facilities and for coordinating site dimensions and tolerances.
- The contractor must also provide for competent testing and commissioning of services as set out in the Building Contract documents, and should be reminded that the time allocated for commissioning is not a contingency period for the main contract works.
- The contractor must obtain the architect's written consent before subletting any work.

Site inspectorate matters

- Clarify that architect's inspections comprise periodic visits to meet the contractor's supervisory staff, plus spot visits.
- Remind the contractor that the site inspectorate must be provided with adequate facilities and access, together with information about site staff, equipment and operations, for their weekly reports to the contract administrator.

- Confirm procedures for checking quality control, e.g. through:
  - certificates, vouchers, etc. as required
  - sample material to be submitted
  - samples of workmanship to be submitted prior to work commencing
  - test procedures set out in the bills of quantities
  - adequate protection and storage
  - visits to suppliers'/manufacturers' works.

Design team matters

- Emphasise that the design team will liaise with specialist subcontractors only through the contractor. Instructions are to be issued only by the contract administrator. The contractor is responsible for managing and coordinating specialist subcontractors.
- Establish working arrangements for specialists' drawings and data for evaluation (especially services) to suitable timetables. Aim to agree procedures which will speed up the process; this sector of work frequently causes serious delay or disruption.

Communications and procedures

- The supply and flow of information will depend upon programmes being established at the start and will proceed smoothly if:
  - there is regular monitoring of the information schedules
  - requests for further information are made specifically in writing, not by telephone
  - the architect responds quickly to queries
  - policy queries are directed to the architect
  - discrepancies are referred to the contract administrator for resolution, not the contractor.
- On receiving instructions, check for discrepancies with existing documents; check that documents being used are current.
- Information to or from specialist subcontractors or suppliers must be via the contractor.
- All information issued by the architect is to be via the appropriate forms, certificates, notifications, etc. The contractor should be encouraged to use standard formats and classifications.

- All forms must show the distribution intended; agree numbers of copies of drawings and instructions required by all recipients.
- Clarify that no instructions from the client or design team can be accepted by the contractor or any subcontractor; only empowered written instructions by the contract administrator are valid, and all verbal instructions must be confirmed in writing. Explain the relevant procedures under the Building Contract. The contractor should promptly notify the contract administrator of any written confirmations outstanding.
- Procedures for notices, applications or claims of any kind are to be strictly in accordance with the terms of the Building Contract; all such events should be raised immediately the relevant conditions occur or become evident.

Meetings

- Always issue an agenda beforehand for all contract administrator meetings, and circulate minutes promptly. Agree with the contractor and design team that:
  - minutes are to be taken as directions for action only where specifically stated and agreed
  - any dissent is to be notified within seven days
  - all persons attending will have authority to act.
- Agree copies and distribution required.

5/SM4: Insurances check
    (actions for the contract administrator)

Insurance in the context of building construction is a highly specialised area, but it is of great importance for the contract administrator. Certain insurance obligations arise from legislation, but the Building Contract will usually contain specific requirements concerning insurance cover against injury or damage caused during the works.

These requirements will have been discussed with the client, and the implications fully explained, prior to tender stage. The cost of insurance premiums will have been taken into account by the tenderers. Responsibility for the required cover, whether taken out by the contractor or the employer, will have been established.

Whereas the checking of policy wording is a matter for insurance experts advising either the contractor or the employer as relevant, it is for the contract administrator to check that the obligations to take out cover have been complied with.

An insurances check is necessary before any work on site is commenced. Although most contractors carry an annual policy, endorsements and some cover can take time to arrange. It may be that in some circumstances it proves impossible to obtain the cover stated, in which case it will be for the parties to the Building Contract to decide the arrangements to apply.

Specialist subcontractors are sometimes mainly responsible for damage which occurs and such an eventuality must be properly covered. The employer pays the cost of insurance in the end and it is important to avoid the risk of double insurance. Cover must be adequate and any figures entered in the Building Contract should be realistic after taking expert advice on the particular circumstances. The mere repetition of some previously quoted sum is a recipe for disaster.

At mobilisation stage it is vital to ensure that the required insurances are in place before work commences.

5/SM5:   Keeping the client informed
(actions for the contract administrator)

The client will expect to be kept informed about the progress of work and given a regular report on the financial situation. Any material changes in design or construction will need prior approval.

How this is best handled will depend on the size of the job, the client's own organisation and the stipulated procedures for the project team. A few clients might prefer to leave matters almost entirely in the hands of the contract administrator, but the majority will expect formal reports at regular intervals. Some clients will expect to be directly represented at site progress meetings. Matters to be kept in mind include the following:

Time

The client will need to be kept informed about programme and progress. This information will be available through minutes of site progress meetings (issued by the contract administrator), copies of correspondence relating to notices of delay, and the award of any extensions of time. It is particularly important that the client is kept informed about any anticipated change to the completion date or the construction cost, as this will have managerial and financial implications for the client.

Quality

The client will need to be kept informed about any problems concerning materials and workmanship (or systems, products and execution) where it becomes necessary to issue contract administrator's instructions. The client should also be advised in good time about such matters as regular maintenance and the need to appoint or instruct staff about installation requirements, control and maintenance of systems. It might also be necessary for the client to take out maintenance contracts for certain installations.

Cost

The client should receive detailed statements of expenditure at regular intervals, with an appraisal of the current position and a forecast of total costs. The client must agree any extra expenditure in advance, whether this is for unavoidable adjustments in design or modifications requested by the client or an adjustment because of provisional sums expenditure. Where possible, it is good policy to have variations costed before the instruction is implemented. Cost reports will normally be prepared by the cost consultant, but where no cost consultant has been appointed (e.g. on minor works) then these might have to be prepared by the contract administrator.

For a typical financial report to the client, see Figure 5/2.

5/SM6:   Site meetings
(actions for the contract administrator)

The usual procedure is for the contract administrator to arrange and chair site progress meetings, and for the contractor to arrange and chair technical meetings. In addition, the contract administrator will call and chair special meetings, including additional design team meetings, for as long as the project requires this. There are also site inspections by the contract administrator, which may or may not be formal and which may take place the same day as the site progress meeting.

As a general rule, meetings should only be called for a clear purpose and should only involve those persons necessary for the successful conduct of the business. All meetings should be properly convened, with a precise agenda issued in advance, and be chaired in a firm and fair manner. All decisions should be clearly minuted.

Contract administrator's site progress meetings

These are essentially policy meetings and should take place at regular intervals (e.g. the first Tuesday in the month). It is sometimes helpful if they are immediately preceded by site visits, but the two should be kept distinct as they serve entirely different purposes. The main business of the meetings will be to receive reports and to agree action necessary as a result. They are not the place to answer routine queries or provide general information. All the people who attend these meetings should have the authority to act.

A standard agenda of items should be maintained, and it is useful to include an 'Action' column. Minutes are normally issued by the contract administrator; this is sometimes done by the contractor, but the contract administrator should be alert to the fact that instructions contained in minutes prepared by the contractor or other person may not carry the same legal effect. Minutes should be issued soon after the meeting to all those named on the agreed distribution list. It is sensible to require that any dissent from the minutes is made in writing within seven days of issue.

For a specimen agenda, see Figure 5/3.

Meetings for special purposes

Even when meetings are called ad hoc for some special purpose there should still be an agenda and a formal minute of decisions taken. Meetings might be needed for various reasons, for example with representatives of adjoining owners or with statutory bodies. It might also be necessary to convene further design team meetings during work on site, and as long as they are needed a consistent agenda and format should be maintained. Such business should not be merged with the contract administrator's site progress meetings.

Contractor's technical meetings

These are technical meetings with the subcontractors and are arranged by the contractor to take place before the contract administrator's site progress meetings. The contract administrator may be asked to attend; if so, they should make a note of any decisions and act appropriately. The contractor should prepare and distribute the minutes.

5/SM7:   Site inspections

These are visits by the architect (as designer) to observe and comment on the contractor's site supervision and examples of work at intervals appropriate to the stage of construction. This is periodic inspection, which should be carried out to the extent determined by the nature of the work, and as agreed with the client in the appointing document. However, it should be noted that there is an obligation (reinforced by case law) for construction professionals to make visits to the site as necessary for the inspection of the works. Although the number of visits can be specified in the architect's agreement, this relates only to fees, and if more visits are necessary they may be chargeable extras. If more frequent visits or constant inspection are required then the client should be recommended to appoint a resident site inspector. It should not be termed or thought of as 'supervision', because this suggests the authority to issue instructions to operatives, which clearly an architect does not possess.

Site visits should be spot checks made without prior warning but should have a specific purpose and as such require preparation beforehand. This might mean devising a plan after studying the most recent reports and minutes of meetings. The architect will then visit the site with the purpose of observing particular parts or items and of checking that specified tests are being carried out and verified. Checks of a general nature might include:

- whether quality complies generally with the provisions of the Building Contract
- whether progress accords with the contractor's master programme
- whether essential parts of the design have been/are being carried out in accordance with the Building Contract provisions.

Such visits should be carried out carefully, and comments systematically noted. Where certificates refer to work, etc. 'properly executed', it is helpful to have a record of notes made at the time of a visit. Queries are often raised during site visits, but all decisions must be issued through the contract administrator in writing.

Reports of site visits should be prepared to a consistent format as soon after the visit as possible. Record photographs (dated), notes and sketches should be attached and carefully filed. These should be retained strictly for in-house use.

For a specimen site visit report form, see Figure 5/4.

5/SM8:   Issuing instructions
(actions for the contract administrator)

Under most building contracts the only person authorised to issue instructions to the contractor will be the contract administrator. It is sensible to establish at the start of the job what constitutes a 'contract administrator's instruction', and it is suggested that only written instructions issued on a standard form should be regarded as valid. The giving of oral instructions, using contractors' site instruction books, or taking the minutes of site meetings as instructions should all be avoided.

The particular form of contract used will state what powers are given to the contract administrator with regard to instructions, and only empowered instructions will bind the contractor. When issuing an instruction it is advisable to check the following:

- that it is empowered under the Building Contract, and that the relevant clause number can be cited
- that the identifying details are entered on the form (e.g. name of project, contractor, date of instruction, serial number)
- that the instruction is precisely worded and its meaning unambiguous
- that the instruction is signed by the authorised person.

A file copy will be retained, and it is also good practice to keep a record of contract administrator's instructions issued for the project.

For a specimen form for contract administrator's instructions issued, see Figure 5/5.

5/SM9:   Dealing with claims
(actions for the contract administrator)

Although the word is frequently used, 'claim' is something of a misnomer as far as contract administration is concerned. The contract administrator has the authority to act where the Building Contract conditions expressly provide for entitlement in certain events, particularly concerning extensions of time and reimbursement of loss and/or expense.

Claims not expressly within the Building Contract provisions or where, for various reasons, a contractor has elected not to follow the procedures or is unable to conform to the express terms would be 'ex-contractual' claims to be pursued in arbitration or litigation.

Extensions of time

Most construction contracts include a mechanism for dealing in a convenient way with events which might affect progress, which are beyond the control of the contractor and which were not foreseeable at the time of tender. For this to be operable there must be a clearly stated date for possession or commencement and a date for completion. There is usually an extension of time provision and a separate provision for dealing with additional costs which might arise.

Extensions of time provisions benefit the contractor in that they are relieved of paying liquidated damages for failure to complete because of stated reasons. The express terms are also very much in the client's interests by keeping alive the right to liquidated damages even though the contract period is extended because of the client's intervention. It is, of course, essential that such intervention is included as an event covered in the Building Contract conditions, and that the architect operates the extensions of time provisions strictly in accordance with the contract requirements.

When dealing with extensions of time, remember the following:

- Respond to each and every proper notice of delay from the contractor – at least it is evidence that the claim has been considered.
- When awarding extensions of time, do so only for the causes specified in the Building Contract. State the causes but do not apportion. Keep full records in case the award is contested.
- Comply strictly with the procedural rules. For example, if the contract requires it, notify every named subcontractor of a decision.
- Observe the timescale if one is stated in the Building Contract. If none is stated, act within a reasonable time.
- Form an opinion which is fair and reasonable in the light of the information available at the time.

Loss and/or expense applications

Monetary claims arising in the context of building contracts are usually made as a result of loss due to regular progress being affected or because of additional costs due to a prolongation of the time on site. The wording in the Building Contract usually identifies events or matters which are recognised as causes. There may be procedures to be followed which exist for the convenience of both parties. It is only these types of claims which the contract administrator has the authority to settle.

For an application to be valid:

• the loss and/or expense must be a direct actual loss
• the works (or a part) must be materially affected
• interference or disturbance to regular planned progress must have occurred
• reimbursement must not be possible under any other contractual provision.

The contract administrator has a duty to decide whether the claim is valid and, if information supplied is not adequate, additional reasonably necessary information must be requested.

Ascertainment of the amount claimed can rest with the contract administrator, but normally the Building Contract allows specifically for this function to be referred to the cost consultant.

When dealing with applications for reimbursement, remember the following:

• The object of these provisions is to put the contractor back into the position they would have been but for the disruption. It is not an opportunity to profit.
• The contractor must make written application at the proper time.
• The contract administrator must form an opinion about whether direct loss and/or expense has been incurred or is likely to be incurred, and that regular progress has been materially affected.
• The burden of proof rests with the contractor. If the notice is not sufficient, more information must be requested.
• Ascertainment is a matter of certainty and not approximation. Particularisation of claims, i.e. 'actual' figures relating to specific items, should be expected.

The importance of keeping good records cannot be emphasised enough.

It is recommended that records should be kept of: site delays observed or noted from reports; defective work observed which might relate to subsequent applications when instructions are issued; 'claims' submitted by the contractor which need to be noted and acted upon.

For specimen record forms, see Figures 5/6, 5/7 and 5/8.

5/SM10: Issuing certificates
(actions for the contract administrator)

Building contracts generally provide for the issue of certificates by the contract administrator. The issue will normally be an obligation, always subject to certain conditions being satisfied. A certificate is simply a statement of fact, and although a letter might constitute a certificate, it is advisable to establish at the beginning of the job that valid certificates will be those issued on a standard form. Refer to the RIBA Agreements Reference Set for guidance on use of the forms. Under the JCT Standard Building Contract 2011 (SBC 11) the following certificates are used:

Interim Certificate

This is for payment to the contractor of an instalment of the contract sum. It might be on a monthly valuation (although the contract administrator when certifying must use skill and care, and not blindly follow the cost consultant's valuation), on a stage or milestone basis as agreed by the parties and in accordance with the contract conditions.

Statement of Retention

These should be attached to the Interim Certificate and show the gross valuation of work done, identification of amounts subject to full retention, half retention and nil retention and the calculation of amounts of retention, which should be transferred to the Interim Certificate.

Section Completion Certificate

These are for use where the Building Contract provides for the work to be carried out in phases.

Statement of Partial Possession

Where the Building Contract makes provision for this, the employer may take possession of a part or parts of the works ahead of Practical Completion of the whole of the works. It requires agreement of the contractor, which cannot be unreasonable withheld.

Notification of revision to Completion Date

For use where an extension of time has been given, work has been omitted or in the final review following Practical Completion.

Non-Completion Certificate

A factual statement, upon which much may depend, e.g. the deduction of liquidated damages by the employer, or the right to deduct damages by a main contractor against a named subcontractor.

Practical Completion Certificate

A statement which expresses that the works have reached Practical Completion. The contractor is relieved from various obligations henceforth.

Certificate of Making Good (in Stage 6)

A statement referring to defects which were made good during the Rectification Period and those which were scheduled within 14 days of the end of the Period.

Final Certificate (in Stage 6)

This is conclusive evidence in respect of the balance due; in respect of the reasonable satisfaction of the contract administrator for particular matters; and in respect of extensions of time and reimbursement or direct loss and/or expense. It is not conclusive evidence that the contractor has met the terms of the Building Contract in respect of materials, goods and workmanship in general.

5/SM11: Preparing for handover
(actions for the contract administrator)

Although not usually referred to in building contracts, the process of completion and handing over the building should nevertheless be subject to careful planning and procedures. These should comprise:

- final commissioning, testing and witnessing of services installations
- pre-completion checks by the contract administrator
- preparation for the formal handing over
- issue of the Practical Completion certificate
- the formal handover meeting.

NOTE

In accordance with Regulation 38 (Fire Safety Information) of the Building Regulations 2010, ensure that the building control body is in receipt of a complete description of the fire safety measures. The absence of this information can be used as a reason for the Building Regulations completion certificate to be withheld.

Normally, the contract administrator can expect to be advised by the contractor when the works are approaching Practical Completion. Sometimes this indication is premature. Sometimes the client will pressure the contract administrator to certify prematurely. The contract administrator should act strictly in accordance with the conditions of the Building Contract. The parties are free to agree an expedient arrangement outside the contract terms if they so wish.

Final commissioning, testing and witnessing of services installations

Commissioning is the process whereby an installation that has reached static completion is brought to the state of full working order for proving. Testing is a matter of checking a commissioned installation and evaluating its performance measured against specified requirements. Commissioning and testing are operations which, on a sophisticated project, might need to be carried out by specialists, will need to be effectively managed, and should be subject to a commissioning specification and system for commissioning. They might also need to be phased, and although the installations will need to be commissioned before handover, some adjustment and testing might not be possible until after installations have been in use for a certain period.

Almost every project includes a service installation, and proper thought is needed at the outset concerning design, installation, inspection and arrangements for commissioning and testing. Many larger client bodies expect particular codes to be observed and stated procedures to be followed. The Chartered Institution of Building Services Engineers (CIBSE) publishes a series of Commissioning Codes which clearly itemise the checks necessary for various installations. The Building Services Research and Information Association (BSRIA) publishes a guide to operating and maintenance manuals for building services installations. Reference to appropriate documents such as these will normally be made when specifying methods of commissioning.

Tender documents should clearly state the level of commissioning and testing which will be required, both before handover and additionally, perhaps with a defects liability period of appropriate duration. Thought should also be given to the need for incorporating special conditions of contract because most standard forms do not make specific reference to such matters.

Where services installations are of a complex nature, it is likely that consultants and specialist firms will be involved, and expert commissioning engineers might need to be brought in. Nevertheless, the main contractor still has the responsibility for overall programming, and for ensuring that the works are finished by the contract completion date. This will usually necessitate commissioning, testing and the preparation of operating or maintenance manuals before handover. Sometimes difficulties arise where these latter operations are not allocated sufficient time, or where the costs entailed have not been fully covered in the contract sum.

A common difficulty is the precise definition of responsibilities. Contract administrators will obviously have a responsibility to see that requirements are properly included for and stated at the outset.

Manufacturers will also have a responsibility, particularly where use of particular components is specified. Inspection of services installations as work proceeds may be largely in the hands of consultants and subcontractors, although the main contractor will ultimately remain responsible for all matters of workmanship and materials. While contract administrators will have a duty to see what appropriate arrangements are made for commissioning and testing, responsibility for carrying out such operations should clearly lie with others.

The following checklist can be used:

Pre-completion checks:

- Warn the contractor to make sure that the building is ready for inspection well before the date of Practical Completion.
- Instruct the site inspectorate to maintain systematic preliminary inspections and to keep the contract administrator informed of progress and any difficulties likely to arise as well as defects discovered.
- Check progress of building control and any other statutory approvals.
- Consolidate a schedule of outstanding items from:
  - the contract administrator's progress meeting minutes
  - the consultants' reports
  - site inspection reports

    – the contract administrator's instructions
    – site visit notes.

These lists are for communication within the design team and for the contract administrator's own records. They should not be issued to the contractor as quality control is the contractor's responsibility and the contract administrator should not be drawn in to taking on this role. If necessary, inform the contractor that the works are not complete according to the Building Contract, and indicate general areas of concern. Remind the contractor to complete record drawings, etc. according to the agreed programme.

Inspection and commissioning:

- In collaboration with the design team, advise the contractor and all subcontractors to coordinate a programme of checks.
- Instruct the site inspectorate accordingly and ensure they check that defective work has been replaced and report any delays anticipated, where relevant asking the client's staff to attend inspections and checks.
- Ask the design team to make detailed inspections and to report back.
- Check that the associated contractors' works are completed.
- Remind subcontractors to complete record drawings, etc. and to prepare maintenance instructions as agreed.
- Make formal arrangements with the client for handover inspections.
- Ensure that Approved Document L compliance checks are carried out.
- Confirm cleaning and maintenance measures under the CDM Regulations.

Preparation for the formal handover

Before the meeting:

- Remind the client of the reasonable standards which are appropriate to the class of work specified. It is the architect/contract administrator's responsibility to certify.
- Inform the client's representative of the basis of the Building Contract (if they have not been personally involved from the start).
- Write to the contractor and all those who are to attend the meeting to let them know the time, date and venue.

Inspecting the buildings and site:

- Hold meeting(s) for inspection and handover.
- Check that the following are ready to hand over as required:
    – building owner's operating manual
    – keys
    – 'As-constructed' Information
    – details of maintenance arrangements
    – Health and Safety File.

- Outline the client's and contractor's responsibilities during the defects liability period.
- Outline arrangements for dealing with any future defects.
- Agree any additional works required by the client.

Additional works (if necessary):

- Liaise with the cost consultant and the contractor to negotiate the basis for pricing.
- Prepare drawings and instructions and obtain the client's approval of these and the related costs.
- Instruct the contractor to proceed (by means of an extension of the Building Contract, or a separate agreed instruction).
- Check that these are covered by the construction phase Health and Safety Plan.

Issue of the Practical Completion certificate

The Practical Completion certificate triggers a sequence of events, namely:

- the contractor's liability for damage to the completed works is ended
- the contractor's liability for any further liquidated damages is ended
- the contractor's liability for insurance of the works is ended
- the contractor's liability for damage to the works as a result of frost is ended
- half the retention money is usually released to the contractor.

A Practical Completion certificate is issued only when in the opinion of the contract administrator (or other person referred to expressly in the Building Contract) the works have reached a state of Practical Completion.

The formal handover meeting

The arrangements listed will be relevant in nearly all cases, including where there is sectional completion or partial possession.

Record attendance, date, etc.

Define purpose of meeting:

- Explain that inspections of the building and site are to establish agreement that work is ready to be handed over to the client for occupation.
- Note defects due to faulty workmanship or materials and issue instructions to the contractor to rectify them, immediately if appropriate.
- Ensure that all the contractor's plant and property have been removed from site.

Tour of inspection:

- Inspect the building and site.

Handover of building

The client accepts the building and site from the contractor, and the contractor hands over the keys.

- Ensure that meters have been read and fuel stocks noted.

Maintenance manuals, servicing contracts, etc.:

- Confirm with the CDM coordinator the contents of the Health and Safety File and the arrangements for delivering it to the client.
- Hand over any further building maintenance information as relevant, including:
  - directory
  - servicing contracts
  - maintenance of plant
  - maintenance of building
  - attention to landscape and planting
  - routine replacement schedules
  - 'As-constructed' Information.

Figure 5/1

Specimen agenda for pre-contract meeting

Job no: Job title:

Agenda for pre-contract meeting

1 Introductions
- Appointments, personnel
- Roles and responsibilities
- Project description

2 Contract
- Priorities
- Handover of production information
- Commencement and completion dates
- Insurances
- Bonds (if applicable)
- Standards and quality

3 Contractor's matters
- Possession
- Programme
- Health and Safety file and plan
- Site organisation, facilities and planning
- Security and protection
- Site restrictions
- Contractor's quality control
  policy and procedures
- Sub-contractors and suppliers
- Statutory undertakers
- Overhead and underground services
- Temporary services
- Signboards

4 Clerk of works' matters
- Roles and duties
- Facilities
- Liaison
- Dayworks

5 Consultants' matters
- Architectural
- Structural
- Mechanical
- Electrical
- Others

6 Quantity surveyor's matters
- Adjustments to tender figures
- Valuation procedures
- Remeasurement
- VAT

7 Communications and procedures
- Information requirements
- Distribution of information
- Valid instructions
- Lines of communications
- Dealing with queries
- Building Control notices
- Notices to adjoining owners/ occupiers

8 Meetings
- Pattern and proceedings
- Status of minutes
- Distribution of minutes

Figure 5/2

Specimen financial report to client

Job no: Job title:

Financial report to client

To end of (month)	(year)	Savings £	Extra £	£
Financial approvals	Contract sum as adjusted			
	Additional approvals to date of last report			
	Total approvals to date of last report			
Adjustments	Contract sum as adjusted			
	including contingencies			
	Cost adjustment on PC sums ordered			
	Cost adjustment on provisional sums			
	Value of Contract Administrator's Instructions issued to date			
	Changes of work anticipated			
Contingencies	Original contingencies sum			
	Estimated proportion			
	absorbed to date			
	Estimated remainder			
Cost of works	Estimated cost of works			
	including contingencies sum			
Reconcilliation	Variations instructed by the employer			
	since last report			
	(a) [addition] estimated cost			
	(b) [omission] estimated saving			
	Additional approvals to last report			
Final estimate	Estimated final expenditure			
	on present information			

Not included in assessments:
VAT, fees, other works (eg piling, landscape, advance orders)

Figure 5/3

Specimen agenda for contract administrator's site progress meeting

Job no: Job title:

Agenda for site progress meeting

                                                            ACTION

1   Minutes of last meeting (or introductions
    if it is the first meeting)

2   Contractor's report

·   General report
·   Sub-contractor's meeting report
·   Progress and programme
·   Causes of delay
·   Health and safety matters
·   Information received since last meeting
·   Information and drawings required
·   Contract administrator's instructions required

3   Site inspection report

·   Site matters
·   Quality control monitoring
·   Lost time
·   Tests observed and verified

4   Engineers' reports

·   Structural works
·   Mechanical works
·   Electrical works

5   Cost consultant's report

6   Communications and procedures

7   Building Contract completion date

·   Likely delays and their effect
·   Review of factors from previous meeting
·   Factors for review at next meeting
·   Revision to completion date
·   Revisions required to programme

8   Any other business

9   Date of next meeting

Figure 5/4

Specimen report form for predictive site visits

Job no: Job title:

Site visit report

Date: No. of visits scheduled:

Visit by: Visit no.:

Purpose

Observed

Checked		Recorded	
Samples		Photos	
Verification of tests			
Vouchers		Video	
Records		Other	

Summary

Work properly executed   ☐   Proceeding in workmanlike manner   ☐

Materials properly stored and protected   ☐   Progress to programme   ☐

Figure 5/5

Specimen record form of contract administrator's instructions issued

Job no: Job title:

Contract Administrator's Instructions issued

Date	CAI no.		Item	Subject	Estimated +/- cost (£)
	1		Gas Main	Quotation ref 8438/63	+1500
	2		Cills	Revised detail drawing L51/03	−750
	3		Opening	First floor revised drawing L51/12	+1000
	4	(1)	Hip tiles	Omit farsand / add Red Bank	+1420
		(2)	Hip irons	Omit / add finials	

1. Use a CAI for all instructions and notifications to the contractor.

2. List all individual items in any CAI.

3. Make sure all instructions are clearly worded and unambiguous.

4. Do not reserve numbers for future issues; do not miss out any numbers. If any error in numbering is found, immediately notify everyone on the distribution list.

Figure 5/6

Specimen record form of site delays observed

Job no:				Job title:	

Record of site delays observed

Date	Delay	Item	Reason	Observed by
6.1.13	1 week	Site clearance	Plant hire equipment late	C of W
17.1.13	1 week	Weather	Heavy snow	C of W
23.2.13	3 days	Foundations	Excavations waterlogged	C of W
10.4.13	2 days	Steelworks	Erectors arrived	H R J
			Problem with crane jib	
			Left site	

1. Record observations in sequence of work element/location, conditions or situation and note the source of information where relevant.

2. Liaise closely with clerk of works and consultants.

3. Check against and coordinate with your site inspection reports.

5

Figure 5/7

Specimen record form of defective work

Job no: _____   Job title: _____

Record of defective work

Date	Item	Contractor notified (date)	Value if deducted (£)	Cleared (date)
1.8.13	Priming to some steelwork unsatisfactory	2.8.13		2.9.13
16.9.13	Nosing to boiler house steps not satisfactory, shuttering poor	16.9.13		12.10.13

1. Describe the work in sequence of work element/location; condition as rejected; rectification required.

2. Check and update this record regularly with clerk of works and design team.

3. Notify cost consultant of any values deducted against valuations made and when items are cleared.

4. Check against and coordinate with your site inspection reports.

Figure 5/8

Specimen record form of claims by contractor

Job no: Job title:

Schedule of claims by contractor

Date	Clause no.	Item	Time/amount: Req'std	Allowed	Date for decision	Date awarded
25.2.13	25	Weather – notice of delay				
		inadequate – more detailed				
		information requested				
		AI No 1				
	25	Gas Main	4 days	2 days		
	26	Consequential loss / expense				

1. Check that contractor uses procedures laid down in the contract.

2. Inform cost consultant, design team, clerk of works immediately any claim is notified.

3. List adequate description and if neccessary open a sub-file to collate the correspondence etc about each claim.

4. Check that your action complies with the time limits stated in the contract.

Handover and Close Out

CONTENTS

Plan of Work and Stage Activities

Supplementary Material

Excerpt from the RIBA Plan of Work 2013

RIBA
Plan of
Work
2013

Stage 6

Handover
and Close Out

Task Bar	Tasks
Core Objectives	Handover of building and conclusion of **Building Contract**.
Procurement Variable task bar	Conclude administration of **Building Contract**.
Programme Variable task bar	*There are no specific activities in the RIBA Plan of Work 2013.*
(Town) Planning Variable task bar	*There are no specific activities in the RIBA Plan of Work 2013.*
Suggested Key Support Tasks	Carry out activities listed in **Handover Strategy** including **Feedback** for use during the future life of the building or on future projects. Updating of **Project Information** as required. *The priority during this stage is the successful handover of the building and concluding the **Building Contract** with support tasks focused on evaluating performance and providing **Feedback** for use on future projects. Fine tuning of the building services is likely to occur.*
Sustainability Checkpoints	• *Has assistance with the collation of post-completion information for final sustainability certification been provided?*
Information Exchanges (at stage completion)	Updated **'As-constructed' Information**.
UK Government Information Exchanges	Required.

Summary

The project team's priorities during this stage will be facilitating the successful handover of the building in line with the **Project Programme** and, in the period immediately following, concluding all aspects of the **Building Contract**, including the inspection of defects as they are rectified or the production of certification required by the **Building Contract**.

Other services may also be required during this period. These will be dictated by project specific **Schedules of Services**, which should be aligned with the procurement and **Handover Strategies**. Tasks in relation to the **Handover Strategy** can be wide-ranging and may include:

— attending **Feedback** workshops

— considering how any lessons learned might be applied on future projects

— undertaking tasks in relation to commissioning or ensuring the successful operation and management of the building.

Mapping to RIBA Outline Plan of Work 2007

Stage 6 maps broadly to the former Stage L services.

6.1   Core Objectives

The project team's scope of services during this stage will be dictated by the appointment documents, which should be aligned with the procurement strategy and Handover Strategy.

Tasks carried out as part of the procurement strategy might include the inspection of defects as they are rectified or the production of certification in relation to the Building Contract.

Tasks in relation to the Handover Strategy can be wide-ranging, and may include:

- attending Feedback workshops

- considering how any lessons learned might be applied on future projects

- undertaking an initial Post-occupancy Evaluation that considers whether the desired Project Outcomes have been achieved, and/or

- undertaking tasks in relation to commissioning or ensuring the successful operation and management of the building.

 Activities in Stage 6 to be undertaken by the architect as contract administrator are annotated 'CA' in the margin.

After Practical Completion / defects liability period

At Practical Completion the client takes possession of the building, half of any retention money is released and the contractor's liability for liquidated damages ends. There is generally a 12-month defects liability period (DLP) which commences at the date of Practical Completion and during which time the contractor must rectify any defects arising if instructed to do so. At the end of the DLP, the contractor must make good any remaining defects within a reasonable period of time. Upon completion of the making good of defects, all retention money must be released, and when all outstanding contractual issues have been resolved, the final certificate can be issued. This marks the conclusion of the Building Contract.

DLP activities are generally for the architect as contract administrator.

Initial occupation period / Soft Landings

Soft Landings activities during the initial occupation period and Post-occupancy Evaluation are additional services. Where they form part of the appointment, certain activities must be carried out from the outset of the project. These activities are noted in this book within the Appointment section of each stage.

For Soft Landings activities the architect should make visits to site to make structured transfer of information to the users and the facilities management team, spot emerging issues and solve problems, and establish a method of providing ongoing assistance for the users.

Post-occupancy Evaluation (POE)

On completion of a project there will always be the need to assemble documents for retention and to compile records. This is an activity appropriate to nearly all projects. A study of such material could lead to an updating of the office systems to take account of lessons learned.

There are then three levels at which further post-completion studies may be carried out. First, an investigation or appraisal that is restricted to an in-house operation. Second, a debriefing exercise that involves other people concerned with the project, which could commence shortly after completion. Third, a full post-project evaluation, but this is unlikely to be possible until several years after completion.

Both in-house appraisals and debriefing are exercises not normally listed in the services provided by the architect and are unlikely to be funded by the client. However, they can provide useful lessons for the members of both the design team and the construction team.

A full Feedback study can be costly; if the client wishes one to be undertaken, it will probably have to be the subject of a separate commission. With partnering arrangements this kind of study is likely to be an essential part of the assessment of whether targets have been met. Full post-project evaluations can be particularly useful to clients who construct more than once, in order to improve the briefing they provide for future projects.

However, this is a sensitive area and confrontation should be avoided at all costs. A full Feedback study will not be a productive exercise in all cases and great care needs to be taken when deciding whether or not it will be worthwhile for a particular project. The architect's professional indemnity (PI) insurers should be informed before such a study is undertaken for the client.

6.2	**Procurement**

6.2.1	Conclude administration of the Building Contract. Refer to 6.5.6, 'DLP activities'.	**CA**

6.3	**Programme**

6.3.1	*There will be a prescribed programme for DLP activities after Practical Completion, usually for 6 or 12 months. A programme for activities for Soft Landings and POE will need to be agreed with the client during an earlier stage, ideally in Stage 1.*

NOTE

6.4	**(Town) Planning**

	There are no (Town) Planning activities during this stage, but the planning process should be reviewed along with other matters in the post-project reviews.	**6/SM2** **6/SM3**

6.5	**Suggested Key Support Tasks**

6.5.1	Information required

DLP activities

6.5.1.1	Check that all information necessary for DLP activities is available, which might include the following:	CA

- copies of the Health and Safety Plan developed by the contractor and certified by the CDM coordinator

- sets of administration forms appropriate for the form of contract being used

- energy performance certificate.

Soft Landings activities

6.5.1.2	Check that all information necessary for Soft Landings activities is available, which might include the following:

- as-installed information for services, construction detailing, etc. (if responsible for producing the energy performance certificate)

- brief from the occupier on their operational requirements

- Part L log book.

POE activities

6.5.1.3	Check that all information necessary for POE activities is available, which might include the following:

- energy use data, e.g. utility bills.

6.5.2 Brief

6.5.2.1 The brief for Soft Landings and POE activities must be agreed at an early stage in the project, ideally at Stage 1.

6.5.3 Appointment

6.5.3.1 Establish scope, content and context for Stage 6.

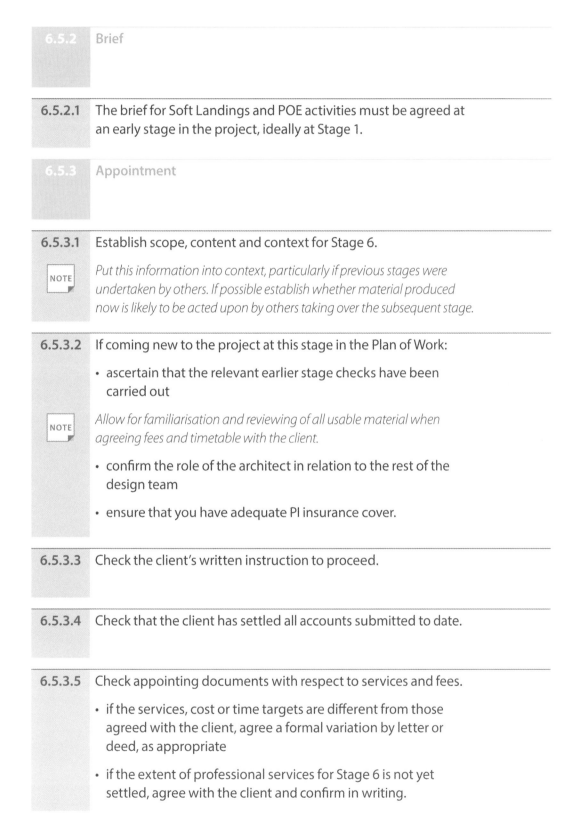

NOTE *Put this information into context, particularly if previous stages were undertaken by others. If possible establish whether material produced now is likely to be acted upon by others taking over the subsequent stage.*

6.5.3.2 If coming new to the project at this stage in the Plan of Work:

- ascertain that the relevant earlier stage checks have been carried out

NOTE *Allow for familiarisation and reviewing of all usable material when agreeing fees and timetable with the client.*

- confirm the role of the architect in relation to the rest of the design team

- ensure that you have adequate PI insurance cover.

6.5.3.3 Check the client's written instruction to proceed.

6.5.3.4 Check that the client has settled all accounts submitted to date.

6.5.3.5 Check appointing documents with respect to services and fees.

- if the services, cost or time targets are different from those agreed with the client, agree a formal variation by letter or deed, as appropriate

- if the extent of professional services for Stage 6 is not yet settled, agree with the client and confirm in writing.

NOTE *Remember that the agreed services must reflect the role of the architect under the form of Building Contract selected. Inform the client in advance if more frequent visits are required than those allowed for in the agreement and which would incur additional expenditure.*

6.5.3.6   Assess the office resources needed for Stage 6 and ensure that they are available and adequate.

6.5.3.7   If accredited for energy performance certificate (EPC) administration, check if the client wants to instruct this and, if so, agree fees.

NOTE *EPCs are required for all buildings when they are constructed, leased or sold. In newly constructed or refurbished buildings the EPC will normally be provided by the main contractor.*

WWW *For information on EPCs refer to the UK Government website at www.gov.uk and search 'energy performance certificates'.*

WWW *For clarification on exceptions for providing EPCs and what they should cover, refer to the relevant guide at www.communities.gov.uk.*

Soft Landings activities

6.5.3.8   Check if the client wants to instruct the design team to undertake continuous commissioning, 'sea trials' and Soft Landings, etc. If so, agree a scope of service for the additional service and fee. Agreement for this service should be confirmed prior to going to tender.

NOTE *A Soft Landings team (designer and constructor) is resident on site during the move-in period to ensure emerging issues are dealt with effectively. The team can then monitor building use and energy performance for the first two or three years of occupation, identifying opportunities both for fine-tuning the building and for improvements in future developments. The process also creates a coordinated route to POE.*

NOTE *Sea trials are where the design team are involved in running the building for the first two years.*

6.5.3.9   If a BREEAM assessment has been commissioned you may need to provide information to the BREEAM assessor in order for the post-occupancy stage of the assessment to be completed.

NOTE

A full BREEAM assessment is undertaken in four to five stages (depending on when the assessor is appointed), comprising: registration, pre-assessment, initial guidance/design stage assessment, construction and post-construction review/final certification. A BREEAM certificate will not be issued until after the post-construction stage of the assessment has been completed.

WWW

For further guidance refer to www.bream.org.

POE activities

6.5.3.10   Check to see if the client wishes to undertake a BREEAM In-Use assessment of the building in operation and agree the scope of the service and the fee.

NOTE

BREEAM In-Use is a scheme to help building managers reduce the running costs and improve the environmental performance of buildings.

6.5.3.11   Check if the client wants to instruct a POE exercise and, if so, agree the scope of service and the fee.

6.5.3.12   Advise the client of the need to employ other consultants and the contractor.

6.5.4   Client

DLP activities

6.5.4.1   Remind the client that responsibility for insurance reverts to them.

	Soft Landings activities
6.5.4.2	If appointed as information manager, assist in the Soft Landings processes and coordinate and release the 'end of construction' BIM record model data.
	Review the Project Performance in use and compare with projected BIM data.
	Invite and coordinate Feedback from all stakeholders in the process and disseminate to all in order to benefit future projects.
6.5.4.3	Check whether the client has issued an instruction for an energy performance certificate prior to selling or leasing the building.
	POE activities
6.5.4.4	If a full Feedback study is planned, agree with the client what access will be available, what the timescale should be and in what form the findings should be presented.
6.5.4.5	If the building is occupied by a public authority or an institution providing a public service to a large number of persons, with a total useful area greater than 1000 square metres, check if the client has issued an instruction for a display energy certificate.
6.5.4.6	Explain to the client the purpose of a debriefing exercise or full post-project evaluation and that their feedback might be a key part of this activity. Discuss to what extent key persons in the organisation could be expected to contribute opinions at a meeting chaired by the architect (see BRE Digest 478 for guidance).
6.5.4.7	Arrange a meeting with key personnel from the client organisation (the building users and maintenance staff). Ensure that you have considered your objectives and what information you want to get from this exercise and have a clear agenda for the meeting.
6.5.4.8	Discuss with the client to what extent the managers and users of the project could be expected to cooperate in completing a questionnaire.

6.5.4.9	Discuss with the client whether authorised photographers would be allowed access after final completion, for Feedback purposes.	
6.5.4.10	Discuss with the client whether it would be permissible for the architect to carry out a survey of the building in use some time after completion.	
6.5.4.11	Check with your PI insurers that you have cover for Feedback activities.	
6.5.5	**Project team**	
6.5.5.1	Involve the project team as required.	
6.5.6	**General matters**	
	DLP activities	
6.5.6.1	Administer the terms of the Building Contract.	CA
6.5.6.2	Collate all documents issued to the contractor, and store them. NOTE *Preparation of 'As-constructed' Information and maintenance manuals is included under Stage 5.*	CA 6/SM1
6.5.6.3	Conduct in-house appraisal of office performance on project.	6/SM2
6.5.6.4	Consider holding a debriefing exercise with the client and other consultants.	6/SM3
6.5.6.5	Check if the building log book for the building operator – required by Part L of the Building Regulations – has been issued. The building log book should be in accordance with the requirements of CIBSE TM31 (refer to www.cibse.org).	

| 6.5.6.6 | Participate in the creation of operating manuals for the building. See BSRIA BG 1/2007TK for recommended contents of these manuals (refer to www.bsria.co.uk). |

Soft Landings activities

| 6.5.6.7 | For residential schemes where the Code for Sustainable Homes (CSH) is required, complete the post-construction review of the CSH assessment so that 'final' code certification can be issued. |

| 6.5.6.8 | For non-domestic buildings, undertake the post-completion stage of the BREEAM assessment if required. |

| 6.5.6.9 | Provide a copy of a building user guide if required. The guide will contain the information that will be relevant to the non-technical building user to explain how the building systems operate to increase comfort levels, etc. This might include an onsite presentation. |

| 6.5.6.10 | Ensure that seasonal commissioning is undertaken, so that HVAC systems are commissioned for both summer and winter conditions, as agreed with the client. |

6.5.6.11	Debriefing and Feedback are management exercises. If it is agreed to extend the commission to include these, establish the scope and content of Soft Landings and POE activities.
NOTE	*Do not allow an exercise to be undertaken if it seems likely that it might result in recriminations – and even arbitration or litigation.*
	Always inform your PI insurers before embarking on any Feedback study.

| 6.5.6.12 | Check whether the design and technical teams would cooperate in debriefing. |

| 6.5.6.13 | Check whether the client would cooperate in debriefing. |
| NOTE | *In-house appraisal is a healthy operation for nearly all projects, but participants must feel able to exchange views freely. Debriefing can become a sensitive matter and will only succeed with the full cooperation of all involved.* |

6.5.6.14	Raise with all consultants the desirability of engaging in a systematic analysis of the management, construction and performance of the project.	6/SM4
6.5.6.15	Arrange a series of debriefing meetings.	
6.5.6.16	Convene debriefing meetings upon completion to evaluate technical matters. Involve all design team members, the main contractor and possibly the client.	
NOTE	*At debriefing meetings, watch out for partisan or defensive attitudes. Honest and objective discussion should not be allowed to degenerate into acrimony.*	
6.5.6.17	Record the discussions.	
6.5.6.18	Formulate overall conclusions from the debriefing.	
6.5.6.19	Make visits to the site to make structured transfer of information to the users and the facilities management team.	
6.5.6.20	Spot emerging issues and solve problems arising.	
6.5.6.21	Establish a method of providing ongoing assistance to the users.	
	POE activities	
6.5.6.22	Consider the desirability of a full Feedback study or a post-project evaluation.	
6.5.6.23	Year 1: • Recalculate capital and revenue target costs at current rates. • Identify the actual capital costs.	

6.5.6.24	Year 2 (and 3):
	• Identify/provide data required for the review.
	• Agree a programme of meetings.
	• Identify the issues, establish causation and consider remedies.
	• Contribute to the output reports and recommendations.
	• If instructed, implement the recommendations.

6.5.6.25	Participate in the BREEAM In-Use assessment process if required.

6.5.7	**Inspections/tests**

6.5.7.1	Refer to 6.1 for the broad scope of inspections required during this stage.

6.5.8	**Consultations, approvals and consents**

6.5.8.1	Seek approvals as required by the building occupier to undertake post-occupancy tests.

6.5.9	**Cost planning**

6.5.9.1	Keep records of time costs for POE activities.

6

6.6   Sustainability Checkpoints

Sustainability Checkpoint 6

Sustainability aims

To support the client in the early stages of occupation and to provide aftercare services as agreed.

Checkpoints

• Has assistance with the collation of post-completion information for final sustainability certification been provided?

Key actions

• Assist with collation of post-completion information for final sustainability certification.

• Observe building operation in use and assist with fine tuning and guidance for occupants.

• Issue declaration of energy/carbon performance in use (e.g. Carbon Buzz)

• If necessary, review the project sustainability features and operation methods with the client, facilities managers and occupants.

• Assist with the fine tuning of building services and operational systems to check that they meet user requirements.

6.7   Information Exchanges

The RIBA Plan of Work 2013 states:

Updated 'As-constructed' Information.

6.7.1   Check that all the agreed outputs have been produced, which might include the following:

DLP activities

• certificate of making good defects

This is issued when defects listed at the end of the defects liability period have been remedied.

- final certificate

The issue of the final certificate brings the authority of the contract administrator, under the terms of the Building Contract, to a close. The contractor's liability continues, of course, until the end of the limitation period.

There might, in addition or alternatively, be contract provisions which refer to statements issued by the contract administrator or by the employer (e.g. in the case of design and build contracts). These should be regarded as requiring the same care and consideration as certificates before being issued. Case law has confirmed that there is no immunity from negligence in certifying.

 - Facilities Management BIM model data, as asset changes are made

 - study of parametric object information contained within BIM model data.

Soft Landings activities

- energy performance certificate

- operating manual/building user guide, if part of scope

- records of trials and their recommendations.

POE activities

- record of conclusions reached at debriefing meetings, distributed to participants

- results of full Feedback study conducted with the client or user client, or everyday users of the building, perhaps several years post completion.

 It is essential that the benefits and lessons learned from appraisals are passed to all members of staff. The office quality plan, manuals and procedures might need amendment or revision as a result.

6.8　UK Government Information Exchanges

6.8.1　Information Exchanges are required.

Supplementary Material

6/SM1: Keeping office records

Once a job is complete, a decision has to be made about which drawings and documents should be kept. No office has the space to keep all project records indefinitely.

A set of project records, properly maintained and completed, should be a useful condensed history of the project – a point of reference for quick comparison of working methods, timescales and costs. Photographs of the work in progress and as completed, presentation drawings and models should also be kept available for prospective clients and for general publicity purposes. However, it is essential to keep proper records of the kind of information that will be required in the event of disputes, in particular:

- the client brief and related correspondence
- the contract documents
- contract administrator's instructions
- minutes of project meetings
- certificates issued
- notes of inspections and surveys
- any crucial 'state of the art' information (manufacturers' key information, current British Standards, codes, etc.)
- progress charts, etc.
- selected working drawings.

It is important to remember that the personnel involved with the project may not be available to give evidence if litigation occurs some years later.

6/SM2: In-house appraisal

Appraise the project under the headings given in the following checklist:

1. Office costs:
   - relate office costs to reserve and profit targets

2. Performance of design team and site inspectorate in terms of:
   - communications with client
   - communications between design team members
   - communications with CDM coordinator
   - communications with contractor
   - design team programming
   - quality of drawings, specifications
   - cost planning, final costs against budget
   - quality control
   - energy effectiveness
   - meeting completion date(s), etc.

3. Contractor's performance in terms of:
   - project management, quality of staff
   - site management, quality of staff
   - health and safety compliance
   - continuity of personnel
   - quality of work
   - effectiveness of programming
   - cooperation in settling claims
   - cooperation over material for the Health and Safety File.

4. Working arrangements between design team and contractor in terms of:
   - architect's site progress meetings, actions on minutes
   - quality control
   - early identification of problems relating to progress, information and quality
   - potential disputes
   - financial arrangements, certificates, dayworks and measurement evaluation.

5. Completed works in terms of:

   - resolution of the brief
   - relation to site and surroundings
   - quality of building, functional and abstract
   - incorporation of mechanical and electrical services into structure
   - energy efficiency
   - wear and tear, maintenance.

Prepare reports:

- Include proposals for long-term reviews; distribute, file as appropriate.

Complete project records:

- Collect all relevant project records and information.
- Collate material and keep available for quick reference and comparison with that of other completed jobs.
- Arrange photographs for record and/or promotional purposes.

6/SM3: Debriefing

Obtaining valuable lessons with the benefit of hindsight is unlikely to be an activity commissioned by most clients, but it is a worthwhile exercise and, for a truly objective report, impartial 'auditors' could be engaged.

Debriefing after completion is something which should happen in all major projects to some extent. A series of meetings convened by the architect who acted as project lead could achieve this, as follows:

- meetings between the architect and CDM coordinator to evaluate matters related to compliance with the CDM Regulations
- meetings between key design team members and the contractor to evaluate design and technical aspects of the project
- meetings between the architect and the contractor to evaluate the management of the construction of the project.

A frank exchange of views might be expected at meetings, and the success of the operation will depend very much on the cooperation of all parties involved. Opinions on, for example, the overall timescale, the effectiveness of cost control, whether contract administrator's instructions including variations could have been avoided, whether drawings production and issue could have been improved, whether site reporting and quality control were effective, etc., might provide valuable lessons for future projects. Obviously, the time spent on this kind of operation and the cost of meetings has to be weighed against the fact that the project is usually a 'once only' occurrence and the particular team might never again be assembled. However, for repeat clients and consultant teams, this exercise will be very useful in establishing working relations for future projects. RIBA research shows that approximately half of architects' workload comes from existing clients.

6/SM4: Post-project evaluation

The more intensive investigations for Feedback, which might not be practicable until several years after completion of the project, could include structured interviews with the client's staff or with users, access to the buildings, and access to information and records held by various team members.

None of these activities should be attempted if there is a risk of inviting acrimony and dispute, although there is significant potential value in terms of continued client relations, learning from Feedback and aiding continuous improvement.

The purpose of a post-project evaluation is to analyse the management, construction and performance of a project. This could entail:

- an analysis of the project records
- an inspection of the fabric of the completed building
- studies of the building in use
- meetings and workshops with the client, consultants and users.

A post-project evaluation should cover:

- the purpose of the study
- the description of the need
- performance against cost, quality and timescale targets
- client satisfaction with the project and the facility
- user satisfaction with the facility
- performance and communication between project participants
  - project sponsor
  - client project manager
  - where relevant, client adviser
  - project team
- overview and recommendations
  - lessons learned
  - major points of action
  - costs
- technical appendices
  - user survey data
  - monitoring data.

6/SM5: Soft Landings

Five stages of Soft Landings

Soft Landings extends the duties of the team before handover, in the weeks immediately after handover, for the first year of occupation, and for the second and third years. The procedures are designed to augment standard professional scopes of service, not to replace them. They can be tailored to run alongside most industry-standard procurement routes. Major revisions to industry-standard documentation are therefore not necessary. The main additions to normal scopes of service occur during five main stages:

1. **Inception and briefing**

   To clarify the duties of members of the client, design and construction teams during critical stages, and to help set and manage expectations for performance in use.

2. **Design development and review (including specification and construction)**

   This proceeds much as usual, but with greater attention to applying the procedures established in the briefing stage, reviewing the likely performance against the original expectations and achieving specific outcomes.

3. **Pre-handover**

   To take place with greater involvement of designers, builders, operators and commissioning and controls specialists in order to strengthen the operational readiness of the building.

4. **Initial aftercare**

   To take place during the users' settling-in period, with a resident representative or team on site to help pass on knowledge, respond to queries and react to problems.

5. **Aftercare**

   In years 1 to 3 after handover, with periodic monitoring and review of building performance.

Soft Landings is effectively a palette of activities which improves the performance outcome of buildings because designers and contractors remain involved with buildings after Practical Completion. They help fine-tune the systems and ensure that occupants understand how to operate their buildings. Designed to dovetail with any existing procurement process, Soft Landings begins at the outset of any project, not just at handover. It includes better briefing, realistic performance benchmarking, reality-checking of design and procurement decisions, a graduated handover process and a period of professional aftercare by the project team. Equally important, it promotes an open and collaborative working culture.

Core principles

In order to provide greater clarity to the industry about the core fundamental requirements of a Soft Landings project, BSRIA has created a set of core principles (Table 6/1). A Soft Landings project is defined by the core principles: the package of principles should be adopted in their entirety in order for a construction project to be deemed a true Soft Landings project.

Table 6/1: Soft Landings core principles

1.	**Adopt the entire process**	The project should be procured as a Soft Landings project, and project documentation should explicitly state that the project team will adopt the five work stages in the Soft Landings Framework to the extent possible
2.	**Provide leadership**	The client should show leadership, engender an atmosphere of trust and respect, support open and honest collaboration, and procure a design and construction process that can be conducted with equal levels of commitment from all disciplines
3.	**Set roles and responsibilities**	In Soft Landings, the client is an active participant, and leads the process at the outset to develop the roles and responsibilities. This should include client representatives, all key design professionals, and the supply chain. The people involved in this process should be the actual individuals who will work on the project

4. **Ensure continuity**   Soft Landings should be continuous throughout the contractual process. It should be made part of all later appointments, and expressed clearly in contracts and subcontract work packages as appropriate. The client and principal contractor should ensure that subcontractors and specialist contractors take their Soft Landings roles and responsibilities seriously

5. **Commit to aftercare**   There should be a clear and expressed commitment by the client and project team to follow through with Soft Landings aftercare activities, and to observe, fine-tune and review performance for three years post completion. The aftercare activities should aim to achieve the Soft Landings performance objectives, and any targets agreed at the design stage

6. **Share risk and responsibility**   The client and principal contractor should create a culture of shared risk and responsibility. Incentives should be used to encourage the project team to deliver a high-performance building that matches the design intentions

7. **Use feedback to inform design**   The client's requirements, the design brief, and the design response should be informed by performance feedback from earlier projects. The desired operational outcomes need to be expressed clearly and realistically

8. **Focus on operational outcomes**   The Soft Landings team should focus on the building's performance in-use. Regular reality-checking should be carried out to ensure that the detailed design and its execution continues to match the client's requirements, the design team's ambitions, and any specific project objectives

9. **Involve the building managers**   The organisation that will manage the finished building should have a meaningful input to the client's requirements and the formulation of the brief

10. **Involve the end users**	Prospective occupants should be actively researched to understand their needs and expectations, which should inform the client's requirements and the design brief. There should be a clear process for managing expectations throughout the construction process and into building operation
11. **Set performance objectives**	Performance objectives for the building should be set at the outset. They should be well-researched, appropriate and realistic, capable of being monitored and reality checked throughout design and construction, and measurable post completion in line with the client's key performance indicators
12. **Communicate and inform**	Regardless of their legal and contractual obligations to one another, project team members need to be comfortable communicating with the entire team in order to achieve the levels of collaboration necessary to carry out Soft Landings activities

Although late adoption of Soft Landings could bring some benefits, clients and aftercare teams should be prepared to face problems with building performance that could have been anticipated and dealt with had Soft Landings been adopted earlier and in its entirety. Graduated handover can be useful in its own right, but far more can be achieved by applying all core principles from the start.

Even on projects that adopt Soft Landings from the outset, cherry-picking of the core principles may introduce risks and fragilities. The risk of underperformance will increase proportionately as core principles are weakened or abandoned. For this reason, the term Soft Landings should not be applied on projects where any of the core principles are missing.

STAGE 7

In Use

7

CONTENTS

Plan of Work and Stage Activities

RIBA
Plan of
Work
2013

Excerpt from the RIBA Plan of Work 2013

RIBA
Plan of
Work
2013

Stage 7

In use

Task Bar	Tasks
Core Objectives	Undertake **In Use** services in accordance with **Schedule of Services**.
Procurement Variable task bar	*There are no specific activities in the RIBA Plan of Work 2013.*
Programme Variable task bar	*There are no specific activities in the RIBA Plan of Work 2013.*
(Town) Planning Variable task bar	*There are no specific activities in the RIBA Plan of Work 2013.*
Suggested Key Support Tasks	Conclude activities listed in **Handover Strategy** including **Post-occupancy Evaluation**, review of **Project Performance**, **Project Outcomes** and **Research and Development** aspects. Updating of **Project Information**, as required, in response to ongoing client **Feedback** until the end of the building's life.
Sustainability Checkpoints	• *Has observation of the building operation in use and assistance with fine tuning and guidance for occupants been undertaken?* • *Has the energy/carbon performance been declared?*
Information Exchanges (at stage completion)	**'As-constructed' Information** updated in response to ongoing client **Feedback** and maintenance or operational developments.
UK Government Information Exchanges	As required.

Summary

This is a new stage within the RIBA Plan of Work. It acknowledges the potential benefits of harnessing the project design information to assist with the successful operation and use of a building.

While it is likely that many of the handover duties will be completed during Stage 6, prior to conclusion of the **Building Contract**, certain activities may be required or necessary afterwards. These should be confirmed in the relevant **Schedule of Services**.

While the end of a building's life might be considered at Stage 7, it is more likely that Stage 0 of the follow-on project or refurbishment would deal with these aspects as part of strategically defining the future of the building.

Mapping to RIBA Outline Plan of Work 2007

Stage 7 is a new stage which includes **Post-occupancy Evaluation** and review of **Project Performance** as well as new duties that can be undertaken during the In Use period of a building.

7

7.1   Core Objectives

This is a new stage, not previously part of the RIBA Plan of Work. It covers the life of the building after handover up to its eventual demolition, a period when the architect and the project team (the client aside, where the client is the end user) are not traditionally involved. However, with an emphasis on using the BIM model to assist in maintenance of the building, its mechanical and electrical systems and the components of which it is constituted, the architect and other designers can play a role. Such activity will also enable better measurement of key performance indicators in use, with consequent benefits for the development of future buildings. It is thus a potential benefit to the profession and to the property and construction industries as a whole.

As such it feeds back to Stage 0, where data from existing buildings can be used to inform the briefing process for their refurbishment and alteration, or indeed for development of other new projects.

The RIBA Plan of Work 2013 states that the activities in this stage are to undertake In Use services in accordance with the Schedule of Services.

While it is likely that many of the handover duties will be completed during Stage 6, prior to conclusion of the Building Contract, certain activities may be required or necessary afterwards. These should be confirmed in the relevant Schedule of Services.

7.2   Procurement

7.2.1   Activities to be carried out in Stage 7 should be identified as an additional service as early as possible, ideally at the outset of the project and agreement of the Schedule of Services.

7.3	**Programme**

7.3.1	A programme for maintenance activities should be set out in the building manuals.

7.4	**(Town) Planning**

7.4.1	There are no (Town) Planning activities as such while the building is in use, but should alteration to the building be required, it is likely that planning permission will be needed.

7.5	**Suggested Key Support Tasks**

7.5.1	Information required

7.5.1.1	'As-constructed' Information and programme of maintenance.

7.5.2	Brief

7.5.2.1	If appointed for this stage, agree the programme of maintenance and scope of work to maintain the BIM model.
BIM NOTE	*Information from work carried out during this stage can be invaluable in informing briefs for future projects.*

| 7.5.3 | Appointment |

| 7.5.3.1 | Agree the terms of the appointment and how fees will be paid. |

NOTE

There are potential benefits to maintaining an ongoing relationship with the client and this should be considered in negotiating services for Stage 7 work. Such a relationship might well lead to further work in future, either in refurbishment or alteration of the building in question or for other building projects. This opportunity should not be overlooked.

| 7.5.4 | Client |

| 7.5.4.1 | *Due to this being a relatively new aspect of work for the architect and the project team it is likely that you will need to assess and carefully explain to the client what the potential benefits are in terms of cost in use of the building and how the BIM model can be used to optimise this. As noted above, developing an ongoing relationship with the client or, if a different person or body, the building occupier will be of benefit and it is worthwhile encouraging take-up of these activities.* |

NOTE

| 7.5.5 | Project team |

| 7.5.5.1 | It may well be necessary to form collaborations with building services consultants or others to provide a comprehensive service for Stage 7. You should engage in discussions with appropriate companies to allow you to offer multidisciplinary services where necessary. |

| 7.5.6 | General matters |

| 7.5.6.1 | Consider the activities required to undertake this work carefully and agree the scope of work with the client, who may be the building occupier, the owner, or a contractor to whom you are providing consultancy services. |

| 7.5.6.2 | Conclude activities listed in the Handover Strategy. |

| 7.5.6.3 | If appointed for this stage, update the Project Information as required in response to client Feedback and modifications in use. |

7.6   Sustainability Checkpoints

Sustainability Checkpoint 7

Sustainability aims

To provide any services relevant to the operation or use of the building as agreed.

Checkpoints

- Has observation of the building operation in use and assistance with fine tuning and guidance for occupants been undertaken?

- Has the energy/carbon performance been declared?

Key actions

- Review controls and performance in each season and update manuals and records to reflect any changes.

- Feed back lessons learned from the post-occupancy review to the client and project team.

7.7   Information Exchanges

| 7.7.1 | 'As-constructed' Information should be updated in response to ongoing client Feedback and maintenance or operational developments. |

7.8   UK Government Information Exchanges

| 7.8.1 | Information Exchanges will be as required. |

Contractor Engagement

CONTENTS

RIBA
Plan of
Work
2013

With Procurement set out as a variable task bar in the RIBA Plan of Work 2013, tendering activities do not have a specific place in the chronology of a project. Tendering activities have therefore been set out here as a separate chapter. Procurement under the RIBA Plan of Work 2013 includes assembling the project team, but this section refers only to contractor and subcontractor engagement.

Traditional procurement

Tendering involves the assembly and coordination of the Developed Design and Technical Design into the tender package. In addition, it is the stage when the final cost plan is prepared by the cost consultant. This is an essential final check – before proceeding to tender – that the design as currently developed still meets the client's budget. It should be noted, however, that the cost plan should be updated regularly throughout the design process, with increasing levels of predictive accuracy. If the estimate reveals any unanticipated problems then some adjustment of the Technical Design may be needed before going out to tender. If this is the case it will require careful management and collaboration from all concerned.

Design and build procurement

In design and build procurement, tendering activities may occur at different points in the Plan of Work. In cases where the client wishes to tender on detailed information, the stages may follow something close to the normal sequence, but in others, where the design and build contract is entered into on minimal information, tendering may follow Stage 2, with Stages 3 and 4 occurring after the Building Contract is let, and sometimes during construction. It can also occur after Stage 3 or even Stage 4. Design and build procurement can also be undertaken as a two-stage process.

Management procurement

With management procurement, the amount of Technical Design information available at the commencement of the project will be limited to the extent that much of the detailed information will be supplied by the works contractors in the form of shop or installation drawings. Nevertheless, the general Technical Design information will originate from the design team, and the process of coordinating and integrating information will continue throughout the construction of the project.

There will often be the need to obtain tenders from specialist subcontractors or suppliers at an early stage. Sometimes it may be advantageous if the main contractor is appointed early to provide pre-construction advice, and then again by a second-stage tender to undertake the full contract works. Obviously, the procurement method adopted – or the size and complexity of the project – can have an effect on tender action and timing. For example, in management procurement there will be a tendering procedure to select the management contractor (or construction manager) followed by separate tendering for each works package. Normally, however, tendering refers to the period when the main contract tenders are invited and evaluated and advice is given to the client on appointing the contractor.

Tenders may be obtained by following one of these routes:

- open tendering: open to all and, in theory, competitive, but generally regarded as wasteful, often unreliable and not in the client's long-term interests

- selective tendering: open to selected invitees only, competitive and appropriate for all forms of procurement, with fair and clear criteria for selection

- negotiated tendering: applicable where price is not the main criterion, and not necessarily competitive, except perhaps where it forms the second step in a two-stage process – this may not be applicable for certain public sector contracts (e.g. those under EU procurement rules).

Tendering will mostly be a one-stage activity, but where the project is particularly large and complex, or where the procurement method makes it desirable, two-stage tendering can be a more efficient and satisfactory way forward.

Regardless of the route chosen, it is important to ensure that tendering is always on a fair basis. Competition should only be between firms which have the necessary skills, integrity, responsibility and reputation to enable them to deliver work of the nature and standard required. Competitive tendering should involve only a realistic number of bids from firms that have been. given the same information and the same realistic period in which to formulate offers.

P

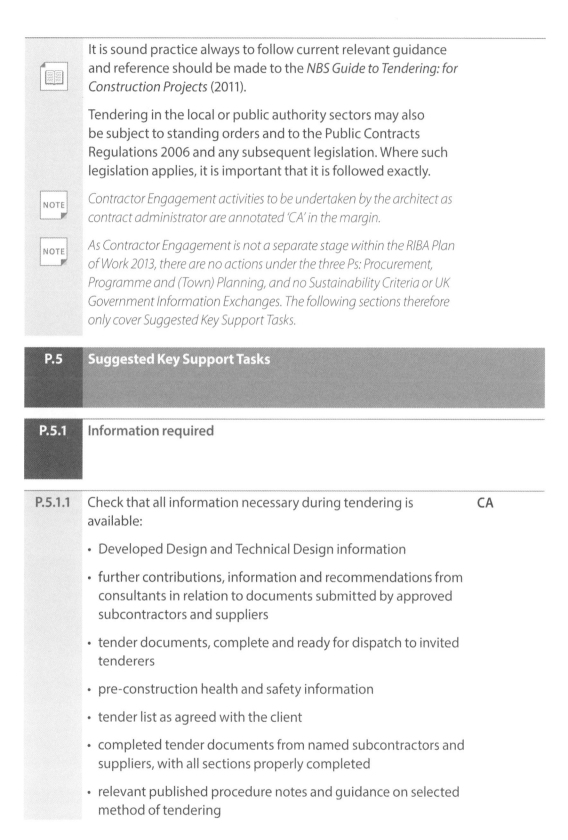

It is sound practice always to follow current relevant guidance and reference should be made to the *NBS Guide to Tendering: for Construction Projects* (2011).

Tendering in the local or public authority sectors may also be subject to standing orders and to the Public Contracts Regulations 2006 and any subsequent legislation. Where such legislation applies, it is important that it is followed exactly.

NOTE

Contractor Engagement activities to be undertaken by the architect as contract administrator are annotated 'CA' in the margin.

NOTE

As Contractor Engagement is not a separate stage within the RIBA Plan of Work 2013, there are no actions under the three Ps: Procurement, Programme and (Town) Planning, and no Sustainability Criteria or UK Government Information Exchanges. The following sections therefore only cover Suggested Key Support Tasks.

P.5 Suggested Key Support Tasks

P.5.1 Information required

P.5.1.1   Check that all information necessary during tendering is available: CA

- Developed Design and Technical Design information

- further contributions, information and recommendations from consultants in relation to documents submitted by approved subcontractors and suppliers

- tender documents, complete and ready for dispatch to invited tenderers

- pre-construction health and safety information

- tender list as agreed with the client

- completed tender documents from named subcontractors and suppliers, with all sections properly completed

- relevant published procedure notes and guidance on selected method of tendering

- completed particulars for the Building Contract and any supplements for the form of contract selected

- pre-tender cost estimate prepared by the cost consultant based on bills of quantities/specifications/schedules of work

- any further conditions imposed by the local building control and fire authorities, particularly relating to construction details and fire prevention, including finishes.

 See the note under section 4.5.1 in Stage 4 regarding the Regulatory Reform (Fire Safety) Order 2005.

P.5.2   Brief

| P.5.2.1 | Ensure that all members of the project team are aware of their responsibilities during the tender process. | CA |

P.5.3   Appointment

P.5.3.1   Establish the scope, content and context for tendering activities.

 Put this information into context, particularly if previous stages were undertaken by others. If possible, establish whether material produced now is likely to be acted upon by others taking over subsequent stages.

If the appointment includes Stage 6 Soft Landings activities, the architect must contribute to the appraisal of tenders/negotiations relative to the Handover Strategy and facilities management matters.

If the appointment includes Post-occupancy Evaluation activities at Stages 6 and/or 7, the architect must identify any changes to targets and their causes.

P.5.3.2   Check that the client's instruction to proceed has been given and confirmed in writing.

P.5.3.3   Check that the client has settled all accounts submitted to date.

P.5.3.4	Check appointing documents with respect to services and fees:	
	• If the services, cost or time targets are different from those agreed with the client, agree a formal variation by letter or deed as appropriate.	
	• If the extent of professional services for the tendering activities is not settled, agree with the client and confirm in writing.	
	• If the methods and levels of charging for the tendering activities are not yet settled, agree these with the client and confirm in writing.	
P.5.3.5	Assess the office resources needed for tendering activities and ensure that they are available and adequate. Agree the arrangement for any additional services in case of design changes or tender renegotiation to meet the cost plan.	

P.5.4   Client

P.5.4.1	Establish any points to be discussed and developed during tendering.	
P.5.4.2	Check whether any necessary contractual information to be supplied by the client is still outstanding.	CA
P.5.4.3	Confirm with the client the details of any preliminary contracts for enabling works, demolition, etc.	CA
P.5.4.4	Confirm with the client the details of any advance appointments of subcontractors and specialists. Ensure that the client has copies of relevant warranties.	CA
P.5.4.5	Arrange with the client for further interviews of potential contractors if appropriate.	CA
P.5.4.6	Confirm with the client the details of any phasing, restrictions and implications.	CA
P.5.4.7	Confirm with the client the details of any proposal for work not forming part of the Building Contract to be carried out by other persons.	CA

P.5.4.8	Confirm with the client the list of tenderers.	CA
P.5.4.9	Confirm with the client the details of Building Contract appendix entries.	CA
P.5.4.10	Confirm with the client the details of any special or optional contract provisions.	CA
P.5.4.11	Confirm with the client and advisers that arrangements for insurance for works, etc. are being made.	CA
P.5.4.12	Check whether the client has confirmed the following: • whether tendering for the particular project is subject to legislative control • the preferred tendering method, any client tender operational requirements and the method for selecting firms to be included on the tender list.	CA
P.5.4.13	Clarify and confirm in writing any outstanding matters related to the tendering procedure to be followed, including procedures to be followed after receipt of tenders.	CA
P.5.4.14	Check with the client that the site will be available to the contractor on the date stated in the documents, and that there is nothing likely to prevent possession or commencement.	CA
P.5.4.15	Check whether the client has given authority for any preliminary tender action for specialist subcontractors and suppliers that will be required, and confirm in writing.	CA
P.5.4.16	Review with the client the appointment of subcontractors and specialists at this stage and whether it might be advantageous to place advance orders for materials, design or fabrication.	CA
P.5.5	**Project team**	
P.5.5.1	Agree input to tendering activities by design team members.	CA

P.5.5.2	Confirm the timetable for tendering activities and note its relationship to the project timetable as agreed with the client.	
P.5.5.3	Confirm the timetable for receipt of any revisions to tender information required from design team members.	CA

NOTE *Establish a cut-off point for revised information to be passed to the cost consultant.*

P.5.5.4	Confirm patterns for communication between the client, the CDM coordinator, the project manager and the lead designer.	CA
P.5.5.5	Confirm the programme and pattern for design team meetings.	CA
P.5.5.6	Integrate and coordinate input from project team members and specialists.	CA
P.5.5.7	Continue to appraise input from specialist firms, including potential subcontractors and suppliers.	
P.5.5.8	Provide final information for pre-construction health and safety information and pass to the CDM coordinator.	
P.5.5.9	Discuss with the CDM coordinator any outstanding matters of designers' contributions to the pre-construction health and safety information.	CA
P.5.5.10	Coordinate production of the Information Release Schedule if appropriate.	CA
P.5.5.11	Confirm with project team members any further arrangements for inviting specialist tenders.	CA
P.5.5.12	Check with design team members their input to main contract tender documents to discover inconsistencies or omissions.	
P.5.5.13	Review with design team members the tenders and accompanying information received from specialist subcontractors and suppliers and, if these are in order, confirm that you have no comments on them.	

P.5.6	**General matters**

Preparing the tender documents and sending out for tenders

P.5.6.1	Obtain from subcontractors and suppliers any outstanding Project Information.	CA
P.5.6.2	Provide final information to the cost consultant for bills of quantities and the pre-tender cost estimate.	CA
P.5.6.3	Consolidate the final detailed information for Technical Design drawings, subcontract specifications and preliminaries (or project management sections) to specifications or schedules of work.	
P.5.6.4	Establish the form of the Building Contract and its conditions.	CA
P.5.6.5	Prepare, coordinate, collate and check the tender documents.	CA
P.5.6.6	Prepare report on tendering activities and submit to the client.	CA
P.5.6.7	Request client's authority to invite tenders.	CA

P.5.6.8	*If procurement is through design and build:*
NOTE	• *for an employer client: check whether the client has confirmed in writing acceptance of proposals and information supplied in Stages 3 and 4 which are to form part of the Employer's Requirements*
	• *for a contractor client: review any client comments on the detail design or development, and note any adjustments which may be unavoidable owing to modifications introduced recently by component manufacturers or specialist subcontractors. Detail design amendments might also be necessary, for example if long delivery times of component manufacturers or specialist subcontractors force substitutions to be made.*
	Check what action is to be taken as a result.

P.5.6.9   Make a final check of information for main contract tenders, including:

- that documents sufficiently explain the requirements and that they are accurate, listed and numbered

- that drawings required under the SMM Measurement Code are ready to accompany bills to tenderers

- that any requirements for a warranty or guarantee bond are made known to tenderers at the time of invitation.   **CA**

P.5.6.10   Make a final check to ascertain whether the selected firms have   **CA**
all completed the tendering questionnaire and any non-collusion
or other similar certificates required by the client.

Key principles of good practice to be adopted when appointing contractors are as follows:

- *Clear procedures should be followed that ensure fair and transparent competition in a single round of tendering consisting of one or more stages.*

- *The tender process should ensure compliant, competitive tenders.*

- *Tender lists should be compiled systematically from a number of qualified contractors.*

- *Tender lists should be as short as possible.*

- *Conditions should be the same for all tenderers.*

- *Confidentiality should be respected by all parties.*

- *Sufficient time should be given for the preparation and evaluation of tenders.*

- *Sufficient information should be given for the preparation of tenders.*

- *Tenders should be assessed and accepted on quality as well as price.*

- *Practices that avoid or discourage collusion should be followed.*

- *Tender prices should not change on an unaltered scope of works.*

- *Suites of contracts and standard unamended forms of contract from recognised bodies should be used where they are available.*

- *There should be a commitment to teamworking from all parties.*

P.5.6.11	Invite tenders for main contract works from contractors on the final tender list.	CA P/SM3 P/SM5
	NOTE *Follow the relevant codes of procedure for tendering to ensure fairness and reliable pricing.*	
	Supply all tenderers with identical information. If queries are raised during the tendering period, deal with them promptly, and notify all other tenderers in identical terms.	
	Do not accept late tenders.	
P.5.6.12	Initiate action for second-stage tendering if relevant.	CA P/SM5
P.5.6.13	NOTE *If procurement is through design and build, make a final check that the Employer's Requirements are complete.*	P/SM2
P.5.6.14	Draft preliminary notes for bills of quantities/specifications/ schedules of work.	CA
	NOTE *This should be done systematically as further materials are chosen and standards of workmanship set.*	
P.5.6.15	Agree with the client and the CDM coordinator the tendering period and procedures to be followed in opening tenders and notifying results.	CA
	NOTE *Allow adequate time for tendering, and for the assessment of tenders. The most acceptable tender must be thoroughly checked for errors, and this takes time. Allow time for checking by the CDM coordinator.*	
P.5.6.16	If necessary, send out preliminary enquiries to firms selected as potential tenderers, as agreed with the client.	CA P/SM3 P/SM4 P/SM5 P/SM6 P/SM7
P.5.6.17	Check that the form of contract to be used has been confirmed with the client in writing.	CA
P.5.6.18	Discuss with the client the need to use supplements to cover, for example, sectional completion, contractor's design and fluctuations.	CA

P.5.6.19	Discuss with the client the appropriate choice for optional provisions in the Building Contract.	
	Advise on the particulars which need to be entered in the appendix to the Building Contract and referred to in the tender documents (e.g. dates, insurances, liquidated damages, option clauses).	CA

P.5.6.20	Confirm with the client the inclusion of any special clauses or amendments to the Building Contract, bearing in mind legal advice obtained.	CA

P.5.6.21	Confirm with the client any arrangements to employ persons direct to carry out work not forming part of the Building Contract during the contractor's occupation.	CA

P.5.6.22	*If procurement is through design and build:*	
NOTE	*• for an employer client: advise on completion and content of tender documents and the final form and content of the Employer's Requirements*	
	• for a contractor client: inspect drawings and information received from specialist subcontractors and suppliers for checking against the Contractor's Proposals, and advise the client.	

P.5.6.23	Obtain the necessary information from firms to be named.	CA
NOTE	*Obtain this information in good time and place reliance on it only after having secured a design warranty in favour of the client.*	
	Check on availability and delivery before including particular materials or sources named in the Technical Design.	

P.5.6.24	Check, in particular, that the client is aware of the requirements of insurance provisions in the Building Contract and that they appreciate the advisability of seeking specialist advice from their insurers or brokers.	CA
NOTE	*It is very important that the client should be fully aware of the insurance requirements well in advance of the tender process.*	

	Contract and tender review	
P.5.6.25	Confirm any outstanding details of the contractual terms – including supplements, optional provisions and particulars – which need to be entered in the appendix to the Building Contract.	CA
P.5.6.26	Discuss with the client the results of any pre-selection interviews or other selection procedures and take any necessary further action.	CA P/SM3
P.5.6.27	Confirm with the client the final tender list and inform all tenderers of their inclusion.	CA
P.5.6.28	Check that the client has finalised all insurance arrangements.	CA
P.5.6.29	Check that all advance orders for design, materials and fabrication by specialist subcontractors and suppliers, as agreed, have been placed.	CA
P.5.6.30	Check that any preliminary contracts for enabling works are under way and on schedule. Administer the preliminary contracts, if authorised.	CA
P.5.6.31	If appropriate, confirm with the client that the appointment of a clerk of works is in hand.	CA
P.5.6.32	Confirm with the client that any arrangements to employ persons direct to carry out work not forming part of the Building Contract are in hand.	CA
P.5.6.33	Review, with other design team members, any further tenders received from specialist subcontractors and suppliers and include in tender documents as appropriate.	CA

P.5.6.34	Amend the Technical Design if necessary following cost checks.	**CA**
	Establish whether changes are to be reflected in the Building Contract documents (which will then differ from the tender documents) or whether amendments are to be the subject of immediate variations under a contract administrator's instruction issued when the Building Contract has been entered into.	
P.5.6.35	Check the effects of any amendments on specialist subcontract work and arrange for adjusted tenders if necessary.	**CA**
P.5.6.36	Record all amendments.	**CA**
	Identify changes clearly on revised documents.	
	Retain and file all original issues.	
P.5.6.37	Manage any questions arising during the tendering process.	**CA**
P.5.6.38	Appraise, with the cost consultant and CDM coordinator, the tenders received and prepare a report with recommendations for the client:	**CA**

- Check with the cost consultant for arithmetical errors in the most acceptable tender; if any are found, use the appropriate stated procedures.

- Inspect draft programmes submitted by tenderers, if required.

- Arrange for the CDM coordinator to inspect material submitted by tenderers relating to health and safety requirements, and to appraise the construction phase health and safety information submitted in the most acceptable tender.

- Check that the tender includes information regarding the contractor's competency.

NOTE *Deal with tender errors, or the need for a reduction, strictly in accordance with recommended procedures.*

P.5.6.39	Prepare and review the tender report with the client and discuss recommendations about acceptance.	**CA**

NOTE *Be wary of a very low tender and explain to the client the possible risks in accepting it.*

P.5.6.40	If the lowest figure is greater than the amount allowed for in the cost plan, discuss with the cost consultant the most appropriate measures for reducing it (such as making alterations to the design), agree the action to be taken with the client and initiate it through negotiation or re-tendering.	CA
P.5.6.41	Assist as necessary with any negotiations following consideration by the client of the most acceptable tender.	CA
P.5.6.42	Continue with appraisal of tenders from specialists. Check that offers are still open for acceptance and that particulars on which they tendered are still correct.	CA
P.5.6.43	Check that the CDM coordinator has certified that the construction phase health and safety information has been developed sufficiently by the firm to be appointed as principal contractor for the construction phase to commence.	CA
P.5.6.44	Notify unsuccessful tenderers of the result when the Building Contract is signed and provide figures when appropriate. NOTE *If procurement is through design and build, assist the client with negotiations following the submission of the Contractor's Proposals and the contract sum analysis, as relevant.*	CA P/SM6
P.5.6.45	Arrange interviews to select the principal contractor if relevant and necessary. NOTE *Pre-tender meetings and interviews should only be held if considered essential, and always with a strictly limited agenda.*	CA
P.5.6.46	If appropriate, arrange for interviews for selection of contractors by negotiation.	CA
	Other general matters to be addressed during tendering	
P.5.6.47	Regularly check progress against the timetable for tendering activities.	

P.5.6.48 Continue resource control procedures for the job (usually monthly):

- check expenditure against the office job cost allocation for tendering activities

- monitor fee income against the projected fee income.

P.5.6.49 Report regularly to the client on fees and expenses incurred and submit accounts at agreed intervals (usually monthly).

NOTE *Check that the client settles all accounts promptly.*

P.5.7   Inspections/tests

P.5.7.1 Arrange for tenderers to have the opportunity to inspect the site   **CA** and/or existing buildings during the tender period.

P.5.7.2 Arrange for tenderers to have the opportunity to inspect   **CA** drawings not issued with the tender documents.

P.5.7.3 *If procurement is through design and build:*

NOTE • *arrange for submission and testing of prototypes designed by contractors or specialist subcontractors, as required by the tender procedure*

• *if applicable, arrange for tenderers to submit any queries to the lead designer for answering before tender submission. Q&A information should then be shared with all tenderers to ensure fairness and that all tenders are based on the same information.*

P.5.7.4 Decide on the method statement required from the appointed contractor on quality management testing, verification, audit and records.

P.5.8   Consultations, approvals and consents

P.5.8.1 Monitor progress on statutory and other consents. Submit additional information if necessary.

| P.5.8.2 | Monitor progress on party wall awards. | CA |

| P.5.8.3 | Check all necessary statutory and other consents have been obtained and that party wall awards are in place. | CA |

NOTE   *If any permissions, consents or awards are still under negotiation during the tendering process this could mean that alterations will be required to the tender negotiations or that start on site will be delayed.*

P.5.9   Cost planning

| P.5.9.1 | Provide information for the cost consultant to prepare a pre-tender cost estimate (or prepare a pre-tender cost estimate if appointed to do so). | |

NOTE   *The pre-tender cost estimate is an essential check prior to inviting tenders. At this point the estimate should be an accurate prediction of the tender figures. The design and tender documents may need to be amended if the estimate does not match the project brief.*

| P.5.9.2 | Review with the client the implications of the pre-tender estimate prepared by the cost consultant. | CA |

| P.5.9.3 | Discuss possible options with the client. Explain implications for timetable and consultants' fees if amendments are required to change (or comply with) the brief. | CA |

| P.5.9.4 | Report to the client on cost matters at agreed intervals. | CA |

NOTE   *If procurement is through design and build:*

• for an employer client: provide revised information if relevant for corrected cost estimates

• for a contractor client: provide revised information if relevant to the contractor's estimators.

P.7	**Information Exchanges**

P.7.1   Before the conclusion of tendering, check that all the agreed outputs have been produced. Outputs might include the following:

- finalised tender documents – probably including drawings, schedules, bills of quantities/specifications/schedules of work, pre-construction health and safety information, terms of bonds and warranties, subcontractor information and tenders. When sending out for tender, any of the following documents and information may be relevant:

  - a list of all tender documents so that the tenderers can check they have received the complete package
  - tender forms and details of procedure to be followed, e.g. type of tender required, submittals required, how the tender should be packaged and identified, to whom it should be sent
  - site information and surveys
  - drawings
  - drawn schedules, e.g. for doors
  - specification
  - bill of quantities
  - list of items to be paid for prior to delivery on site
  - schedule of works
  - schedule of rates
  - activity schedule
  - Information Release Schedule
  - Health and Safety Plan
  - programmed dates for proposed work
  - details of any phased commencement or completion
  - details of the Building Contract terms and conditions, including insurance provisions
  - details of advance payment arrangements
  - details of any bonds or guarantees required from the contractor or to be provided by the employer
  - details of any warranties to be provided

Refer to P/SM1 for a comprehensive schedule of information to be   **P/SM1**
provided.

- information prepared specially for use in self-build or semi-skilled operations

- information for issue to specialist subcontractors and suppliers in connection with tender invitations

- information which is not necessarily part of the tender package for use in dealings with third parties, landlords, tenants, funders, etc. (e.g. in connection with leases, boundaries, party walls, etc.).

4/SM2
4/SM3
4/SM4
P/SM1

NOTE

If procurement is through design and build:

• for an employer client: detail design information for incorporation into Employer's Requirements (part of Stages 3 and 4)

• for a contractor client: general arrangement drawings, interface details, performance specification and other technical information (part of Stage 4 and Contractor Engagement).

Outputs required after tenders have been received might include the following:

- main contract tenders and report with recommendations

- tenders received from specialists with appropriate forms and numbered documents where appropriate.

NOTE

If procurement is through design and build:

• for an employer client: report for the client on the appraisal of Contractor's Proposals and contract sum analysis

• for a contractor client: report for the client on the appraisal of tenders submitted by specialist subcontractors and suppliers; final material for incorporation into Contractor's Proposals and in connection with contract sum analysis.

Supplementary Material

P/SM1:   Tender documentation checklist

NOTE

There is a separate list for Employer's Requirements in design and build procurement in P/SM2.

The Construction Project Information Committee's (CPIC) *Production Information: A Code of Procedure for the Construction Industry* gives the following guidance on drawn information to be issued to tenderers. It covers contracts with and without quantities, sets out the definitions and rules relating to drawn information in the *Standard Method of Measurement of Building Works*, seventh edition (SMM7), and gives guidance on how those requirements may be satisfied.

Prior to tendering, drawn information is used mainly for the measurement of quantities. On 'with quantities' contracts SMM7 requires drawn information to be provided to tenderers to give:

- an overall picture of the project to allow assessment of the cost significance of the design and inform decisions about methods of construction
- detailed information about parts of the work where this information is more effectively communicated graphically rather than by a lengthy description in the bill of quantities.

The requirements for provision of this information are dealt with in detail below. Drawings selected from those normally available for construction of the project should satisfy the SMM7 requirements (except for dimensioned diagrams).

Apart from the specific requirements for provision of drawings, SMM7 allows descriptive and specification information to be given on drawings or in the specification provided that a specific cross-reference is given in the bill of quantities' description of the item (SMM7 General Rule 4.2).

The following types of drawings are referred to in SMM7:

- location drawings
- component drawings
- dimensioned diagrams.

Location drawings

The SMM7 rules for Preliminaries/General conditions require certain location drawings to accompany the bill of quantities. These are defined in General Rule 5.1 as follows:

(a) Block Plan: shall identify the site and locate the outlines of the building works in relation to a town plan or other context.

(b) Site Plan: shall locate the position of the building works in relation to setting-out points, means of access and general layout of the site.

(c) Plans, Sections and Elevations: shall show the position occupied by the various spaces in a building and the general construction and location of principal elements.

The architect's smaller scale location drawings will normally satisfy this requirement. The majority of work sections in SMM7 commence with a statement of the information to be provided specifically for that type of work. The requirements will normally be met by the architect's location drawings referred to above. If not, other drawings produced by the architect, structural, mechanical and electrical engineers etc. should be provided.

SMM7 applies equally to all with-quantities projects. However, when deciding which drawings to include to comply with the rules, the type, size and relative complexity of the particular project will need to be considered. For example, the scope and location of foul drainage above ground for a simple single-storey building may be adequately defined by the general arrangement floor plan showing the sanitary appliances, whereas more detailed drawn information will be required for this work in a more complex building.

In addition to the requirements concerning location drawings there are other SMM7 rules which, although not specifically referring to drawings, can often be complied with to best advantage by giving information on drawings referenced from the bills of quantities. An example is Section D20 Excavating and filling, which requires details of:

- groundwater level
- trial pits or borehole details stating their location
- features retained
- live over- or underground services, indicating location.

Component drawings

Component drawings are required by General Rule 5.2 to show the information necessary for the manufacture and assembly of components.

Dimensioned diagrams

Dimensioned diagrams are required by SMM7 General Rule 5.3 to show the shape and dimensions of the work covered by an item. They may be used at the discretion of the cost consultant as an alternative to a dimensioned description except in those cases where there is a specific requirement for a dimensioned diagram. Dimensioned diagrams may be prepared by the cost consultant or, on their behalf, by the architect. They can also be extracts from the architect's or engineer's drawings reproduced at a suitable size for incorporation in the bills of quantities.

Dimensioned diagrams should not appear in documentation other than the bills of quantities. However, there may be occasions where it is more appropriate to issue the architect's or engineer's drawings with the bills of quantities rather than produce dimensioned diagrams. In such instances it will be necessary to identify the drawings in the bill description.

Preparation of tender documents

The tender documentation will include the bills of quantities, the tender drawings, the project specification (as appropriate), the form of tender and the letter of invitation. The bills of quantities will list the drawings from which the bills have been prepared, and copies of these should be kept as a record. It is good practice to indicate which of the drawings listed accompany the tender documents.

As much of the drawn information as possible should be contained within the bills of quantities to minimise the problem of expensive reproduction of drawings. The provision of copy negatives or similar methods rather than prints will also assist in keeping down tendering costs.

It will be of assistance to contractors if, when domestic subcontractors are named in bills of quantities, the drawings and the specification relevant to their work are sent to them direct, obviating the need for all tendering contractors to do so when they can see from the bill that this has been done.

P/SM2:   Design and build documentation

Employer's Requirements

The Employer's Requirements document is the basis for obtaining tenders and is created during the pre-construction work, typically Stages 2 to 4 (or such other stages as may be agreed for the project) prior to inviting tenders. It might comprise the following information:

Preliminaries and contract conditions
- JCT DB11 Schedule 2 Supplemental Provisions
  - Named subcontractors
  - Bills of quantities
  - Valuation of changes – contractor's estimates
  - Direct loss and/or expense – contractor's estimates
- Pre-construction information pack

Design information
(all or part may be by way of performance specification)
- 1:100 plans, sections and elevations
- 1:500 site layout, including critical setting-out data
- 1:50 room layout plans
- Site – extent, external works and access
- Landscape design
- Fire compartments and escape routes
- Engineering services mains and risers
- Plant spaces
- Drainage – main runs
- Enabling works

Specification
- Quality – aesthetics
- Constraints
- Materials and workmanship (or systems, products and execution)
- Technical standards
- Building owner's manual – operation and maintenance
- Health and Safety File

Schedules
- Equipment including sanitary and storage fittings, user outlets, etc.
- Commissioning and testing

Other information
- Brief
- Client's health and safety policy
- Site constraints (covenants, etc.)
- Topographical surveys
- Geotechnical report
- Existing engineering services and/or main supplies
- Planning consent – outline/detailed/reserved matters
- Statutory consultation records
- Room data sheets.

The amount of information to be included in the Employer's Requirements can vary enormously. A straightforward project requiring a relatively simple design solution which can be left largely to the contractor may need little more than basic details of site and accommodation. With a more complex problem, or a design which needs sensitivity of detail, the Employer's Requirements might extend to a full scheme design.

The number and detail of documents that make up the Employer's Requirements will be influenced by considerations such as:

- how much design control the employer wishes to retain, for example in the interests of maintenance programmes or because of functional requirements
- whether the employer regards the process as more of a develop and construct operation, where only constructional details are left in the hands of the contractor
- whether the contractor's standard unit types will form the basis of the scheme
- whether the employer will require design continuity via novation or a 'consultant switch'
- whether the employer has appointed a CDM coordinator and whether the pre-tender Health and Safety Plan exists.

Generally, the Employer's Requirements will always need to include basic information, such as the following:

- site information and requirements (e.g. boundaries, topography, known subsoil conditions, existing services)
- site constraints (e.g. limitations of access, storage) and relevant easements or restrictive covenants
- topographical surveys
- geotechnical reports
- planning permission obtained or conditions known (contractors will not usually tender until outline planning permission has been obtained)

- reports on other statutory consultations
- existing Health and Safety Files, client's health and safety policy documents
- functional nature of the building(s) (e.g. kind and number of units) and accommodation requirements
- schematic layout of the building (or more developed design as appropriate)
- specific requirements as to forms of construction, materials, services, finishes, equipment, etc.
- specification information, probably including performance specifications
- room data sheets
- equipment and fitting schedules
- details of special programming requirements (e.g. phased completion)
- contract data or special requirements (e.g. named subcontractors, 'as-built' information)
- requirements concerning contractor's design liability, insurance cover, design team, requirement to use employer's designers, etc.
- clear statement of the extent of information and detail to be included in the Contractor's Proposals
- content and form of the contract sum analysis
- if JCT DB11 is to be used, information related to supplementary provisions.

It is generally accepted that too specific an approach to design and constructional matters, or the specifying of proprietary systems and materials, may reduce the contractor's design liability in the event of a failure.

Contractor's Proposals

These will be in direct response to the Employer's Requirements. Architects acting as consultants to a contractor client will first need to check the information provided to establish whether it is adequate. While contracts like the JCT DB11 absolve the contractor of any liability of the adequacy of the design or other information in the Employer's Requirements, this is subject to the requirement that any inadequacy found is brought to the notice of the employer immediately. Therefore a query list is often necessary to obtain clarification on matters of conflict or omission.

Submissions sometimes take the form of an A3 brochure and typically include the following:

- design drawings (e.g. site layout, floor plans, elevations, principal sections, some detailed drawings, landscaping)
- structural details (e.g. foundation and structure general arrangement drawings)
- mechanical services (e.g. layouts of ducts, pipe runs, schematic indications for all systems)

- electrical services (e.g. floor layouts showing lighting, power, alarms)
- specifications (e.g. particular for trades prescription and performance, general specification for workmanship, materials, finishes)
- programme (e.g. bar chart)
- method statements (e.g. general organisational matters and, in particular, the health and safety information proposals).

The tender figure will usually be required to be made separately. With it will be the contract sum analysis.

The structure of the contract sum analysis will be in accordance with the Employer's Requirements. A typical breakdown could be as follows:

- design work
- preliminaries
- health and safety provisions
- demolition
- excavation
- concrete
- brickwork and blockwork
- roofing and cladding
- woodwork
- structural steelwork
- metalwork
- mechanical and plumbing services
- electrical services
- glazing
- painting and decorating
- drainage and external works.

P/SM3:   Selective tendering lists

The first stage in the tender process is the compilation of the tender list. Although this may not be finalised until the activities set out in this section occur, some preliminary enquiries can be made as soon as the overall scope, nature and approximate timescale of the work are known.

There are three steps in the selection of a contractor:

1. qualification, in which potential contractors are assessed as to their general skills and performance to undertake a given type or range of projects

2. compilation of a tender list, in which the field of qualified contractors is refined to a short tender list of comparable, competent contractors who are willing and able to tender for a specific project

3. selection of successful tenderer, in which tenders are sought from those on the tender list and assessed to identify the preferred contractor.

During the period of qualification, potential contractors will normally be required to provide information about their firms and their track records. Architects will then wish to take up references and make further enquiries about those who seem suitable for inclusion in the final tender list. It is advisable to maintain a file or record of all enquiries to contractors and subcontractors and their responses.

The following sections provide detail on compiling lists of potential contractors.

List of contractors for larger projects

The preliminary list will be compiled from previous experience and after discussion with the client, the cost consultant and other consultants. If a wider pool is needed, enquiries could be made of registering bodies or from www.constructionline.co.uk. A questionnaire can then be sent to all those on the preliminary list to ascertain their interest in, and suitability for, the project.

The questionnaire might be expected to cover:

• name and details of company
• business status of company, names of directors, etc.
• financial status, share capital, etc.
• details of quality system and accreditation
• details of insurers and liability insurance
• construction turnover and details of contracts completed recently
• particular skills and experience of relevance to the proposed project
• the personnel who would be available for the proposed project
• names of three referees
• health and safety policy and procedures
• policy on discrimination.

At this initial stage the tenderers should be informed of:

- the job name and location
- nature, scope and approximate value of the works
- the proposed dates and duration of the works
- the procurement method and contract form
- any contractor responsibility for design or other particular skills or experience sought
- the selection process and criteria to be used
- details of the tender procedure to be followed; e.g. whether any particular code or principles will be followed, the numbers of tenders to be invited, the anticipated dates and period of tendering.

The completed questionnaire should be signed by a director of the company. On larger projects the questionnaire might also be followed by an interview. It should then be possible to finalise the tender list. It may be wise to identify one or two contractors as reserves, in the event that, nearer the tender date, one of those on the list can no longer tender. Those on the list and reserves should be informed and any changes to the list notified to them immediately.

List of contractors for small projects

On smaller projects, contractors are generally selected by reputation or from previous experience and after consulting the client, office records, other consultants and other sources. It would still be good practice to write to all potential contractors requesting up-to-date information about their firm and a reference, and enquiring as to their current availability and anticipated workload. This would help to ensure that the tender process runs smoothly and that only suitable contractors are invited.

Standing list of approved contractors

It is often a good idea to develop a 'standing list' of approved contractors that can be drawn on at the preliminary stage of a new project. This may be particularly helpful where the office is often involved in repeat – or very similar – projects. The list could be compiled once responses to a questionnaire sent to potential tenderers have been received. Shortlists of tenderers for future particular projects can then be drawn up as and when required.

The questionnaire might be expected to include the information shown above, with additional entries to indicate the type of work in which the firm is experienced and whether they would be interested in tendering for non-traditional procurement contracts.

P/SM4:   Selective tendering: Specialist subcontractors and suppliers

1.   Identify items

During the Developed Design and Technical Design stages, items where a measure of control over choice needs to be exercised should be identified. These might include, for example:

- materials or named suppliers
- acceptable subcontractors, restricted to listed names
- named subcontractors, as provided for by the Building Contract.

Where subcontractors or suppliers have been named under procedures laid down in the particular contract, there is usually a requirement or opportunity to use a standard design warranty in favour of the employer. However, where subcontractors or suppliers are referred to in items in the bill or specification, and are intended to be domestic appointments, then the contractor will have no liability for their design input. In such cases, the employer's interests might need to be protected by a warranty, should this be available. The client's consent should always be obtained in writing where subcontractors have a design input which might be regarded as having been subcontracted by the architect.

The purpose of tendering should be identified, e.g. whether it is to obtain information necessary to complete detail design, to obtain a realistic basis for a provisional sum, or to facilitate advance ordering, where desirable.

2.   List suitable firms

Compile a list after discussion with other members of the design team and the contractor (if appointed). Refer to office records of previous experience and check out references if necessary.

3.   Make preliminary enquiries

Consult the cost consultant and other consultants to establish a timetable for inviting tenders so as to provide necessary information for inclusion in bills/specifications/schedules. Check that current information is obtained concerning the financial status of firms and that they have adequate resources. Send a preliminary invitation to tender, or to ascertain willingness for inclusion in a list of subcontractors or as a named supplier. If approximate dates and figures can be given at this stage, it should be possible to obtain a reliable response. It may be sufficient to make initial enquiries by telephone, but a letter can be written if considered appropriate.

P

4.   Invite tenders

Use the correct standard forms appropriate to the form of contract and check that all relevant information is entered before sending.

Check the information to be issued with the tender form, in particular the numbered documents (e.g. drawings, schedules, bills or specification) relevant to the subcontract works. They should adequately define the work to be tendered for. A covering letter may or may not be considered necessary.

If the subcontract work is such that no particular form or set of procedures is required under the terms of the main contract, then send tender information under a suitable enclosing letter.

In the majority of cases, domestic subcontract works will be entirely a matter between the main contractor and their selected subcontractors. However, if the Building Contract makes provision for the architect to select subcontractors, who will nevertheless be domestic, and the contract does not require any practitioner form to be used, the architect may need to write letters of invitation to them.

There may also be situations where the architect wishes to include the name of domestic subcontractors in main contract tender documents, if the Building Contract does not preclude this.

5.   Deal with tenders

Tenders should be opened as soon as possible after the date for receipt. Check that everything specified has been included. Note any omissions or added conditions and pass to the relevant consultants for comment, and to the cost consultant for cost checking.

Once a selection has been made, approve the selected tender on behalf of the employer.

Notify unsuccessful tenderers at once, but do not give tender figures until a decision to proceed with the successful tenderer has been reached.

Where there is a direct subcontractor/client agreement, and only if considered desirable in the particular circumstances, issue instructions concerning advance ordering of design works, materials or fabrication. Do not do this before obtaining the client's agreement in writing.

After the appointment of the main contractor, meticulously follow the procedures set out in the main contract for instructing the acceptance of the subcontract tender. Before issuing the instruction, check that the offer is still open for acceptance, and that the particulars on which the tender was based have not changed.

P/SM5:   Selective tendering: Main contract – traditional procurement

1.   Decide whether one- or two-stage tendering is required

The one-stage procedure operates on the assumption that full information is available to tenderers at the time of tendering. The tender figure is then the price for which the contractor offers to carry out and complete the works shown on the drawings and described in the contract bills/specification/schedules.

Two-stage procedures allow the selection of the contractor by means of a first-stage competitive tender based on 'pricing documents' relating to preliminary design information. There will then follow negotiations when the design is completed and bills of quantities are priced on the basis of pricing provided in the first-stage tender. This procedure is only suitable for large, complex projects, where there could be advantage in collaborating with the contractor during design stages.

2.   Make preliminary enquiries

Send a preliminary invitation to tender to selected potential contractors. This will enable contractors to decide whether they will tender, and allow them to programme tendering staff effort. The letter of invitation should have attached to it a description of the project, relating to the form of contract it is intended to use, together with all information that might be necessary for a contractor to assess whether they are competent and interested in undertaking the project. It is essential that full details are sent in this preliminary enquiry.

3.   Invite tenders

Send formal letters to tenderers informing them of the date for issuing tender documents and the closing date for submission of tenders. Documents may be dispatched by first class post or made available for collection if the number of documents is considerable.

A standard form of tender should be issued, and all tenderers clearly told that tenders will be submitted on exactly the same basis. Adequate time for tendering will be determined in relation to the size and complexity of the job.

Any particular requirements of the client concerning, for example, guarantee bonds or a certificate of non-collusion should be clearly stated in the formal invitation.

4. Deal with tenders

Tenders should be opened as soon as possible after the date for receipt, and strictly in accordance with the procedures agreed with the client. Qualified tenders should be rejected if it is considered that the qualification affords an unfair advantage, or the tenderer should be given an opportunity to withdraw the qualification.

The priced bills of quantities should be submitted at the same time as the tenders, but in separate sealed envelopes clearly marked with the tenderers' names. Bills from unsuccessful tenderers should be returned unopened.

Tenders under consideration should be referred to the CDM coordinator to check adequacy of allocated resources in respect of health and safety requirements.

Examination of the priced bills of the lowest tenderer should be undertaken immediately by the cost consultant, who should report on arithmetical errors.

Unsuccessful tenderers should be informed as quickly as possible, and once the Building Contract has been let, every tenderer should be sent a list of firms who tendered (in alphabetical order) and a list of tender prices (in ascending order). It should not be possible to cross-reference the lists.

P/SM6:   Selective tendering: Main contract – design and build procurement

1.   Make preliminary enquiries

Send a preliminary invitation to tender to selected potential contractors. This will enable contractors to decide whether they will tender, and allow them to programme tendering staff effort. The letter of invitation should have attached to it a description of the project, relating to the form of contract it is intended to use, together with all information that might be necessary for the contractor to assess whether it is competent and interested in undertaking the project. It is essential that full details are sent in this preliminary enquiry. In particular, for design and build, the letter of invitation should clearly state whether this is a one-stage or a two-stage process and the extent to which the contractor will be expected to design the works and carry professional indemnity insurance.

The letter should have attached to it information relating to planning requirements, e.g. whether the project is within a conservation area, etc.

Tenderers will also need to know the basis for awarding the Building Contract (e.g. on price alone) and, if not, the extent to which other considerations will be taken into account, such as design quality, maintenance or running costs.

2.   Arrange interviews

It is particularly important to arrange for interviews in the context of design and build. Matters to be raised might include:

- construction forms and methods favoured
- time considered appropriate for tendering and mobilisation
- design liability and insurance arrangements
- professional and technical support available to the contractor
- design and construction programme envisaged by the contractor.

The interviewing panel should include the client, the CDM coordinator and appropriate professional advisers.

3.   Invite tenders

Send formal letters to selected tenderers either enclosing the tender documents in duplicate or informing them of the date for collection. The extent of these documents will depend on whether the tendering is one or two stage, but should include everything that is intended to form part of the final agreement (see P/SM2 for a checklist of what might be included in Employer's Requirements).

A standard form of tender should be issued. Adequate time for tendering will depend on the size and complexity of the project, and whether this is a one- or two-stage submission.

4.   Deal with tenders

Tenders should be opened as soon as possible after the date for receipt and strictly in accordance with the procedures agreed with the client.

With a one-stage procedure where price is stated to be the sole criterion, supporting design proposals and pricing documents should be submitted at the same time but under separate cover.

With a two-stage procedure the tender will also include an undertaking to enter into second-stage negotiations on the basis of the first-stage tender sum.

The examination of the Contractor's Proposals and pricing documents will be undertaken by the employer, the CDM coordinator and other professional advisers, to establish that the proposals are consistent with the Employer's Requirements.

Unsuccessful tenderers should be informed as quickly as possible, and all documents received should be treated as confidential, and returned.

P/SM7:   Selective tendering: Main contract – management procurement

1.   Make preliminary enquiries

Send a preliminary invitation to tender to selected potential contractors. This will enable contractors to decide whether they will tender and allow them to programme tendering staff effort. The letter of invitation should have attached to it a description of the project, the form of contract it is intended to use, the anticipated duration of the project pre-construction and construction, together with all information that might be necessary for the contractor to assess whether it is competent and interested in undertaking the project. It is essential that full details are sent in this preliminary enquiry.

With management contracting, the emphasis will be on ascertaining the nature and extent of the contractor's management skills and experience.

2.   Arrange preliminary interviews

Because of the large or complex management nature of projects usually procured by this method, it might be necessary also to hold preliminary interviews at this stage. This will enable the employer to gain a better understanding of the philosophy and management structure offered by some of the potential firms, to an extent not obtainable solely through written enquiries.

3.   Invite tenders

Send formal letters to selected tenderers. Tender documents should contain:

- clear conditions for the submission, so that all tenderers provide the same amount of information
- proposed timescales for the pre-construction and construction periods
- a clear indication of the assessment and interview procedures that will form part of the overall assessment.

Criteria to be satisfied will normally include:

- management service offered
- key personnel for the project
- financial competencies, both in respect of fees and ability to manage costs
- conditions of engagement
- programmes
- method statements.

P

4.   Deal with tenders

Tenders should be opened as soon as possible after the date for receipt, and strictly in accordance with the procedure agreed with the client.

A detailed evaluation of each submission should be prepared. When the written submissions have undergone preliminary evaluation they can be assessed by the employer. It will then be necessary to interview each tenderer. This will enable them to explain their proposals in detail, clarify any points in the submission which need comment, and allow the employer to meet the key personnel that the tenderer proposes to use. Further interviews may be necessary before a decision is reached.

Unsuccessful tenderers should be informed as soon as possible.

Bibliography

Association for Project Safety (2007)
Design Risk Management
RIBA Publishing

Association for Project Safety (2007)
Guide to the Management of CDM Co-ordination
RIBA Publishing

Billington M J, Bright K and Waters J R (2007)
The Building Regulations Explained and Illustrated
Blackwell Science

British Standards Institution (BSI) (2013)
PAS 1192-2:2013: Specification for Information Management for the Capital/Delivery Phase of Construction Projects using Building Information Modelling

Chappell, D (2011)
DB11 Contract Administration Guide: How to Complete the DB Contract and its Administration Forms
RIBA Publishing

Chappell, D (2011)
IC11 Contract Administration Guide: How to Complete the IC Contract and its Administration Forms
RIBA Publishing

Chappell, D (2011)
MW11 Contract Administration Guide: How to Complete the MW Contract and its Administration Forms
RIBA Publishing

Chappell, D (2011)
SBC11 Contract Administration Guide: How to Complete the SBC Contract and its Administration Forms
RIBA Publishing

Clamp H, Cox S, Lupton S and Udom K (2012)
Which Contract? Choosing the Appropriate Building Contract 5th edition
RIBA Publishing

Collins, J and Moren, P (2009)
RIBA Good Practice Guide: Negotiating the Planning Maze
RIBA Publishing

Construction Project Information Committee (CPIC) (2003)
Production Information: A code of procedure for the construction industry
(available to view online at www.cpic.org.uk)

Construction Industry Board (1997)
Briefing the Team: A Guide to Better Briefing for Clients
Thomas Telford Publishing

Finch, R (2011)
NBS Guide to Tendering: For Construction Projects
RIBA Publishing

Health and Safety Executive (HSE) (2007)
Managing Health and Safety in Construction: Construction (Design and Management) Regulations 2007 Approved Code of Practice
(available to download free from the HSE website: www.hse.gov.uk)

HSE (2010)
HSG 168 Fire Safety in Construction
(available from the HSE website: www.hse.gov.uk)

Institute of Clerks of Works (2006)
Clerk of Works and Site Inspector Handbook
RIBA Publishing

Luder, O (2012)
Good Practice Guide: Keeping Out of Trouble
RIBA Publishing

Lupton, S (2011)
Guide to DB11
RIBA Publishing

Lupton, S (2011)
Guide to IC11
RIBA Publishing

Lupton, S (2011)
Guide to MW11
RIBA Publishing

Lupton, S (2011)
Guide to SBC11
RIBA Publishing

North, G (2005)
Anstey's Party Walls and What to Do with Them 6th edition
RICS

Ostime, N and Stanford, D (2010)
Architect's Handbook of Practice Management
RIBA Publishing

Phillips, R (2008)
A Client's Guide to Health and Safety for a Construction Project
RIBA Publishing

Philips, R (2012)
RIBA Good Practice Guide: Fee Management
RIBA Publishing

Race, S (2012)
BIM Demystified
RIBA Publishing

RIBA (1999)
Engaging an Architect: Guidance for Clients to Quality Based Selection

RIBA (2005)
RIBA Code of Professional Conduct

RIBA (2012)
Guide to Letter Contracts for Very Small Projects, Surveys and Reports
RIBA Publishing

RIBA and Phillips, R (2012)
Guide to RIBA Agreements 2010 (2012 revision)
RIBA Publishing

Sawczuk, B (2013)
Creating Winning Bids
RIBA Publishing

Sinclair, D (2013)
Assembling a Collaborative Project Team
RIBA Publishing

Sinclair, D (2013)
Guide to Using the RIBA Plan of Work 2013
RIBA Publishing

Standard Method of Measurement of Building Works (SMM7) seventh edition
(1998)
RICS

The Party Wall etc. Act 1996: Explanatory Booklet
(available from www.planningportal.gov.uk)